EPIDEMIC

Examining the Infected Roots
of Judaism and Christianity

To
James & Joy -
May the Blessing of
Our Lord overtake you -

Isa 61:1-10

S Marlen
Poppy

Dedication

To Brenda, my incredible wife, who taught me more about the grace and mercy of God than anyone, and who is trying to teach me to love myself. And to my children, who taught me that my wife is the second greatest gift God ever gave me.

Acknowledgments

I want to thank all the teachers who have been such a blessing in my life. First, to my heavenly Father and His Holy Spirit that blessed me with a child-like mind that continually hungers for more of the truth and for more of Him, and to His Son who allowed my heart to be redeemed and my mind to be renewed. Second, to my earthly teachers, especially my father, who taught me to love, honor and respect all men. To my mother, who taught me to love God. To Lauren Tourville, who taught me the basics and saw many sunrises with me. To Marlene Geiser, who taught me to love my heritage and sent me on one of the most fascinating journeys of my life. To Rabbi Joseph, who taught me to love our culture. To Dr. R. E. Anderson, who taught me to love the scriptures with zeal and authority.

To my Jewish Brethren: I am so indebted and honored to have *any* Hebrew blood flowing through my veins. I am so thankful for the strength, commitment and unfailing love that I have experienced with my Jewish friends and family. I am proud of so many of the accomplishments, sacrifices and undying passion that come with this heritage.

To my non-Jewish brethren: All of my life I have fought a demon of inferiority. As my journey with God intensified and I am allowed to walk closer and closer to Him, I realize that we are all His children and that no man is any better than another. I have also realized that there is only one class of man. When we pray, we say "Our Father…" We are all His children and He loves us all. Let no man belittle you, for the Almighty Himself chose your gender, race and heritage! None of us are inferior to any other. Blessed be His name!

Special Thanks to Marlene Geiser, Brenda Houck, John Gardner, Matt Jacobson, Brian & Melissa Frink, Sarah Lowe, Gordon Emerson, Ted Pearce, Michael Lederer, Nehemia Gordon, Yochanan Marcellino, all who have made special contributions in many ways. And many thanks to David Green, who provided the chapter pages artwork.

I don't have the words or space to thank Sandy Bloomfield enough. She made many special contributions to the content, organization, and final edit of this work. She, with the others, worked very hard to knock many rough edges off this old Texas Country Jew Boy and helped make this difficult work as palatable as possible. Thanks!

Finally, a very special thanks to Bob Dylan for the albums *Slow Train Coming* (1979) and *Saved* (1980). These two albums, containing the incredible songs *Gotta Serve Somebody, Slow Train, Gonna Change My Way of Thinking,* and *When You Gonna Wake Up* were, and are, a continual inspiration to me. I have the songs on my computer and listen as I write and work. Dylan's courage and insight from over 30 years ago are just astounding, and his songs are probably more relevant today than they even were then. He was way ahead of his time, and though I don't know what happened on/to his spiritual journey, I can testify that what he produced in these two packages came straight from heaven, and blessed and inspired me. Thanks, RJ.

*T*he essential element for both successful fly fishing and successful religious systems is identical: Deception. Without deception, no fish would deliberately bite down on a hook. Without deception, no reasonable person would intentionally trade the opportunity for an intimate loving and life-giving relationship with the Creator of his or her soul — to accept, in its place, entrapment in a manmade system of rules and regulations. Have you ever wondered why your church or synagogue does not do many of the things the Bible teaches, but instead spends time, energy and money doing things which are nowhere to be found in the Bible? The Torah was given by G-d to Moshe (Moses) roughly 3,400 years ago. Y'shua (Jesus) came and taught about 2,000 years ago. Over the course of thousands of years, religious teachers and tyrants have seriously screwed things up. They have replaced the loving instructions of the Creator G-d with the empty traditions of men. Those traditions, whether they be Judaic or Christian, have several things in common. They also seem strangely consistent with religious practices found in "another" religious system; an ancient system which G-d, together with His prophets and disciples, warned our ancestors to reject. This book reveals the origins of many widely accepted religious practices. If you are interested in being set free from the bondage of false religious systems and their manmade traditions, then this book is for you. However, if you are convinced that your religious traditions are truly from G-d, if you love those traditions and find strength and security in them, and if you intend to never give up those traditions, then this book is especially for you.

Richard A. Erb, Jr., Attorney at Law
Gillette, Wyoming

EPIDEMIC

Examining the Infected Roots of Judaism and Christianity

Dr. Russ Houck, Ph.D. Th.

Negev Publishing

EPIDEMIC
Examining the Infected Roots of Judaism & Christianity
© Copyright 2009 Dr. Russ Houck, Ph.D. Th. Corsicana, TX

2nd Printing 2010

Published by Negev Publishing, PO Box 84, Corsicana, TX 75151
Contact: Info@russandbrenda.com
Printed in the United States of America
Library of Congress Catalogue
ISBN 978-1-61623-123-1
Unless otherwise noted, Scripture quotations are from the *King
James Version* Bible.

Note:
*Special formatting has been used for citations with credit given to all
authors of articles, excerpts, and quotations used.*

Book Cover:
John Diffenderfer

EP-I-DEM-IC:

adj.
1. Spreading rapidly and extensively
by infection and affecting many
individuals in an area or a
population at the same time 2.
Widely prevalent:
n.
1. An outbreak of a contagious
disease that spreads rapidly and
widely.
2. A rapid spread, growth, or
development.

CONTENTS

PART 6: THE REFORMATION ERA *AD 1400 – c. 1700*

PART 7: AGE OF ENLIGHTENMENT ERA *c. AD 1800*

PART 8: THE LAST ERA BEFORE THE MILLENNIUM

FINAL THOUGHTS: HOW TO WALK WITH GOD

FOREWORD

EPIDEMIC is a book that I wish had been written years earlier because it would have saved me a lot of time and trouble. It is a book full of truth—truth that may be inconvenient to some, but truth that is sorely needed. It serves as an appeal to the people of God to understand and "contend for the faith which was once delivered unto the saints" (Jude 1:3). Dr. Houck's perspective on this "original faith" may be considerably different than the one you currently adhere to. While there are other books that are critical of the religious status quo, very few of them address both Christianity and Judaism, and almost none of them offer valid solutions.

Truth does not have an agenda. Truth is reality. It is simply the way things are, not the way we want them to be. All of us will be successful if we address the world according to the way things really are. Yeshua said that His disciples will "know the truth and the truth will make you free" (John 8:32). But we must remember that truth demands a response. It often demands that we rethink the way we've been taught and make hard choices. It may require that we repent, and this process of repentance can be quite uncomfortable in the short term. It takes humility and courage; yet in the end it's worth it all as we are set free from the bondage of deception.

I would compare the call of Dr. Russ Houck to that of the prophet Jeremiah. On one hand he is called to "build and to plant," and on the other he is called "to pluck up, break down, and overthrow" (Jer. 1:10). It is the "overthrowing" part that proves challenging and problematic. Russ does say some things that may offend those who have personal agendas, or who place their faith in religious dogma and tradition, but he does so because he has a heart that yearns for restoration. His ultimate goal is that the God of Abraham, Isaac, and Jacob be glorified, and that God's people would worship in spirit and in truth. Prophetic ministry was never concerned with being politically correct.

Its emphasis has always been correction, and it is born out of zeal for holiness and righteousness. It is not for the faint of heart.

Albert Einstein was the preeminent scientist of his time; yet, until the end of his life, he continued to search for the Unified Field Theory and the related Theory of Everything. He sought to explain the nature and behavior of all matter and energy in the universe. In some way, this is what every true believer hopes to achieve — to understand and explain the whole plan of God in regard to humanity. It is an ambitious endeavor, and over time every one of us discovers that we are not up to the task. While Dr. Houck has not succeeded in this respect, his work goes a long way in advancing the cause and setting things straight. This book leads God's people to ask the right questions, and this is the all-important step in acquiring the right answers.

We are at a place in history where Jews and Christians need each other desperately. God has us on a collision course in a good way, and we need to recognize this. The truth underlying this statement goes much deeper than people realize. The sovereignty of God and His eternal plan of redemption have brought us to this place, and we need to enter in. People from both religious camps must be completely honest. It's time to be zealous for God, not for our respective "teams." It's time to admit that both Jews and Christians have truth, and both Jews and Christians have error. The challenge is to correctly discern which is which and move forward. Above all, both groups must begin to see each other as witnesses of the same God and heirs of a common destiny. It is not the scriptures that have divided us, but infected mindsets and distorted understandings.

The time is short. Dark clouds have been building on the horizon for some time, and a storm is about to break upon the nations. Everything that can be shaken will be shaken, and all that will remain is that which our Heavenly Father has established. As the Scripture says, the day will come when the children of Israel "will no longer defile themselves with their idols, or with their detestable things, or with any of their transgressions; but I will deliver them from all their dwelling places in which they have sinned, and will cleanse them. And they will be My people, and I will be their God" (Ezek. 37:23). This book was written with that goal in mind.

Hale Harris, President, B'nai Ephraim International
Ft. Smith, Montana

PREFACE

There are many times I'll pick up a book just to "pick it apart," even though I know just by its title that I will not agree with it. It helps me to understand those who think and believe differently than I do. Growing up in an Orthodox Jewish environment has made my beliefs in Judaism rock solid, even prior to my year of education in Israel. Well, from the title of this book I was certain that it would confirm what I already knew, and life for me would go on as usual.

I had not counted on being intellectually challenged and stimulated by Dr. Houck's book. Though we do not agree on all points, he has left me feeling there's a lot more about my own belief system that I can no longer simply take for granted. Honestly, I had not noticed that the Torah or the Tanach never mentions the name of the religion or faith that G-d is calling His people to believe. I always assumed it was Judaism—what else could it be, right? I never realized how much of Judaism's shaping actually occurred in the exile following the destruction of the first Temple in 586 BCE.

Before reading *EPIDEMIC*, I was never challenged by my teachers with questions like: "What were the changes to Judaism's tenets for Torah-living once the Temple was destroyed and the Jewish people were out of Israel?" "WHY is this among the least documented eras of Jewish history?" "What happened in Babylon?" No minority culture has ever survived unscathed or unchanged in a majority environment. Never. Why are the names of our months not Hebrew names? Why do we still have prayers in Aramaic, the language we learned in Babylon? An even BIGGER issue for me is, *"What exactly did we take out of Babylon when we left?"*

So why had I not asked myself this question before: "Is there a relationship between what occurred there with the rabbinical establishment, and the fact that a mere 70 years later when they were allowed to return to the Land, only a minority of Jews did so?" Or, "How did this 'religion of Judaism,' as constituted in Babylon, match up to the rebuilt Temple system when the exiles returned?" These are only some of the perplexing questions that have been careening in my head since reading this book. Although we might not see eye to eye on every issue, Dr. Houck has certainly planted seeds for further honest inquiry into the integrity of my "Orthodox" beliefs. Do I believe there was a systematic plan or plot to hijack the Judaic system? No, but certainly something happened, despite the fact it is rarely, if ever, discussed. Now I'm committed to finding out what it was...

This book IS a tough read for any truth-seeking Orthodox Jew, or for that matter, like-minded Christians. However, it is HONEST and asks important questions. In an age like ours, where just about everything that can possibly be corrupted has been corrupted, and whatever can go wrong has, it is time to look into ourselves and our belief systems if we are to worship G-d in truth and draw closer in our relationship to Him. My personal quest now is to find out where the roots of my faith, commonly referred to as "Orthodox Judaism" originated. Moreover, I have a burning desire to find out how to get back "there," to the "true" Orthodox foundations. At least, I want to find out and recognize what might not have come from what G-d Himself had intended.

We live in an age of deceptions, frauds and corruptions, yet some still pursue truth and meaning in their lives. To these questors I strongly recommend they read the book and wrestle with its implications. The scholarship, background, readability and intensity of this book is truly worth many times the discomfort it may cost us about our beliefs. I commend Dr. Houck on sharing his personal journey to the truth; at whatever price that may prove to be.

EPIDEMIC may intrigue, encourage, challenge or anger you. One thing is certain - you will not be able to ignore the issues it raises. May we all draw inspiration from this courageous work, and may it bring us closer to the one true G-d of Abraham, Isaac and Jacob. Although it has already cost me much sleep thinking about it, "A heart-felt thank you, Dr. Houck!"

- *David Greenfeld, Teaneck, New Jersey*

In the Beginning ...

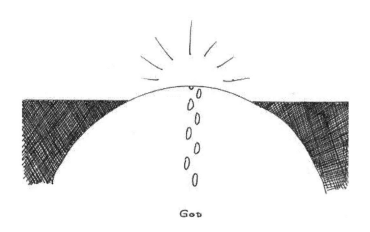

GOD

INTRODUCTION

There is an epidemic gripping the planet. It began when man was driven from the Garden of Eden, and has grown in scope and malignancy to this very day. Once the infection sets in, it attacks both the hearing and sight of victims and eventually settles in the brain, resulting in a dangerous delusion: that self-invented acts will make that individual holy and acceptable to God. Spiritual blindness increases over time. Hearing of the spirit becomes impossible. Feverish fits of passion are symptomatic, and frequently displayed as the individual seeks to convince himself — and others — that he is not infected. This condition is extremely contagious and has morphed over the centuries into many virulent strains. The infection is religious in nature and deadly in its mission.

We will attempt to explore the early symptoms and historical outbreaks of this infection. We also need to examine the faith we think we understand, defining the terms and asking some basic questions to make sure we, ourselves, are not infected.

CRUCIAL DEFINITION: COVENANT
A vehicle created BY GOD to define both His relationship with man and the rules man must abide by to maintain that relationship. Covenant—not religion—was the vehicle God chose to define his relationship with, and to, man. (Man-made covenants were patterned after God's design.)

UNTHINKABLE POSSIBILITIES That We Need To Think About:

What if you found out that... both Judaism and Christianity were not actually Biblically based religions — that is, that neither were birthed in Jerusalem — but rather had their origins in Babylon and Rome? I'll clearly show you this in the historical record.

*How would you feel if...*you discovered that many of their major doctrines and practices were of man-made paganism and not from the Holy Scriptures? I'll show you where.

*What if you discovered that...*much — if not all — of the New Testament was originally written not in Greek, as popularly believed, but in Aramaic and Hebrew? And that several scriptures were added to the Greek text to "help" prove certain Roman Catholic doctrines that Protestants never removed? We will cover many of these.

*What if you learned that...*Protestant denominations were really just Roman Catholic sects?

*What would you think if...*you discovered that *all religion,* including *yours,* was an infection and that Judaism and Christianity are just varying strains and degrees of it?

*What would you do if...*you learned that that there is a diabolical conspiracy to keep you from knowing and understanding the truth? And that this conspiracy makes the Illuminati, the Tri-Lateral Commission, and the CFR look like the Cub Scouts?

Why the conspiracy? *Because the truth will set you free!* Free from what? Free from the bondage of deception. From the Garden of Eden to this very hour, the serpent has done all he can to twist and distort what God has said. His campaign to inject fleshly, religious corruption into the spirit-to-Spirit relationship with our Creator has been spectacularly successful to date.

CRUCIAL POINT: *God has never—nor will He ever—create, sanction, or commission a single religion in the entire record of time. NOT ONE! Religions are man-made—all of them, including YOURS! Go ahead! Throw a fit. Throw the book on the floor and jump up and down on it. Scream and yell. Call me all those names. I'll wait...Okay, let's get back to work.*

But despite the enemy's best efforts, truth remains the antidote. And we can have as little or as much of this antidote that we desire! Each revelation of truth reduces the infection and brings us one step back toward God. Truth is like an injection. It sometimes stings, but if it's the right injection for the problem, healing begins. Because the infection did not occur overnight, it generally requires more than one injection to restore wholeness. This look back into our history is designed to allow you to see how some of these distortions came to be, and why many "injections for the infection" are critical if we hope to see the Body of Believers fully healed and restored.

> *But the hour cometh, and now is, when the true worshippers shall worship the Father in spirit and in truth: for the Father seeketh such to worship him. 24 God is a Spirit: and they that worship him must worship him in spirit and in truth (John 4:23-24).*

> *There is one body, and one Spirit, even as ye are called in one hope of your calling; 5 One Lord, one faith, one baptism, 6 One God and Father of all, who is above all, and through all, and in you all (Eph 4:4-5).*

> *My people perish from a lack of knowledge (Hos 4:6).*

WHO AM I TO SAY SUCH THINGS? *Just A Man On A Quest...*

Although I'm ethnically Jewish on my father's side, I spent my early years without any religious training or affiliation. Then, at nine years of age, my mother became a Christian and I was dragged to more types of religious services than you can imagine. Later, I began my professional life as a mechanical engineer for the largest construction company in the world. Engineers are analyzers and problem solvers. It's a constant vigil, asking, "Why?' and working to provide a safe environment while maximizing development investment. Early on they tell you that an education is not to teach you everything you need to know but, rather, where to find what you need. It's an interesting paradigm that has stayed with me. I still ask, "Why?" and still want to know how things work. Eventually I became a Christian, entered the ministry, and studied theology with a passion. I received my B.A. in Theology from the School of Biblical Theology in San Jacinto, California, with a major in eschatology. I received my Masters in Eschatology and my Ph.D. in Biblical Philosophy from Homestead College of the Bible in Orlando, FL.

This study is the result of more than 20 years of ministry and 6 years of focused, in-depth research in the United States as well as Rome, Vatican City, and Jerusalem. Many years ago, after deciding to study my Jewish roots, I arranged an appointment with the rabbi of our little community, Rabbi Ernest Joseph. He was the only rabbi in town and he happened to be Orthodox. I told Rabbi Joseph that I was a Christian believer, but that I had a burning desire to know and understand the Jewish religion and customs. When I asked him to teach me my Jewish heritage, he graciously agreed.

Rabbi Joseph was always very candid. One day, when I asked him about the origin of the *kippah* (*yarmulkes,* or skullcaps) he responded, "Paul, the apostle! Paul told Christians not to pray with their heads covered. So, about 300 years ago, we Jews came up with the yarmulkes to be anti-Christian." I was taken aback. "Don't worry," he said, "Both sides have done it. Many of our traditions were intentionally developed to be anti-Christian." And many of yours were, and still are, anti-Semitic." (Note: There are differing views on the origin and initial purpose of the head covering, the kippah, which we will cover more in-depth at the end of Section 4 on Messianic Judaism.) Later, as I revisited early church history, I discovered that what he said about the "many doctrines" designed to be anti-Semitic was true—blatantly true! This work reflects some of those cases.

Not long ago, the leader of a Dallas Messianic Jewish congregation asked me to come and teach a series on the paganism in Christianity. I smiled and said, "Sure—if you will allow me to teach on the paganism in Judaism as well."

A curious stare followed. "The *what?* I didn't know..."

Recognizing all the pagan practices in Christianity is no problem if you're Jewish. Messianic Jews find it easy to throw stones at Christians for their Christmas trees, Easter Bunnies, and Sunday Sabbaths. Christians, on the other hand, know little or nothing about Judaism, so it is difficult to respond in kind. Ignorance of Judaism is also one of the reasons why most Christians find it hard to witness to Jews.

Isn't it amazing how each religious group is convinced of its own infallibility as they proclaim all others either ignorant or corrupt? Each is certain they have the purest form of truth while everyone else suffers from a lack of light. *But what if it turned out we were ALL infected with this religious virus to some degree? What if we all needed "Injections for the Infections"?*

THE GREATEST QUESTION: How to Know and Walk with God

The goal of this study is not to prove or disprove any person, view, sect, belief, tradition, or religion. We will, however, dig through historic records and reveal the origins of several religions and many doctrines—a process that will undoubtedly be a shock to some. Our sincere intention in this study is to know and comprehend, as much as is humanly possible, the God of Israel, of Abraham, Isaac, and Jacob, as well as the individual called Yeshua, a Hebrew name which means "salvation now, in the present tense." In Christian theology, Yeshua is usually translated "Jesus."

In addition to understanding who the God of Israel is, we will explore the question, *How does God exist?* Throughout history, there have been debates within the Jewish and Christian communities on the manner and mode in which God exists, and I am sure they will continue. Until the time of *Yeshua* (Jesus), Jews recognized only two types of religions: their own, as the correct one, and pagan. Most Jews still feel that way today. I believe this is one of the primary signs of the infection: thinking you or your group has a corner on the truth—and closing down your mind and spirit to continued dialogue and revelation with the two witnesses of truth: the Word and the Spirit.

HOW DOES GOD EXIST? (The Jewish Answer):

Summarizing the Jewish view is this concept: "God exists alone, as Creator of the universe; His Holy Spirit *Ruach ha Kodesh,* is an inseparable part of the Father and He will send the 'Anointed One,' the Messiah King, to deliver Israel from its oppressors and establish a perpetual government." This is an extremely simplified doctrinal statement, but it is the one we will use for the purpose of this study.

When the Temple was destroyed in AD 70, the Pharisees, Sadducees, and many other sects of Pre-Judaism survived. Judaism officially became a religion, "Rabbinic Judaism" in AD 157. Today Judaism is represented by the Orthodox, Ultra-Orthodox, Hassidim, Conservative, Reform, and Messianic Jews in the rabbinical camp, as well as the Karaites and other splinter groups in the non-rabbinical camp. While all these groups have varying doctrines about how to live and worship and obey God, they all—except the Messianics—share the same root monotheistic doctrine about the nature and existence of God as declared in Deuteronomy 6:4: *Hear oh Israel, the Lord our God, the Lord is one.* This represents the simplest form of monotheism.

HOW DOES GOD EXIST? (The Christian Answer):

Three distinct teachings of God's nature have been widely propagated in Christendom. **Trinitarianism**, which states that God is made up of three distinct Persons who are coequal, coeternal, and are yet one, became the "Christian Standard" after the Council of Nicea in AD 325. The basic formula adopted by that council soon became the doctrinal foundation upon which Roman Catholicism was built.

Trinitarianism was postulated specifically to oppose **Arianism**, which states that *Yeshua* (Jesus) was created by God; that he was above the angels, but not truly God. Propagated by Arius, a bishop of Alexandria in the fourth century, the Arian doctrine still finds adherents in today's Jehovah's Witnesses.

In the early 20th century, **Modalism** (or Sabellianism), re-emerged. Modalism, which claims that the Father came as the Son and returned as the Holy Spirit, is often called the "Oneness" doctrine (the "Jesus Only" doctrine is a variant) and is the least known and propagated of the three. A form of monotheism, Modalism made a brief appearance in the second century, then died until resurfacing in the Apostolic and United Pentecostal denominations in the early 1900's.

There are other views on the nature of God such as the one taught in Mormonism, which teaches that God evolved from a man, but for this study we will examine only four: the basic three that have evolved in Christendom and the one taught in Judaism.

SO, WHAT DOES THIS MEAN?

As a result of these differing teachings regarding the nature of God, the following questions may naturally arise:

1. If the Jewish view is correct (God alone exists with his inseparable Spirit), who was *Yeshua* (Jesus)?

2. If the Trinitarian view is correct (three coequal, coexistent, coeternal persons of the Godhead), how is *Yeshua* (Jesus) the only begotten of the Father, and when was He begotten?

3. If they are *three distinct persons*, wouldn't *Yeshua* (Jesus) be the Son of the Holy Spirit and not the Father, since it was the Holy Spirit that overshadowed Mary when she conceived?

4. If the Modalist view is true, where the Father came down to the earth as the Son, then went back to heaven and returned to earth as the Holy Spirit, a serious problem exists: God didn't actually have a Son! Did the Father give His only Son...or did He give Himself?

5. If the Arian view is correct (Yeshua (Jesus) is a created being above the angels, but not truly God), the question once again revolves around who was actually sent as the world's sacrifice: Did the Father give His only begotten Son as He states; or did He instead give one of His creations?

OUR DIRECTION

We will allow Scripture to answer questions that different doctrines present as we explore this fascinating subject. At the time of this writing, my Messianic Jewish brothers are debating this very subject, and it seems to be a point of considerable contention. I pray that this study will help as we explore our heritage. After many years of research, I've come to the conclusion that anything can be taught and learned; however, truth can only be grasped if the Spirit reveals it: *Not by might, nor by power, but by My Spirit, saith the Lord of hosts (Zec 4:6).*

We will examine some of the problems with different texts, versions, and languages. Historical records have become readily available to us all with the advent of the internet. Many intentional changes have been made to both manuscripts and translations. I personally believe that the original scriptures are divinely inspired and inerrant, but as with any work in which man involves himself, they have been rendered "less holy." Each group has added its slant to the process, making it increasingly difficult for the student to discover the intent and precise meaning of many of the original passages.

MY HEART

Before we get into the study, I feel it necessary to state that this is a work done in love, without animosity (despite my zeal) directed toward any particular view or group. I know and love brothers and sisters that hold all of these views; I will not condemn them or myself for trying to discover all we can about our God. I feel that no matter how persuasive or sophisticated the arguments, I repeat: *only the Holy Spirit can bring true revelation to any of us.* We all attempt to evaluate the arguments and make decisions based on the information available to us and through our experiences. Peter and Paul disagreed on many points, but they dared not "dis-fellowship" each other; for they knew that they were both servants of the same Master. I think we would do well to learn from them, for *who art thou that judgest another man's servant (Rom 14:4)?*

The more we learn, the more we realize that we are not much better off than the hapless men in the story of the blind men and the elephant. The blind men were each taken to a different part of the massive animal to experience what an elephant was like. The first touched the trunk which he declared was like a snake, another touched a sharp tusk and he announced that elephants were like spears, the third man touched an ear and insisted that elephants were like a huge palm leaf, one touched the side which he exclaimed was a wall, and one touched the tail which prompted him to disagree with all his friends and proclaim that elephants are indeed just like a rope. Could it be that we are like the blind men? Have we all seen "a part" of God?

OUR LIMITATIONS

> *For my thoughts are not your thoughts, neither are your ways my ways, saith the LORD. 9 For as the heavens are higher than the earth, so are my ways higher than your ways, and my thoughts than your thoughts (Isa 55:8-9).*

This tells me that I'm not capable of *totally* understanding God. We only understand three dimensions. How many are there—four? Five? Six? We don't know. In the book of Revelation we read of the slain Lamb that has the seven Spirits of God who have seven eyes. These images, along with so many others, are of another world. We are confined to a limited existence in God's world—for example, we are subject to "time" and God has taught us that He is not. So there are aspects and dimensions we cannot comprehend about God. However, He left many revelations about Himself throughout the scriptures, knowing we would find what He purposed us to find. Using the scriptures and canonized books that have been made available to the masses, let us prayerfully explore and see what He will reveal to us about Himself.

OUR MISSION & PURPOSE: TO WALK WITH GOD

And Enoch walked with God; and he was not; for God took him (Gen 5:24).
They heard the voice of the Lord God walking in the Garden (Gen 3:8)...

In the beginning, man walked and talked with God. To do that, he had to be holy. After the fall, man was no longer holy — he was infected. God has been trying to make man holy ever since that day so He can walk and talk with him once again. As we explore this work, it won't be difficult to see God wooing man back toward that relationship in so many ways.

CRUCIAL POINT: *Walking with God is our ultimate purpose, and if we are faithful to pursue TRUTH and continue in it, TRUTH will cure the infection and eradicate the lies and false teachings that keep us from doing so. Walking with God is what we were created to do!*

You may not agree with the ideas brought forth in this book. You may dismiss it as fiction, or even heresy. However, if through this work and the examination of historical records you find a way or see a path in which you can walk closer with God, then we have accomplished what we set out to do. We call it "Injections for the Infection!"

PART 1

UNDERSTANDING THE INFECTION

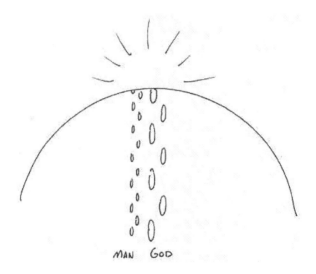

MAN   GOD

YHWH'S COVENANT BASICS

COVENANT – *The vehicle(s) God chose to define his relationship with, and to, man.*

As we travel through this teaching it should become clearer and clearer that God's only true religion is not a religion at all. The only way God ever defined His relationship with mankind was through His covenants. The ones we know of are:

> 1) Edenic (Adamic) Covenant
> 2) Noah's (Noahic) Covenant
> 3) Abrahamic Covenant
> 4) Mosaic Covenant
> 5) Everlasting Covenant (with possible additions to this Covenant during the Millennium period).

There is a Davidic Covenant that is referenced but there are no details to examine.

THE EDENIC COVENANT ERA: c. 4000 BC to 1200 BC

I refer to the period commencing after the fall and up to the time of Abraham as The Edenic Era. This period includes both the Edenic (Adamic) and the Noahic Covenants. While some students are not aware of the Edenic Covenant, most scholars agree that there had to be a covenant made with Adam and Eve either before or after the fall. It seems more likely that it was made after the fall and instituted when YHWH killed the animals and provided coverings for them. The details are not available to us but three distinct teachings from this first covenant are:

1) *Instruction on how and what to sacrifice*. If this had not been in place, Cain's sacrifice could not have been rejected since there would have been no standard by which to judge it. (We'll cover more details on this in the following text.)

2) *A code of conduct on how to treat one another*. This code, similar to the Ten Commandments, had to exist because without the law there is nothing to measure sin against. Murder is not murder if you have never been told what it is and that it's not acceptable.

3) *Clean vs. unclean*. In Genesis 7:2, we see Noah being instructed to take a certain number (7 sets male and female) of the "clean" animals and another number (2 sets male and female) of the "unclean" animals. How did Noah know which animals were clean or unclean? The command is given with no explanation—as though the hearer knows what is expected. The Edenic Covenant must have had this information in it since without it everyone from Adam to Noah might have sacrificed unclean animals to the Lord.

Because we know that God never changes, it's fairly easy to guess that the Edenic Covenant would be similar to the Mosaic Covenant with possibly less detail and the exclusion of the Levitical (priesthood) system. Everything regarding the details is conjecture, but evidence of its existence is overwhelming.

THE NOAHIC COVENANT ERA: 1600 BC—EVERLASTING

The covenant God made with Noah added several very distinct things. Gen. 9:2 tells us that the animals would now be afraid of man. In Gen. 9:3 God gives Noah the right to eat meat. In Gen. 9:4 God tells them not to eat anything with blood still in it (like we all do today from every commercial, non-kosher butcher house in the world). Gen. 9:8-10 re-establishes God's covenant with Noah and "every living thing." In Gen. 9:11 God declares there will never be another flood to destroy all the earth and all flesh. We read in 9:12-15 where God adds the "token" or sign of His covenant — the rainbow — and finally in Gen. 9:16 God declares that this is an everlasting covenant between Himself and all flesh.

The curious part of this covenant is that God doesn't put any conditions with the deal. He does command them to not eat anything with blood still in it or to shed innocent blood, however those are not conditions but rather commands.

> **CRUCIAL POINT:** *Some covenants are conditional and some are not. Noah's Covenant looks to be an additional set of conditions added to the original. (*Writer's opinion! I also believe that during the Millennium, YHWH will add some "additional items" to the existing Everlasting Covenant.)*

In the Garden we see that there is a conditional covenant in place. "Do not eat of the fruit...or you will die!" In the Mosaic Covenant, in Deu. 28:1-14, God tells of the blessings that will overtake those obeying the Mosaic Covenant. Deu. 28:15-68 tells of the curses that will overtake those who disobey the Mosaic Covenant. It is a conditional covenant.

THE ABRAHAMIC COVENANT ERA: EVERLASTING

Abraham's (Abram's) Covenant is unique. It is the only one that gives us a record of God coming down to Earth and literally walking through the blood to personally establish a covenant with a man. Abram had so much favor with God that it records God repeatedly "coming to him" to discuss a situation or notify of an event.

God not only walked through the blood for Himself, He put Abram to sleep and walked through it for Abram's part, as well. Abram was not worthy to walk through the blood with God so this is the example God gives us all. Instead of requiring an equal contributor, He took it all on Himself. *He* would make the covenant for us and *He* would provide everything necessary to renew our relationship with Him. And *He* would make us Holy and acceptable to Him, so *we could walk with him*.

Then, if that wasn't enough, YHWH executed a fascinating "name change" for *each* of them: He added the middle part of His name to Abram and Sarai's and then added Abraham's name to Himself. Abram would now be Abraham, Sarai would be Sarah, and YHWH became...The God of Abraham! (Now, I don't know what gets you excited but to think of having that much favor with the Creator of the universe that He would forever connect Himself to your name—that God would identify Himself *as Abraham's God*—WOW! It's incredible.)

Do you realize that God is still, to this very day, continuing to fulfill the promises He made to Abraham by adding us to Abraham's seed?! It's just overpowering to me to realize that a man could be this important to God.

THE MOSAIC COVENANT ERA: Approx. 1200 BC — AD 30

We will cover in some detail the covenant that is referred to as the Mosaic Covenant, also known as the Covenant of The Law. While this study is not primarily a review of the covenants, we must realize a never-changing truth: that God *only* works inside the covenants that He makes — not the ones we try to make for Him (religion). We will cover various aspects of the Mosaic Covenant in the following chapters.

The reason we are starting this book with the subject of covenants is that everything else must be approached from this foundation. The questions we must continue to ask ourselves today are, "What are the differences between the covenants?" as well as, "Which covenant am I walking in?" and, "What applies to me?" The question of which covenant we are to operate under and what that looks like is one of the most misunderstood topics in the Body today. As we go through this study, we'll begin to see God's answers for us emerge and take on a new significance as we seek to purge the man-made aspects of our faith and be restored to His original and best plan for His covenant people.

THE FIRST OUTBREAK

The Same Old Lie

> *And the serpent said unto the woman, Ye shall not surely die:*
> *5 For God doth know that in the day ye eat thereof, then your*
> *eyes shall be opened, and ye shall be as gods, knowing good*
> *and evil. 6 And when the woman saw that the tree was good*
> *for food, and that it was pleasant to the eyes, and a tree to be*
> *desired to make one wise, she took of the fruit thereof, and did*
> *eat, and gave also unto her husband with her; and he did eat. 7*
> *And the eyes of them both were opened, and they knew that*
> *they were naked; and they sewed fig leaves together, and made*
> *themselves aprons (Gen 3:4-7).*

I'm so amazed at the power and the pattern in these five
simple scripture verses, and am reminded as Solomon said:
there is no new thing under the sun (Ecc 1:9). How true it is!
Note the pattern of the five-step Edenic paradigm:

1. **God says:** When God speaks, it's always a
    revelation to man.
2. **The serpent said:** Someone else interprets what God
    said *(God knows you'll be better off; it's for your own*
    good...)
3. **They believe the serpent and disobey God.** *(The*
    infection sets in.)
4. **They share it and recruit others.** *(A new religion*
    emerges through which they infect followers.)
5. **They immediately set about to "cover" themselves.**
    (They create religious traditions to make themselves look
    and feel holy.)

Isn't it interesting that all religions seem to have
followed this same pattern? No sooner does someone
receive a revelation than the serpent slips in and says, "Yes,

but…" They listen to the lie, are infected with a deceptive virus, and then create all kinds of doctrines and -isms to add to God's original word. They gather to themselves disciples who must follow their teachings, and finally, they build denominations to perpetuate their teachings and cover themselves with traditions and rules. The result? The Epidemic rages on.

Rabbinic Judaism and modern Christianity are prime examples of religions built on these five exact steps. As we explore how this pattern evolved in both and document some of the most flagrant examples, keep in mind the five-step Edenic paradigm. Remember, all religion was created by man and is part of the infectious epidemic of our planet. Each doctrine, as it develops, becomes one more infectious strain of the same demonic plague.

Signs of Infection

> *And in process of time it came to pass, that Cain brought of the fruit of the ground an offering unto the LORD. 4 And Abel, he also brought of the firstlings, of his flock and of the fat, thereof. And the LORD had respect unto Abel and to his offering. 5 But unto Cain and to his offering he had not respect. And Cain was very wroth, and his countenance fell. 6 And the LORD said unto Cain, Why art thou wroth? and why is thy countenance fallen? 7 If thou doest well, shalt thou not be accepted? and if thou doest not well, sin lieth at the door. And unto thee shall be his desire, and thou shalt rule over him. 8 And Cain talked with Abel his brother: and it came to pass, when they were in the field, that Cain rose up against Abel his brother, and slew him (Gen. 4:3-8).*

Do you realize that Cain was infected? Let's examine this as closely as we can to see what actually happened here.

The first thing we must understand is this was a fall season first-fruits offering. There were five different types of offerings during the pre-everlasting covenant periods. Sin offerings always required blood. First-fruits, on the other hand, were either barley (spring), or wheat (fall), whether it was the Feast of First-fruits offering (during Passover) or just the regular fall first-fruits offering. Only at the fall first-fruits offering were the first-fruits animals offered from herds and crops offered from the harvests. From this we can see Cain and Able were making their annual fall first-fruits offering.

> *3 And in process of time it came to pass, that Cain brought of the fruit of the ground an offering unto the LORD. 4 And Abel, he also brought of the **firstlings**, of his flock and of the fat, thereof. And the LORD had respect unto Abel and to his offering...*

There is no doubt what this is. It is Abel's fall first-fruits offering:

> *"Abel, he also brought of the firstlings of his flock."*

Most teach that the reason God rejected Cain's offering was that it had no blood in it, but that is not what we are seeing here. First-fruit offerings are of any harvest and do not require shed blood. In fact, the spring first-fruits offering (during Passover) was comprised *only* of grain. In the fall, if your first-fruits are of animals, then it would require blood. We see that Abel's offering was an animal so we know this would have been in the fall, not in the spring. Cain was a farmer and Abel was a herdsman, therefore, Cain's first-fruits offering had to be grain. The problem could only be one of four things: the offering was blemished, the quantity was too little, it was prepared wrong, or the offering was comprised of something unclean. Cain must have offered defective, spoiled, or unusable grain, or he was offering too little, or the preparation of the grain was incorrect, i.e. adding or omitting something to it outside of the instructions given. Lev. 2: 12-16 gives a complete system on how to offer a meal offering.

Additionally, Cain and Abel had been instructed on how to present their offerings. This is part of the evidence that there was an Edenic Covenant in place during this time.

> *5 But unto Cain and to his offering he had not respect. And Cain was very wroth, and his countenance fell. 6 And the LORD said unto Cain, Why art thou wroth? and why is thy countenance fallen? 7 **If thou doest well, shalt thou not be accepted?***

Notice that God did not say to Cain, "Let me show you the correct way to make your offering." If Cain had not been instructed prior, the Lord would obviously have done so before Cain was rebuked. This is just more of the evidence for the Edenic Covenant. It was clear that Cain knew what the *correct way* was, but he chose a different way. I wonder what the serpent whispered in Cain's ear? All he had to do was to offer it God's way, but instead of "hearing" the rebuke and repenting, he let pride, arrogance and jealousy rise up in him. The infection led to the next steps: anger and hatred!

> *…And Cain talked with Abel his brother: and it came to pass, when they were in the field…*

What do you think Cain and Abel were talking about? Was Cain trying to get Abel to side with him and justify his unacceptable sacrifice? Did Abel remind Cain that all he had to do was repent and do it God's way and it would be okay?

Or could it be that something even more troubling for Cain was taking place? In verse 7, we see an interesting statement:

If thou doest well, shalt thou not be accepted? and if thou doest not well, sin lieth at the door. And unto thee shall be his desire, and thou shalt rule over him.

Although most teach that the verse is saying that Cain's desire would be towards the sin, it is also quite possible that this is saying that the positions of the two brothers would be exchanged. Was Abel rubbing it in that he was now the head of the clan? We don't know.

Did the rejection Cain felt for his infected actions merge with passion and Cain's anger get the best of him? How infected do you have to be to murder your own brother? Not a stranger, or enemy combatant, but *your own brother?*

The first murder we have recorded was not over greed, power, land, wealth or a woman — it was an infected man who was rebellious in his heart and jealous of God's approval of another.

Let's look at the stages of the infection. All it takes for an infection to spread is to believe a lie about God, or what God said. This is the basis of the infection and it is *the legal access or right* Satan uses to begin his work in your heart and mind.

THE FIVE STAGES OF INFECTION

☠ **STAGE I INFECTION –** *Believing the Lie*
Cain was infected before he offered his sacrifice to the Lord.
Obviously, someone or something (Satan?) had convinced
him that his method of sacrifice should be counted just as
good as God's way. Just like Eve, his mother, the infection
set in when he believed the lie. *The bacterium that creates the*
infection is the lie! If we believe the lie, it enters our minds
and begins to develop into the infection. If we reject the lie,
the bacteria can't enter.

☠ **STAGE II INFECTION –** *Deafness to the Rebuke*
As the infection spreads, one of the first symptoms is that it
becomes hard to "hear the truth." It was the Lord Himself
who rebuked Cain. Not a preacher or prophet. Yet instead of
repentance, we see anger. It was the Lord who rebuked
Adam and Eve but instead of repentance, we see the blame
game. Adam blamed Eve, and Eve blamed the Serpent. If we
don't repent at this stage then the infection accelerates.

☠ **STAGE III INFECTION –** *Blindness and/or Rebellion*
Cain didn't go back to God and repent, instead he went to
his brother in the field and confronted him. Anytime you
head toward your brother with anger in your heart, you had
better check your motives. He was blaming someone else
and hatred took hold. At the third stage, the infection can go
several directions depending on the individual and the
strain of infection. This rebellion can be aimed at God or
man. If it is at God it results in a "forget you!" attitude, or it
may take the religious route, which is arguably the most
dangerous of all.

☠ STAGE IV INFECTION – *Delusion and Cover-Up*

This is the ranting and clamoring stage. *8 And Cain talked with Abel his brother: and it came to pass, when they were in the field, that Cain rose up against Abel his brother.* If Abel had caught the infection along with Cain, they could have gotten angry together, rebelled and started a new religion. Obviously, that didn't happen. Also, if the infection has taken the religious route, self-righteousness and bitterness start to take over. This is where many false doctrines, religious traditions and religions are developed to cover up the infection.

☠ STAGE V INFECTION – *Grand Scale Epidemic*

Finally we see the infection break out into the full-blown "*TWIB*" epidemic: Cain murders his own brother. If the infection takes the religious route, there is no end to the deviant things that can be done "in the name of God!" The progression of religious infection upon reaching Stage V is a distortion of the mind so drastic that the infected person believes they are doing God a favor by brutalizing or even killing someone else. Not all infections reach the Stage V level. In fact, most only reach Stage II or III. Yet, more people have been murdered due to this religious infection than any other cause ever known to man.

> **CRUCIAL POINT:** The Crusades, the Inquisition and the Holocaust were all products of this Stage V infection. The final "end times" persecutions and massacres will be the culmination of this deadly epidemic at Stage V levels.

NOTE: While everyone can point at radical Islam and shout, "Stage Five! Infection! Infection!" remember this: Christians have killed more Jews and Arabs than anyone else, all in the name of God! Also, it was rabbis who wrote in the Talmud that any Jew who taught a gentile Torah was worthy of death, and any gentile who tried to keep Torah was worthy of death. So let's stop pointing at others until we've examined ourselves to see how infected we may actually be.

RELIGIOUS INFECTION SYMPTOMS

This is a little self-test; a kind of "check-up" to measure exposure to the virus. Infection symptoms include:

- A sense of self-righteousness
- A continual desire to justify one's self or deeds
- Belief that man-made acts make one holy and acceptable to God
- Increasing blindness to error, sin or rebellion
- Spiritual hearing that dulls until spirit is unable to receive any correction
- Fits of passion that may erupt as person tries to convince others that they are not infected
- A sense of superiority toward anyone not infected with the same strain

If any symptoms are present in someone you know or love, seek *the Injection for the Infection!* Be especially wary of the following, which mark infection carriers:

- The inability to repent
- Love of mankind dissipating
- Anger increasing

PART 2

MOSAIC COVENANT ERA
1200 BC - c.AD 200

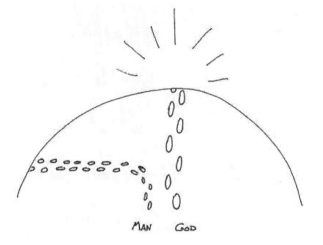

MAN   GOD

THE HEBREW OUTBREAK

The Mosaic Era starts around 1200 BC and technically fades out between 400 BC to about AD 157. However, there are several milestones that many can hang dates and events on to argue the exact time.

Jews will argue that it's still intact under the leadership of the Rabbinic Jews. Reality shows us through the history of the Jewish scripture and records that it was a process, not an event. All of the Minor Prophets' books are records of God's rebuke and effort to cause the Hebrew descendants of Abraham to return to the covenant. It was by their own rebellion that they were cast from the land we call Israel. We will lay out the details of the process throughout this section.

Christians will argue that "spiritually" the Mosaic Era ended when the Everlasting Covenant was ushered in by *Yeshua* (Jesus). We will examine this in more detail at the end of this section as many of the details are the subject of this study.

NOTE: Many people don't realize that demons have strongholds in different areas of the country and of the world including Egypt, Babylon (Iraq), Rome and Greece. From these areas the worst religious infections have sprung. Remember this as we explore the historic roots of Judaism and Christianity.

THE COVENANT ISRAEL REFUSED

If we are to discover the true God of Abraham, Isaac, and Jacob, we must examine both the religious experiences of those men and the religious beliefs that developed among their descendants. So much is determined by the covenants and so much is misunderstood, so that is where we need to begin. You may or may not be aware of some of the truths or facts that are exposed in this section. Again, nothing written here is intended to demean or belittle anyone....there is *no new* thing *under the sun (Ecc 1:9); All we like sheep have gone astray (Isa 53:6)...*

Let's look at the covenant the children of Israel were originally offered when they were camped near Mount Sinai.

> *Ye have seen what I did unto the Egyptians, and* how *I bare you on eagles' wings, and brought you unto myself. 5 Now therefore,* **if ye will** *obey my voice indeed,* **and keep** *my covenant,* **then ye shall be** *a peculiar treasure unto me above all people: for all the earth is mine: 6 And* **ye shall be** *unto me* **<u>a kingdom of priests</u>**, *and* **<u>an holy nation</u>**. *These are the words which thou shalt speak unto the children of Israel (Exo 19:4-6).*

Most of us have read this many times but might have missed the greatest point, which was what had been offered to the Israelites *before* the Mosaic Covenant was given. They were offered the *Kingdom of God, the covenant of personal relationship, a holy priesthood, hearing God's own voice* — the greatest privilege of any humans on Earth!

If you examine the details of the promised covenant, you'll see that the children of Israel were offered the same covenant spoken of in Jeremiah 31! This is a covenant where each individual is in a personal relationship with God — and where God will do the teaching, not man.

> *Behold, the days come, saith the LORD, that I will make a new covenant with the house of Israel, and with the house of Judah: 32   Not according to the covenant that I made with their fathers in the day* that *I took them by the hand to bring them out of the land of Egypt; which my covenant they brake, although I was an husband unto them, saith the LORD: 33 But this* shall be *the covenant that I will make with the house of Israel; After those days, saith the LORD, I will put my law in their inward parts, and write it in their hearts; and will be their God, and they shall be my people. 34   And they shall teach no more every man his neighbour, and every man his brother, saying, Know the LORD: for they shall all know me, from the least of them unto the greatest of them, saith the LORD: for I will forgive their iniquity, and I will remember their sin no more (Jer 31:31-34).*

What does the New Covenant do to and for the believer? *Revelation 1:6* tells us:…*and hath made us kings and priests unto God and his [Yeshua's] Father;* (a better translation would be <u>kingly priests</u> instead of kings and priests).

God had Moses start the process of cleansing. They were told to wash their clothes and abstain from sex. The abstinence of sex was required of the priests while performing their duties unto the Lord. Then, God came down the mountain with a display of power and might, and He gave the Ten Commandments (pre-covenant) to the children of Israel direct from His own mouth. (Exo 20:1-17). Imagine the anointing of that moment filled with earthquakes, lightning and thunder as the Word of God came directly from Him. But instead of embracing the Almighty with humility and reverence, they ran from Him. These are the same people who saw all the plagues in Egypt, and the Red Sea part for them yet swallow the entire Egyptian army. These are the ones God spared and brought out of bondage. What was their response to the personal covenant God offered them?

"You talk to God for us!"

> *And all the people saw the thunderings, and the lightnings, and the noise of the trumpet, and the mountain smoking: and when the people saw it, they removed, and stood afar off. 19 And they said unto Moses, Speak thou with us, and we will hear: but let not God speak with us, lest we die. 20 And Moses said unto the people, Fear not: for God is come to prove you, and that his fear may be before your faces, that ye sin not. 21 And the people stood afar off, and Moses drew near unto the thick darkness where God* was *(Exo 20:18-2).*

They refused it! Can you believe it? Why were the Israelites afraid of the God Who had done so much for them? Why did they tell Moses that he should be their priest and speak to God for them? Why didn't they want a personal relationship with the God of Abraham? They were already infected from the religions in Egypt, stubborn and stiff-necked, wanting to continue in their wicked ways. Add to the religious infection the cultural infection of hundreds of years of slavery. When they saw how strong and powerful this God was, did they realize in their hearts that they were in no condition to assume the priestly role in relation to this ground-shaking, lightning-flinging powerhouse; maybe both? Instead of accepting God's offer, they considered themselves — not realizing that God Himself would do the purifying — and refused the privilege of personal covenant.

How many times have we refused what God wanted for us because of our own carnal condition? How many times have we refused the calling of God in our own lives because we were looking at our inadequacies instead of what God was able to make out of us?

As the infection spreads, the same nakedness that Adam and Eve felt in the Garden befalls man and creates inferiority complexes that impact our relationship with God. This spiritual breach generally manifests in two ways: first, individuals lose the confidence to directly interact with or return to God. Second, there are those who suffer delusions of a calling to a false priesthood.

Most people actually want someone to be their "priest." Before long, the priest becomes addicted to his inflated sense of importance and increasing power over the people. The people become comfortable with the priest acting as intermediary between them and God, and the infection worsens.

The Million Dollar Question

What would God have done if the children of Israel had accepted the offered covenant? Would He have sacrificed *His own Lamb* for the people? If they had become a nation of Holy Priests at that time, would the Millennium have begun and Israel been priests for the rest of the nations? It is an amazing scenario to ponder.

Had the children of Israel accepted the covenant of personal relationship, God would not only have had to make priests out of all of them, but He would also have had to make them *holy*. In order to make them holy, He would have had to make a sacrifice to purify them. For any man to be a priest, there must be a purifying process so the presence of God doesn't kill him. They had come from Egypt and were all infected with the religious demons of the Egyptians, who had developed a complex religious system complete with priests and temples. From Joseph forward, the descendants of Abraham were exposed and infected. We will never know what acceptance of the covenant would have meant for all of us, but we do know what happened next.

God Is Forced Into the Creation of the Levitical Priesthood

THIS CHANGED EVERYTHING! In refusing the covenant, the everlasting covenant, they yoked themselves and their descendants with 1,200 years of the inferior Levitical system. Instead of accepting God's sacrifice for them, they ended up living in an ongoing sacrificial system. Under that system, they had no personal relationship with God, and they were forced to support a priesthood that continually spiraled downward and ended up in corruption.

Over and over again, the Levitical system failed. It always did and it always will; to this very day, every time people lift up a man to be their "go-between," he fails the people and, as the appointed priest, becomes corrupt. This is something that occurs everywhere in every religion — many a good man falls prey to the deception of trying to be someone else's priest, often without even realizing what he is doing.

CRUCIAL POINT: *The children of Israel were offered the same individual priesthood that is offered in the New Covenant. They were offered a covenant that would make each one of them...a Holy Priest! As a Holy Priest they could offer the Passover Lamb in their own home, because only a Priest could kill the Lord's Passover Lamb. By refusing this covenant they forfeited their priestly rights.*

It's important to realize that from the beginning, God has been continually and without variance offering man a personalized, individual priesthood. He doesn't want anyone between you and Himself — *no one!* He wants to be your God. He doesn't want a priest, a rabbi, a pastor, a prophet, or even an apostle to be a mediator between you and Himself. When we grasp that single point, we will be miles ahead of where we are today.

In the garden, when God created man, no one spoke to God for Adam. No one buffered the relationship or the conversation. That's the way God made it, and that's the way He wants it! He wants to walk with you!

DEFILEMENT OF THE ACCEPTED COVENANT

As we continue to set up our history lesson, let us consider the following:

- When the Children of Israel accepted the Covenant on Mt. Sinai, did it make them a nation of kingly priests? *NO!*
- Did they become a holy people? *NO!*
- Did it regenerate their minds and hearts? *NO!*

This is the exact spot where they made the Mosaic covenant with God, then 40 days later, while Moses was on the mountain, they demanded Aaron make a golden calf. Then and there they, the children of this Mosaic Covenant, *proclaimed that calf as their god!* Anyone who believes that Israel became a "nation of Holy Priests" doesn't get it at all.

The Sinai Covenant, or Mosaic Covenant (referred to as the Covenant of the Law) was established because the freed Hebrew slaves refused the covenant offered to them. It was

> **CRUCIAL POINT:** *Man's fallen nature causes him to sin, and nothing he tries to do can fix that. Sin makes man unholy, infected, and unacceptable to God. God wants to fix that. Satan's "Big Lie" has always been that there are things men can do to fix themselves. It's a trap; a deception; the very seed of the infection.*

established to prove to us all that no other covenant—other than the everlasting covenant of the Kingdom, referred to as the Covenant of Grace—could regenerate man's heart to qualify him as a holy, kingly priest of the God who lives and breathes. There is no religion or system capable of doing that, although every religious system on the planet teaches its converts the lie that they can. The Mosaic Covenant was established to teach men that all sin had to be paid for—in blood—and that nothing a priest did could regenerate their hearts, fix them, or make them holy.

As we move into the defilement of the covenant, look at the five-step Edenic Paradigm in action:

1. **God says:** *I want to make you a Kingdom of Priests!*
2. **The serpent says:** *God is too holy and too powerful for you to deal with. You have to become holy by your works, first. You'll be better off if someone else was your priest.*
3. **They believe the serpent:** *"Moses, you speak to God for us!" (Infection?)*
4. **They share it with others:** *They have Aaron make them a golden calf. Another religion is born.*
5. **They set about to "cover" themselves:** *They blame Moses for everything that goes wrong.*

In Leviticus 18:26-28 the children of Israel were warned about keeping God's covenant:

Ye shall therefore keep my statutes and my judgments, and shall not commit any of these abominations; neither any of your own nation, nor any stranger that sojourneth among you: 27 (For all these abominations have the men of the land done, which were before you, and the land is defiled;) 28 That the land spew you not out also when ye defile it, as it spued out the nations that were before you.

Song of Curses

Moses' last "song" was dedicated entirely to the curses that the children of Israel would bring upon themselves because of their defilement of the covenant that they committed to keep. They weren't even in the land yet! Read Deuteronomy 31:24 through 32:43. It will break your heart to realize what kind of people they were: the same kind we were, before our hearts were regenerated!

> *And I brought you into a plentiful country, to eat the fruit thereof and the goodness thereof; but when ye entered, ye defiled my land, and made mine heritage an abomination (Jer 2:7).*

> *Hear ye this, O priests; and hearken, ye house of Israel; and give ye ear, O house of the king; for judgment is toward you, because ye have been a snare on Mizpah, and a net spread upon Tabor (Hos 5:1).*

Over and over again, the Israelites defiled themselves and the covenant they made with God. Even when their homes, children, and fortunes were destroyed and they were taken into exile, they would not serve the God of Abraham. The infection kept them from repentance.

> *And I saw, when for all the causes whereby backsliding Israel committed adultery I had put her away, and given her a bill of divorce; yet her treacherous sister Judah feared not, but went and played the harlot also. 9 And it came to pass through the lightness of her whoredom, that she defiled the land, and committed adultery with stones and with stocks. 10 And yet for all this her treacherous sister Judah hath not turned unto me with her whole heart, but feignedly, saith the LORD. 11 And the LORD said unto me, the backsliding Israel hath justified herself more than treacherous Judah (Jer 3:8-11).*

Of the more than 600,000 adult men who left Egypt as slaves, only *two* entered the Promised Land (*Exo 12:37*).

What does that say to us? These people could not move from the mindset of slavery into that of freedom. Even though they were crying out for God to free them, their mental capacity was hindered from accepting their newfound liberty and living in it. There is a difference between being a freed slave and a free man; it's an attitude and a belief. This attitude is key in forming your personality and your destiny. Free men don't think or act like slaves, or vice versa. From Genesis to Revelation, we find men infected with spiritual and religious bondage and we find God setting them free. Unfortunately, most of us still act like slaves instead of kingly priests.

RABBINIC JUDAISM PROPHESIED

I want to make a point that I will repeat at the end of this section. Without question, God used Rabbinic Judaism as cement to hold the Jewish people together for nearly two thousand years. Please examine this section in that light.

> *And I will turn your feasts into mourning, and all your songs into lamentation; and I will bring up sackcloth upon all loins, and baldness upon every head; and I will make it as the mourning of an only Son, and the end thereof as a bitter day. 11 Behold, the days come, saith the Lord GOD, that I **will send a famine in the land, not a famine of bread, nor a thirst for water, but of hearing the words of the LORD: 12 And they shall wander from sea to sea, and from the north even to the east, they shall run to and fro to seek the word of the LORD, and shall not find it** (Amos 8:10-12).*

This is one of the most heartbreaking prophecies in the scriptures concerning the children of Israel. God declares that He will cause their ears to be shut! They will run everywhere, looking, but because God has closed their ears, they will not be able to recognize the truth, even when they hear it!

Israel Pollutes the Feasts

Even an atheist would be impressed with the detail that Moses used in recording both the medical treatment of the unclean and the intricate details in which the feasts were to be kept. How could a man, over 3200 years ago, create a calendar with a feast system that is a complete *type and shadow* of the Mosaic and the Everlasting Covenants, as well as a comprehensive end-time "program of events"?

The Hebrew children were notorious about keeping the feasts incorrectly. They continually varied from the simple system that God had given to them. Is it wise to add to or take away from what God directs? When Israel kept the feasts correctly, they prospered. When they did not, they were cursed. It was almost as if God had hidden a spiritual thermometer in the feasts. Also, notice that when they polluted and changed the feasts, God called them "their feasts" or "her feasts," not "*My* feasts." Compare Isaiah 5:11-14 and Leviticus 23:2-4.

> *Woe unto them that rise up early in the morning,* that *they may follow strong drink; that continue until night, till wine inflame them! 12 And the harp, and the viol, the tabret, and pipe, and wine,* **_are in their feasts_: but they regard not the work of the LORD, neither consider the operation of his hands.** *13 Therefore my people are gone into captivity, because they have no knowledge: and their honour men are famished, and their multitude dried up with thirst. 14 Therefore* **hell hath enlarged herself,** *and opened her mouth without measure: and their glory, and their multitude, and their pomp, and he that rejoiceth, shall descend into it (Isa 5:11-14).*

Did you realize that the passage of scripture that refers to "Hell enlarging herself" is tied to the people who pollute of the feasts of God?

God Prophesies the Destruction of Israel and the Feasts

For she did not know that I gave her corn, and wine, and oil, and multiplied her silver and gold, which they prepared for Baal. 9 Therefore will I return, and take away my corn in the time thereof, and my wine in the season thereof, and will recover my wool and my flax given to cover her nakedness. 10 And now will I discover her lewdness in the sight of her lovers, and none shall deliver her out of mine hand. **11 I will also cause all her mirth to cease, her feast days, her new moons, and her Sabbaths, and all her solemn feasts**. *12 And I will destroy her vines and her fig trees, whereof she hath said, these are my rewards that my lovers have given me: and I will make them a forest, and the beasts of the field shall eat them (Hos 2:8-12).*

> *And now, O ye priests, this commandment is for you. 2 If ye will not hear, and if ye will not lay it to heart, to give glory unto my name, saith the LORD of hosts, I will even send a curse upon you, and I will curse your blessings: yea, I have cursed them already, because ye do not lay it to heart. 3 Behold,* **I will corrupt your seed, and spread dung upon your faces,** *even* **the dung of your solemn feasts**; *and one shall take you away with it (Mal 2:1-3).*

"The dung of your solemn feasts." God calls their solemn feasts fecal excrement? This is about as clear as one can get. God gets angry when you pollute His way of doing things. Yes, I said angry. Don't let anyone tell you that God sits on His throne without any emotion just because *He knows the end from the beginning (Isaiah 46:9).* He does know, but He still gets angry and He still gets happy. Did you ever think about a way that you could make God smile? Try it sometime. See if there is something you can do to put a smile on your Heavenly Father's face. Remember also that there is never a better way than God's way!

PART 3

JUDAISM'S INCUBATION ERA
200 BC - AD 150

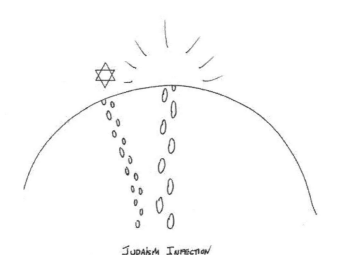

JUDAISM INFECTION

THE BIRTH OF JUDAISM: 200 BC - AD 150

Now, how could things get any worse? Would you believe that a group of Jews, exiled in Babylon as judgment for disobedience, decided to create a new religion based entirely on their view and understanding of what God "really meant" when He gave the written law to Moses? They didn't call it a new religion, but offered it as a new and improved way of doing things! They had a "better revelation!" They didn't need God's system, they had a better one, called *Pharisee-ism!* This was the beginning of a true epidemic outbreak! When men claim they have a *better revelation,* it's usually a bad sign!

This group in Babylon claimed that on Mt. Sinai, God simultaneously gave the written law and "the oral law" (an interpretation of the written law) to a group that was there with Moses. They claimed that this group of Hebrews memorized the entire oral law perfectly and without flaw, then trained new generations to do the same and pass it on down through succeeding generations—a process that they claimed continued for around 1,200 years. This same group from Babylon claimed they finally wrote it all down, calling it the Mishnah (part of the Babylonian Talmud), and then declared that this new book was equal to the written law that Moses received. They began writing this down in approximately 60 B.C., but did not complete their written work of the oral law until nearly 200 AD. This oral law—which they and their adherents claim to have memorized without flaw—has evolved into a work about the size of three sets of encyclopedias. The Mishnah, the original oral law, was the size of one set of encyclopedias.

Now, if you're Jewish, you're asking, "Yeah? So what's your point?" If you are a Christian, you're saying, "Do *what?*

Stop kidding me!" For the skeptics, I have included a reference to a website that verifies my assertions.

NOTE: Website addresses and content change without notice, but at the time this material was reviewed the content was as stated. A few unedited paragraphs follow for those of you without Internet access. I have made comments and underlined several of the statements for emphasis.

AISH is the leading rabbinical yeshiva in Israel. The following excerpts were taken from the article ***CRASH COURSE IN JEWISH HISTORY*** **by Rabbi Ken Spiro, at http://www.aish.com/literacy/**

QUOTE PART 11

>   <u>After the original revelation</u>, Moses spent 40 days listening to God talking to him, dictating to him the 613 commandments of the Torah (which are encapsulated in Ten Statements, the so-called "Ten Commandments") and also the principles how to apply these commandments **(which are referred to as the Oral Law).**
>   **Note that the Oral Law was given first. And the Oral Law has been exclusively in the domain of the Jews**. The Christians adopted the Written Law -- the Torah and other parts of the Hebrew Bible as part of their scriptures -- **but the Oral Law stayed uniquely Jewish. Because it is the Oral Law that tells us how to live as Jews.**
>   **I cannot emphasize strongly enough how significant the Oral Law is. One can't live as a Jew without it.** It's going to become a very important issue when we look at splinter sects in Judaism later on in Jewish history.

Not only does the author claim that God gave the Hebrews an oral law but that He gave it to them before the written law! The oral law teaches them how to be Rabbinical Jews, not descendants of Abraham.

PART 26

Keep in mind that at this time the Talmud has not yet been compiled. Knowing how to live a Jewish life depends on knowing the commandments of the Torah and their interpretations which have been passed down orally - in short, knowing what is known as the Written Torah and the Oral Torah, both of which date back to Moses' teachings at Sinai.

It is impossible to understand the Written Torah without its Oral complement. For example, when the Written Torah states: "And these words which I command you today shall be upon your heart ... and you shall write them upon the door-posts of your house and upon your gateways," it is the Oral Torah that explains which "words" the Written Torah is referring to, and that these words should be penned on a small scroll and affixed to the door frame. **Without the Oral Torah we wouldn't know about the mezuzah and countless other ways of day-to-day Judaism.**

COMMENT: Do you notice the frequent repetition of: "Without the oral you can't understand the written?" Now, how hard is it to understand, "Thou shalt not!"?

The group that promoted the story of the oral law became known as Pharisees. When you read the New Testament, you will find discourses between them and the Sadducees. The Sadducees were temple priests who fought to keep the Levitical system with all its rituals and sacrifices intact. The Pharisees sought to replace the entire Biblical system with their new, oral law interpretations. They claimed that they had received "a better revelation!" They were infected!

History of the Jews Part 28_ JEW VS. JEW

When the Greeks attack Judaism they do it with the help of a certain splinter sect of the Jewish people -- the Hellenized Jews.

These were Jews who were sucked into Greek culture. And it is no wonder why. Greek culture was the major culture milieu of the ancient world.

We see this as a pattern in Jewish history. A world culture comes along which is enlightened and progressive and is changing the world, and some of the upper class Jews always get into it. Why? Because they are rich, sophisticated, and have lots of spare time. Then they say to the rest of the Jewish people: **"Let's get modern. Forget this ancient Jewish stuff."** (We will see this pattern repeated in Spain, and in Germany, and even today in America.)

At this time, we have a small but very vocal and powerful group of Jews, who align with the Greek authorities and who become Hellenized. They do everything the Greeks do.

They send their children to the gymnasium, and they reverse their circumcisions - a very painful operation - since so much of Greek stuff is done naked and the Greeks would consider them mutilated otherwise.

To make matters worse, the schism between the Hellenized Jews and mainstream Jews is paralleled by another schism -- between two factions of religious Jews.

It begins when two teachers named - Zadok and Bysos - begin preaching a new form of Judaism, **devoid of belief in the Divinity of the Oral Torah**. Their followers are called the **Sadducees** and Bysosim, though it is the Sadducees that go down in history. The mainstream observant Jews, who keep Jewish law as it has always been practiced, are called ironically **"Pharisees,"** meaning "separatists," to distinguish them from the others.

Since the **Sadducees do not believe that the Oral Torah comes from God, they maintain that they are only obligated to keep the laws of the Written Torah, which they read literally**. But **so many of the laws of the Written Torah are incomprehensible without the Oral Torah.** Their answer? Each man for himself - anyone can decide what it means and act accordingly.

The Sadducees find natural allies among the Hellenized Jews, as Rabbi Berel Wein explains:

The **Sadducees** were always more acceptable in the eyes of the Hellenist Jews than **their rabbinic foes**. The alliance of the Hellenists and the Sadducees against traditional Judaism guaranteed constant turmoil in Jewish life throughout the time of the Second Temple and even thereafter. (*Echoes of Glory*, p. 38)

(We'll discuss the Sadducees in greater detail when we come to the Roman Empire and its domination of the Jews.)

This is how the ancient historian Josephus in his *Contra Apion* explains the beliefs of the Jews at this time:

> The **Pharisees [who are considered most skillful in the exact explication of their laws and are the leading school]** ascribe all to fate and to God and yet allow that to do what is right or to the contrary is principally the power of men, although fate does cooperate in every action. They say that all souls imperish but that the souls of good men only pass into other bodies while the souls of evil men are subject to eternal punishment.
>
> **But the Sadducees** are those that compose the second order and exclude fate entirely and suppose that God is not concerned with our doing or not doing what is evil. They say that to do what is good or what is evil is man's own choice and that the choice of one or the other belongs to each person who may act as he pleases. They also exclude the belief in immortality of the soul and the punishment and rewards of the afterworld.
>
> **Moreover, the Pharisees** are friendly to one another and cultivate harmonious relations with the community, but the behavior of the Sadducees towards one another is to some degree boorish, and their conversation with those that are of their own party is barbarous as if they were strangers to them.
>
> **You can see how the Sadducees** were influenced by Greek thought. They are part of the reason that the High Priesthood and the Temple service became so corrupt (as many of the priestly class, an upper class at that time, became Sadducees). And this is why the Talmud says that so many High Priests died during the service of Yom Kippur.
>
> The corruption of the Temple and the forced Hellenization and persecution finally becomes too much to bear for **mainstream**

observant Jews. When they finally revolt against the Greeks, they
take on their collaborators among the Jews as well.

The revolt of the Maccabees - which we celebrate today as
Chanukah - is as much a story of a civil war between Jews as against
Greece. It's not a war for national liberation, nor is it a struggle for
physical freedom - it is a struggle of ideas.

Part 31

The Sadducccees, a religious group of the wealthy, who
collaborated with the Romans in order to keep their power base, now
controlled the Temple, much to the chagrin of the mainstream
Jewish majority, the Pharisees, and of the extreme religious
minority, the Zealots. **Part 39**

In a time of chaos, the rabbis decide that they must do the
unprecedented -- write down the Oral Law.

At various times during the Hadrian persecutions, the sages were
forced into hiding, though they managed to reconvene at Usha in 122
CE, and then in a time of quiet managed to re-establish again at
Yavneh in 158 CE.

With so much persecution and unrest, with the Jewish people
fleeing the land of Israel, the rabbis knew that they would not be able
to keep a central seat of rabbinic power alive for long.

(End Quote)

Now, with all due respect, may I say that the foregoing is as
fine an example of bias and revisionist history as you will
find anywhere. It is a collection of politically convenient lies
about themselves (Pharisees) and the Sadducees. They
flipped the story to make themselves look as good as they
could. What's really sad is the scholars know this and
condone it, which only proves how bad the infection is. It is
so bad that to truly believe this, one has to be a reprobate.

I hope that the slant given to history by Rabbinical Jews
and the way in which they debased the Sadducees — simply
because they rejected the oral law as a fabrication — is clear

to you. The Pharisees (Rabbinical Jews) were the newcomers, *not* the Sadducees, yet they refer to themselves as "traditional" and "mainstream observant Jews". The majority of what is taught as historical fact concerning the Sadducees and the oral law is a complete fabrication by the Rabbinical Jews. In Texas, it is a classic case of what would be called "a bald-faced lie."

While it is true that the priesthood had been corrupted, it was the hearts of the men, not the system, that were wrong. Untold millions of Jews have believed this fabrication of the oral law and the rabbinical mandates for over 2,000 years and they fight to the death in defense of these doctrines. While they, Rabbinical Jews, claim they were given the Talmud, or "oral tradition", before Moses was given the written law (Torah) on Mt. Sinai, its first historical mention is in Babylon around 200 BC, with the Pharisees.

The Karaite Jews (a Jewish sect of Israel) still attempt to follow in the Sadducees' footsteps, claiming their religious lineage. Who are the Karaite Jews? Here is a quotation from *Crash Course in Jewish History*, Part #43, by Rabbi Ken Spiro, again with his rabbinic slant on the evolution of the Karaites:

> "During the long history of Babylonian Jewry, sometimes the *Reish Galusa* wielded more power, sometimes the *Gaonim.* Much depended on the political climate and the personalities involved. Generally, however, the position of the *Gaon* was determined by scholarship, while the position of *Reish Galusa* was depended on lineage (as the *Reish Galusa* was traditionally the descendant of King David.)
>
> And it was a dispute over lineage that gave rise to a splinter sect in 8th century Baghdad -- a splinter sect that came to be known as the Karaites.
>
> When Shlomo, the *Reish Galusa*, died childless in 760, two of his nephews Hananiah and Anan vied for the position. Hananiah got the job and Anan went off to start his own religion.

The sect that Anan started in some ways was similar to the Sadducees. Like the Sadducees, the Karaites didn't recognize the authority of the Oral Torah and hence they read the Written Torah literally. (Their name, Karaites, comes from the Hebrew verb, *kara*, meaning "read.")

As a result of their literal reading of the Torah, the Karaites came to observe Shabbat in total darkness, unable to leave their homes all day except to go to the synagogue. They did away with the observance of Chanukah because it is not mentioned in the Written Torah, as well as with the separation of meat and milk for the same reason.

One might think that this sect would have little appeal, and initially it did not. But, with time, the Karaites began to attract those Jews who wanted to dismiss the opinions of the rabbis; this turned out to be a huge draw.

That is, until the great sage, the Sa'adiah Gaon entered the picture. Sa'adiah Gaon is famed for his writings, particularly the *Book of Belief and Opinions*, and for his critiques of the Karaites which made mincemeat of their beliefs.

His arguments stopped the spread of Karaitism which could have overwhelmed the entire Jewish world. It was so popular at one point that in the 10th century the majority of Jews in the Land of Israel were Karaites.

However, the Karaites never recovered from the assault of Sa'adiah Gaon on the logic of their beliefs. Their numbers shrunk with time, though unlike the Sadducees, they never completely disappeared.

The Karaites claim to be in the direct lineage of the Sadducees while the Rabbinical Jews claim they are offshoots of the rabbinical movement. You can read the views of the former on their web site at www.karaitejudaism.com The fact is, the Karaites are the only Jewish religious group *trying* to be "biblical."

Another fact is that the Hebrews continually disobeyed God from the time they left Egypt. Of the 600,000 men who left Israel, only two even made it into the Promised Land by believing God instead of what they saw, and taking hold of their freedom. (Exo 12:37)

Truly, the history of the Hebrew nation is one of disobedience. Remember the words of Amos:

*Behold, the days come, saith the Lord GOD, that **I will send a famine in the land, not a famine of bread, nor a thirst for water, but of hearing the words of the LORD 12 And they shall wander from sea to sea, and from the north even to the east, they shall run to and fro to seek the word of the LORD, and shall not find it.** (Amos 8:11b-12)*

Shortly after the words of Amos were prophesied, the Pharisaical movement was birthed in Babylon. And, to this day, the majority of them have not found "the word of the LORD."

In general, most Christians today seem to think that Rabbinic Judaism is the Jewish religion as it was back in "the Bible days," but without the sacrifices. It's not even close. Instead, it is a complete pagan system imported from Babylon that overthrew the existing system. I've been asked over and over again by Christians, "So how do the Jews obtain forgiveness without the sacrifices?" In response, many of my Jewish brethren say that Rabbinic Judaism is the natural progression from the biblical religion that God put in place.

But…is it?

THE MESSIAH MYTH

If it wasn't a conspiracy, it was the world's greatest labeling error. Was it deliberate or did it just happen? *Is Yeshua (Jesus) "The Messiah"? Is He the reigning seed of David?*

I will ask two questions at the end of this section: "Who would concoct such a lie?" and, "Why would they?"

The time was right for *"The Messiah"* to come. Rome was in a successive line of occupiers who had trampled the Holy Land and the Holy People. Israel needed its deliverer to show up and drive the heathen Gentiles out of the land. The Sadducees had corrupted the temple along with the sacrifice and offering system while the Pharisees were moving in from Babylon and setting up schools all over Israel. They needed their prophesied Messiah!

What kind of Messiah were they expecting? A Messiah King, of course, who would set up the eternal throne of David and make Israel the most powerful nation on earth. But who shows up at this critical point of history? *Yeshua* (Jesus), a gentle teacher from the Galilee region cut from the average Hebrew cloth. How could He be The Messiah? The Lion of the tribe of Judah? The King of all Kings? The ruling Prince from the seed of David and the root of Jesse who would deliver Israel from her enemies and make her the capital of all the world?

One must realize that the word *Messiah* in Hebrew simply means *anointed one*. There were many "anointed ones" in the Tanach or Old Testament: Moses, David, the prophets, even Satan is referred to as the anointed cherub in Ezekiel 28. However, there was one who was prophesied to come to be *The Messiah Prince*, (Daniel 9) the Anointed Deliverer, *The Messiah King* Who would rule Israel forever.

This became a *Jewish idiom* and carries with it a complete definition.

The confusion occurs because most do not understand the difference between a cultural idiom and a translation.

The word *Messiah* only appears twice in the Tanach (Old Testament), both times in Daniel 9 of the King James Version. The phrase *"anointed one"* not at all. However, the word *"anointed"* appears 96 times.

Please catch this: the Hebrew cultural idiom, "The Messiah" is a **very specific title for a specified time.**

CRUCIAL POINT: *"The Messiah" is a Jewish or Hebrew idiom. It carries the connotation of "The King." It is the title of the world ruler during the Millennium era and is applicable only during that era. One can be anointed without being "The Anointed One," or The Messiah King. This is not an exercise in semantics; it will prove to be very crucial as we examine this subject. Wherever we use the title "The Messiah" we will also designate "King."*

There are many prophecies about the Messiah King; we will examine only two of these from Isaiah 11 and Amos 9:

> And there shall come forth **a rod out of the stem of Jesse**, and a Branch shall grow out of his roots: ²And the spirit of the LORD shall rest upon him, the spirit of wisdom and understanding, the spirit of counsel and might, the spirit of knowledge and of the fear of the LORD; ³And shall make him of quick understanding in the fear of the LORD: and he shall not judge after the sight of his eyes, neither reprove after the hearing of his ears: ⁴**But with righteousness shall he judge the poor, and reprove with equity for the meek of the earth: and he shall smite the earth with the rod of his mouth, and with the breath of his lips shall he slay the**

<u>*wicked*</u>. *⁵And righteousness shall be the girdle of his loins, and faithfulness the girdle of his reins.* <u>**⁶The wolf also shall dwell with the lamb, and the leopard shall lie down with the kid; and the calf and the young lion and the fatling together; and a little child shall lead them. ⁷And the cow and the bear shall feed; their young ones shall lie down together: and the lion shall eat straw like the ox. ⁸And the sucking child shall play on the hole of the asp, and the weaned child shall put his hand on the cockatrice' den.**</u> *⁹They shall not hurt nor destroy in all my holy mountain: for the earth shall be full of the knowledge of the LORD, as the waters cover the sea. ¹⁰And in that day there shall be a root of Jesse, which shall stand for an ensign of the people; to it shall the Gentiles seek: and his rest shall be glorious. ¹¹And it shall come to pass in that day, that the Lord shall set his hand again the second time to recover the remnant of his people (Isa 11: 1-11),*

*In that day will **I raise up the tabernacle of David** that is fallen, and close up the breaches thereof; and I will raise up his ruins, and I will build it as in the days of old: ¹²That* <u>**they may possess the remnant of Edom, and of all the heathen,**</u> *which are called by my name, saith the **LORD that doeth this.** ¹³Behold, the days come, saith the LORD, that the plowman shall overtake the reaper, and the treader of grapes him that soweth seed; and the mountains shall drop sweet wine, and all the hills shall melt. ¹⁴And **I will bring again the captivity of my people of Israel, and they shall build the waste cities, and inhabit them; and they shall plant vineyards, and drink the wine thereof; they shall also make gardens, and eat the fruit of them.** ¹⁵And I will plant them upon their land, and* <u>*they shall no*</u>

> *more be pulled up out of their land which I have given*
> *them, saith the LORD thy God (Amos 9:11-15).*

Are the underlined events and situations occurring
now? Were they occurring when *Yeshua* (Jesus) was walking
the earth; after the resurrection or ascension? No! No! No!
They have never occurred. Not yet, anyway. There are
dozens of prophecies like these, not just two. If *"The
Messiah"* (King) comes and there is even one prophecy left
unfulfilled I—and many others—will have a real problem
on our hands.

CRUCIAL POINT:

First Conclusion: All "Messianic" prophecies referring to "The
Messiah" (King) were and are, **future tense**, referring to the reign
of the "The Messiah" (King) during the millennium era.

Second Conclusion: Therefore, no one was, is, or could be "The
Messiah" (King) since it is the title of **the future World ruler** during
that future "Messianic era."

While these are wonderful prophecies, all these
scriptures are referring to the reign of "The Messiah" (King),
the Lion, *during the Millennium period!* Whoever He is, He
will reign during the "Millennium," as it is referred to. Since
this is future-tense, it should be obvious to all that Yeshua
(Jesus) *did not* fulfill these prophecies concerning *"The
Messiah"* (King), in His first visit to the earth. Nor has
anyone else.

More Evidence He Wasn't *"The Messiah"*

So, what do we do with *Yeshua* (Jesus)? If He wasn't *"The
Messiah" (King)*, was He a false Messiah? What, and Who
was He? *What are the prophecies concerning Yeshua (Jesus)?* A
critical part of this mystery is understanding past, present

and future. Who *was* He, in the past? Who *is* He, now? Who will He *be*, in the future?

In John 12:34 we see the people in *Yeshua's* (Jesus') day having a hard time comprehending the same thing: that *Yeshua* (Jesus) did not come to fulfill the Messianic prophecies their nation was waiting for and yearned to see.

> *The people answered him, We have heard out of the law that Christ abideth for ever: and how sayest thou, The Son of man must be lifted up? Who is this Son of man? 35Then Jesus said unto them, Yet a little while is the light with you. Walk while ye have the light, lest darkness come upon you: for he that walketh in darkness knoweth not whither he goeth. 36While ye have light, believe in the light, that ye may be the children of light. These things spake Jesus, and departed, and did hide himself from them (John 12:34).*

They didn't get it! They were quoting Messianic scriptures of *"The Messiah"* (King) future-tense. You can clearly see throughout scripture that Yeshua (Jesus), was trying to prepare the people and His disciples for His own death. They didn't grasp the specific mission of *Yeshua* (Jesus)! Many people today don't get it, either.

How Was He Introduced By God To The World?

> *And Jesus, when he was baptized, went up straightway out of the water: and, lo, the heavens were opened unto him, and he saw the Spirit of God descending like a dove, and lighting upon him: 17 And lo a voice from heaven, saying, This is my beloved Son, in whom I am well pleased (Mat 3:16).*

This passage indicates that His introduction to the entire world, by God, is that He is the Son of God. Not *The Messiah* (King). This establishes our first reference to *Who* He was, past-tense and *What* He is present-tense (during His visit to earth). He is the Son of the Almighty!

In His Own Words

In addition to the prophecies written about *Yeshua* (Jesus), it is important to look closely at His own words, His words to His disciples, His words to the High Priest, and finally, to Pilate.

We also have to stop and deal with several scriptural variants in this section that we cover in detail in Part 5, *Constantine Steals The Bible*. The *Shem-Tob's (Tov's) Hebrew Gospel of Matthew* has many critics and fans alike. While documenting its history and arguments for accuracy is beyond the scope of this work, I want to use two of the commentary excerpts from George Howard's published work for contrast. The first is dealing with Matthew 16:16, the second with 16:20. Here, we really get into a can of worms. Why must we open these cans? Because truth bears record of itself and our spirit seeks to know these truths, no matter the "fit" of the outcome in relation within a beloved belief or doctrine.

To His Disciples –Who Do You Say That I Am?

The King James version reads like this:

> *Simon Peter answered: Thou art the Christ, the Son of the living God. ¹⁷And Jesus answered and said unto him, Blessed art thou, Simon Barjona: for flesh and blood hath not revealed it unto thee, but my Father which is in heaven. ¹⁸And I say also unto thee, that thou art Peter, and upon this rock I will build my church; and the gates of hell shall not prevail against it. ¹⁹And I will give unto thee the keys of the kingdom of heaven:*

Now, what we are about to see is that Peter didn't actually say all that. Let's look at the George Howard's Hebrew Gospel commentary first (translation reference points are in brackets):

> This leaves only 16:16 where the Hebrew contains a clear statement from Peter and accepted by Jesus that Jesus is the Messiah. The text reads: "Simon, called Petros, answered and said: You are the Messiah, that is, Kristo, the Son of the living God, who has come into this world."
>
> If this text is allowed to remain as it now stands, it would be difficult to escape the conclusion that the author agrees with the identification of Jesus as the Christ/Messiah. But, it should be noted that the Hebrew text has been tampered with. The phrase "that is, Kristo", is clearly an addition (see p. 183 above) designed to bring the Hebrew into agreement with the Greek and Latin, which read [] respectively.
>
> There is also evidence that the word "Messiah" [] is an addition. In a subsequent comment, Shem-Tob alludes to this verse in a form lacking the word "Messiah." His comment reads: "Why is it surprising that Peter should say that he is 'the Son of God'?" []. If this represents Shem-Tob's original reading, his present text is again characterized by a modification designed to bring it into harmony with the Greek and Latin canonical texts.
>
> The reading: "You are the Son of God," was known elsewhere in Jewish Christian circles, occurring, in a slightly expanded form, in the Pseudo-Clementine Homilies (17.18.2; ch. 16.15.2): [], "You are the Son of the living God." Compare John 6:69, where the Old Latin b reads *tu es Filius Dei,* "You are the Son of God," and the Old Syriac Sy" reads "You are the Son of God."
>
> Although not totally certain, I tentatively conclude that the author of the Hebrew text never equates Jesus with the Christ/Messiah (Pg 218).

So we have evidence that the text was tampered with and added to. What was added? The words *Messiah* and *Christ!* Why? The translators are part of the problem. They decided to add *Messiah, Lord* and *Christ* in almost every place they could find *Yeshua's* (Jesus') name. Why? It's part of the religious infection. We will cover it more in section 5. For now, let's stay with the Messiah myth.

Our next "translation error" occurs just 4 verses down.

> In 16:20 the Greek reads: "Then he strictly charged the disciples to tell no one that he was the Christ" (RSV). The Hebrew reads: "Then he commanded his disciples not to say that he is the Messiah." The Greek is an injunction to secrecy—not to reveal Jesus' Messiahship; the Hebrew appears to be an injunction against claiming that Jesus is the Messiah (GH pg 217).

The commentary's Hebrew seems pretty clear here—that *Yeshua* (Jesus) was actually commanding His disciples not to start the rumor that He was the Messiah. This is in strong contrast to *"keeping it a secret"* as our interpreters would have us believe.

So, where does that leave us? Peter's revelation was that *Yeshua* (Jesus) was the Son of the Living God. This is a very heavy revelation. Being the Son of God is one of the requirements <u>to be</u> *The Messiah (King), in the future!*

> *I will declare the decree: the LORD hath said unto me, Thou art my Son; this day have I begotten thee. 8 Ask of me, and I shall give thee the heathen for thine inheritance, and the uttermost parts of the earth for thy possession. 9 Thou shalt break them with a rod of iron; thou shalt dash them in pieces like a potter's vessel. 10 Be wise now therefore, O ye kings: be instructed, ye judges of the earth. 11 Serve the LORD with fear, and rejoice with trembling. 12 Kiss the Son, lest he be angry, and ye perish from the way, when his wrath is kindled but a little. Blessed are all they that put their trust in him. (Psa 2:7-12).*

What Peter, and everyone else, didn't realize was *Yeshua* (Jesus) had two different anointings. The first was to be *The Anointed Lamb* who came to fulfill the spring feasts (present-tense) and the second to be *The Messiah (King), the Lion,* who would fulfill the fall feasts (future-tense). While Peter could have been thinking, "You are the Messiah, too!" He had just been instructed by *Yeshua* (Jesus) not to go out telling people that! Peter could tell them that *Yeshua* (Jesus) was the Son of God, but not the Messiah! Why? Because He wasn't—yet! *Yeshua* (Jesus) tried to teach His disciples the difference.

Now, if *Yeshua* (Jesus) was going to be *"the reigning Messiah"* (King), flesh and blood would have been able to reveal it to *everyone*. This is part of the "mystery of God" referred to in the scriptures. If *Yeshua* (Jesus) had become *The Messiah (*King), there would have been an earthly ceremony, He would have been declared King of Israel and He would have ruled the world from that point on! Everyone on the planet would have known!

To The High Priest

When *Yeshua* (Jesus) was asked of the high priest who He was in Matthew 20:63, *Jesus held his peace. And the high priest answered and said unto him, I adjure thee by the living God, that thou tell us whether thou be the Christ, the Son of God.* ⁶⁴*Jesus saith unto him, Thou hast said: nevertheless I say unto you, Hereafter shall ye see the Son of man sitting on the right hand of power, and coming in the clouds of heaven.*

When the high priest *commanded Yeshua* (Jesus) to answer him "by the living God," *Yeshua* (Jesus) had no choice but to answer him truthfully. To deny any of these would have been a lie. He (1) was anointed by God to be the Lamb, (2) is the Son of God, and (3) is the One who <u>*will be*</u> *The Messiah(King)* when He returns to fulfill the fall feasts (future-tense). So, to the High Priest's question, there was only one correct answer: *I Am!*

Notice what else *Yeshua* (Jesus) says to the High Priest. "You will 1) see me sitting on the right hand of power and 2) coming in the clouds of heaven." *Yeshua* (Jesus) just told the High Priest the next two phases of His own Ministry. He was going to go and sit next to Father, as the anointed Lamb of God, "until His enemies be made His footstool." **Then**, he [High Priest] would see *Yeshua* (Jesus) return in the clouds, as *The Messiah* (King) (future-tense)! Wow! No wonder the High Priest lost it. Even though he didn't totally understand it he knew *Yeshua* (Jesus) was making the claim that He was the one who would be *The Messiah* (King).

To Pilate

Notice both the question and the answer. It's a very different question from a very different paradigm.

> In John 18:33, when Pilate asked if Yeshua (Jesus) was King of the Jews, He answered him, *Sayest thou this thing of thyself, or did others tell it thee of me?* [35]*Pilate answered, Am I a Jew? Thine own nation and the chief priests have delivered thee unto me: what hast thou done?* [36]*Jesus answered, My kingdom is not of this world: if my kingdom were of this world, then would my servants fight, that I should not be delivered to the Jews: **but now** is my kingdom not from hence.* [37]*Pilate therefore said unto him, Art thou a king then? Jesus answered, Thou sayest that I am a king. To this end was I born, and for this cause came I into the world, that I should bear witness unto the truth. Every one that is of the truth heareth my voice.*

Here Pilate asks a crucial question and *Yeshua* (Jesus) gives an even more crucial answer. Pilate asked if he was the *King* of the Jews, not the anointed one, or *Messiah* of the Jews. Did *Yeshua* (Jesus) change his story with Pilate? Or was it simply a different question? *Yeshua* (Jesus) did not come to be *The Messiah* (King). His own words were "My Kingdom is (present-tense) not of this world!" How much clearer can you get?! *Yeshua* (Jesus) makes it clear that He is a King, "My Kingdom…" but he also makes it clear that it is not over the Jews. "Not of this world!" Thus, He stated he did not come to Earth to be *The Messiah* (King) (future-tense)! When *The Messiah* (King) comes, His kingdom will be of this world and He will be the King of the Jews! All future-tense!

In John 4:26, *Yeshua* (Jesus) answers the Samaritan woman when she starts talking about what Messiah would do when he came, with "I am." He knew who He was and basically told her that He was the one who would be The Messiah. He could answer her questions even before He became *The Messiah* (King). You'll notice that none of His disciples were with him when He told her. She was a foreigner and unaware of all the semantic issues we experience today. She had needs, and Yeshua (Jesus) met them.

OK, SO HE WAS NOT *"THE MESSIAH"* (KING) — THEN WHO/ WHAT WAS HE?

When John the Baptist saw *Yeshua* (Jesus) coming he proclaimed, "Behold the *Lamb of God* that takes away sins." Why didn't he didn't cry out "Behold the *Messiah*!" or "Behold the *King*"?

> *The next day John seeth Jesus coming unto him, and saith,* **Behold the Lamb of God, which taketh away the sin of the world**. *³⁰This is he of whom I said, after me cometh a man which is preferred before me:* **for he was before me.** *³¹And I knew him not:* **but that he should be made manifest to Israel, therefore am I come baptizing with water.** *³²And John bare record, saying, I saw the Spirit descending from heaven like a dove, and it abode upon him. ³³And I knew him not: but he that sent me to baptize with water, the same said unto me, upon whom thou shalt see the Spirit descending, and remaining on him,* **the same is he which baptizeth with the Holy Ghost.** *³⁴And I saw, and bare record that* **this is the Son of God.** *³⁵Again the next day after John stood, and two of his disciples; ³⁶And looking upon Jesus as he walked, he saith, Behold the Lamb of God (John 1:29)!*

The ministry of John the Baptist was a very specific one. It was prophesied four hundred years earlier, in Malachi 3:1, that a messenger "would come and prepare the way before me."

> *Behold, I will send* **my messenger,** *and* **he shall prepare the way before me***: and the Lord, whom ye seek, shall suddenly come to his temple, even* **the messenger of the covenant,** *whom ye delight in: behold,* **he shall come,** *saith the LORD of hosts… God…3:3 And he shall sit* **as a refiner** *and* **purifier**

*of silver: and **he shall purify the sons of Levi, and purge them** as gold and silver, that they may offer unto the LORD an offering in righteousness (Mal 3:1).*

As you can see, this prophecy is about a redeemer who is coming to refine and purify the people. It doesn't even hint of *"The Messiah"* (King).

I don't know if you realize how critical John's mission was. It was John the Baptist's responsibility to "prepare the way," clear the path," make clear the mission," — however you want to put it, it was his job to introduce *Yeshua* (Jesus) to the Hebrew world and *explain* his ministry. So reexamine in detail all the words of John the Baptist and see what he said about *Yeshua* (Jesus). You won't find messiah or king anywhere.

Also, a concept to examine was that **Yeshua (Jesus) had to fulfill the prophecies in 2 steps, just as pictured in the spring and the fall Feasts of the Lord.** Unfortunately, everyone was expecting him to do it all at once.

While Isaiah 61 foretells of the ministry of Messiah, it did not communicate *how* this would be accomplished. Remember, they were expecting *The Messiah King* to accomplish this.

The Spirit of the Lord GOD is upon me; because the LORD hath anointed me to preach good tidings unto the meek; he hath sent me to bind up the brokenhearted, to proclaim liberty to the captives, and the opening of the prison to them that are bound; 2To proclaim the acceptable year of the LORD and the day of vengeance of our God; to comfort all that mourn; 3To appoint unto them that mourn in Zion, to give unto them beauty for ashes, the oil of joy for mourning, the garment of praise for the spirit of heaviness; that they might be called trees of righteousness, the planting of the LORD, that he might be glorified.

When *Yeshua* (Jesus) came into His hometown and read this scripture, we see Him stop at a very interesting place:

The Spirit of the Lord is upon me, because he hath anointed me to preach the gospel to the poor; he hath sent me to heal the brokenhearted, to preach deliverance to the captives, and recovering of sight to the blind, to set at liberty them that are bruised, ¹⁹*To preach the acceptable year of the Lord (Luke 4:18).*

He stops after reading the first half—or the part that was to be completed in *the spring feasts (present-tense)*. The remaining part of the prophecy would be fulfilled later, when He returns to complete *the fall feasts (future-tense)*.

Here is another key to understand this mystery! The spring feasts — Passover, Unleavened Bread and First-fruits — are *personal* feasts that involve the individual, not the nation. *The fall feasts* — Trumpets, Atonement and Tabernacles — were for the nation. This is a picture, a type and shadow we will begin to see in the ministry and in the timing of *Yeshua* (Jesus).

CRUCIAL POINT: *Yeshua (Jesus) was not The Messiah (King), the Lion. But He WAS The (Anointed) Lamb. The (Anointed) Sacrificial Lamb sent to take away their sins and PREPARE them for their Messiah King.*

The following prophecies foretold of the suffering *the Anointed Lamb* must endure. There are those who will do anything to deny that *Yeshua* (Jesus) fulfilled any prophecy and to them there is nothing that can be said or done, despite the reality. Clearly, however, *Yeshua* (Jesus) fulfilled the smallest details so that you would have to reject the facts to deny Him as *the Anointed Lamb*.

> *My God, my God, why hast thou forsaken me? Why art thou so far from helping me, and from the words of my roaring? 13 They gaped upon me with their mouths, as a ravening and a roaring lion. 14 I am poured out like water, and all my bones are out of joint: my heart is like wax; it is melted in the midst of my bowels. 15 My strength is dried up like a potsherd; and my tongue cleaveth to my jaws; and thou hast brought me into the dust of death. 16 For dogs have compassed me: the assembly of the wicked have enclosed me: they pierced my hands and my feet. 17 I may tell all my bones: they look and stare upon me. 18 They part my garments among them, and cast lots upon my vesture (Psa 22:1).*

> *I became also a reproach unto them: when they looked upon me they shaked their heads (Psa 109:25).*

> *As many were astonied at thee; his visage was so marred more than any man, and his form more than the sons of men: 15So shall he sprinkle many nations; the kings shall shut their mouths at him: for that which had not been told them shall they see; and that which they had not heard shall they consider (Isa 52:14).*

> *Who hath believed our report? And to whom is the arm of the LORD revealed? 2For he shall grow up before him as a tender plant, and as a root out of a dry ground: he hath no form nor comeliness; and when we shall see him, there is no beauty that we should desire him. 3***He is despised and rejected of men; a man of sorrows, and acquainted with grief: and we hid as it were our faces from him; he was despised, and we esteemed him not. 4Surely he hath borne our griefs, and carried our sorrows: yet we did esteem him stricken,***

smitten of God, and afflicted. ⁵But he was wounded for our transgressions, he was bruised for our iniquities: the chastisement of our peace was upon him; and with his stripes we are healed. ⁶*All we like sheep have gone astray; we have turned every one to his own way; and the LORD hath laid on him the iniquity of us all.* ⁷*He was oppressed, and he was afflicted, yet he opened not his mouth: he is brought as a lamb to the slaughter, and as a sheep before her shearers is dumb, so he openeth not his mouth.* ⁸*He was taken from prison and from judgment: and who shall declare his generation? For he was cut off out of the land of the living: for the transgression of my people was he stricken.* ⁹*And he made his grave with the wicked, and with the rich in his death; because he had done no violence, neither was any deceit in his mouth.* ¹⁰*Yet it pleased the LORD to bruise him; he hath put him to grief: when thou shalt make his soul an offering for sin, he shall see his seed, he shall prolong his days, and the pleasure of the LORD shall prosper in his hand.* ¹¹*He shall see of the travail of his soul, and shall be satisfied: by his knowledge shall my righteous servant justify many; for he shall bear their iniquities.* ¹²*Therefore will I divide him a portion with the great, and he shall divide the spoil with the strong; because he hath poured out his soul unto death: and he was numbered with the transgressors; and he bare the sin of many, and made intercession for the transgressors (Isa 53:1-12).*

And after threescore and two weeks shall Messiah be cut off, but not for himself:…(Dan 9:26(a)).

And I will pour upon the house of David, and upon the inhabitants of Jerusalem, the spirit of grace and of supplications: and they shall look upon me whom they have pierced, and they shall mourn for him, as one mourneth for his only son, and shall be in bitterness for him, as one that is in bitterness for his firstborn (Zec 12:10).

And one shall say unto him, what are these wounds in thine hands? Then he shall answer, those with which I was wounded in the house of my friends. ⁷Awake, O sword, against my shepherd, and against the man that is my fellow, saith the LORD of hosts: smite the shepherd, and the sheep shall be scattered: and I will turn mine hand upon the little ones (Zec 13:6).

I'm confident these were some of the same scriptures that Paul was using in the book of Acts when he was teaching the people how *Yeshua* (Jesus) had suffered as written.

In the Book of Revelation, the word Lamb is used 25 times. In Chapter five, the word is used four times.

*⁶And I beheld, and, lo, in the midst of the throne and of the four beasts, and in the midst of the elders, stood **a Lamb** as it had been slain, having seven horns and seven eyes, which are the seven Spirits of God sent forth into all the earth… ⁸And when he had taken the book, the four beasts and four and twenty elders fell down before **the Lamb**, having every one of them harps, and golden vials full of odours, which are the prayers of saints. ⁹And they sung a new song, saying, Thou art worthy to take the book, and to open the seals thereof: **for thou wast slain, and hast redeemed us to God by thy blood out of every kindred, and tongue, and people, and nation; ¹⁰And hast made us unto our God kings and priests: and we shall reign on the earth.** ¹¹And I beheld, and I heard the voice of many angels round about the throne and the beasts and the elders: and the number of them was ten thousand times ten thousand, and thousands of thousands ¹²Saying with a loud voice, **Worthy is the Lamb that was*** *slain to receive power, and riches, and wisdom, and strength, and honour, and glory, and blessing. [13]And every creature which is in heaven, and on the earth, and under the earth, and such as are in the sea, and all that are in them, heard I saying, Blessing, and honour, and glory, and power, be unto him that sitteth upon the throne, **and unto the Lamb** forever and ever. (Rev 5)*

Whether or not you understand how *Yeshua* (Jesus) will be *The Messiah (King)*, it should be obvious that He *was* and *is* the Lamb of God. He *is* (present-tense) the *Sacrificial Lamb*. In one sense it is like calling the President-elect, "The President" when he is not yet in office. That's not semantics, it is a specific title for a specified time, just as "The Messiah" is a Hebrew idiom for a specific title during a specific period.

John, the Levite who was filled with the Holy Spirit in his mother's womb, tells us *who* he was, *what* he was, *what* his first mission was, and *what* his ultimate mission was.

CONCLUSIONS ABOUT WHO *YESHUA* (JESUS) IS:

WHO? He is the Son of God!

WHAT? He is the Lamb of God!

HIS SHORT-TERM MISSION? Take away the sins of the world and establish the New Covenant.

HIS LONG-TERM MISSION? Create a Kingdom of Priests to be filled with the Holy Spirit of the Living Breathing God under the Everlasting Covenant sealed in His blood.

Realize that when *Yeshua* (Jesus) did all these things, it "sealed the deal" and gave Him the right *to be* the Messiah King when He returns at the end of this age.

With these two revelations, that 1) *Yeshua* (Jesus) was the Anointed Lamb and 2) He was the Son of God, you could have eternal life and the keys that unlock the other mysteries.

CRUCIAL POINT: YHWH has always provided both <u>the covering</u> and <u>the lamb</u>—from the Garden of Eden, to Mt. Zion, to Calvary! Yeshua's (Jesus') blood became our covering when He became the sacrificial Lamb of God.

CONCLUSION ABOUT WHAT *YESHUA* (JESUS) WILL BE:

When The Millennial Reign begins, also known as the Messianic era, *Yeshua* (Jesus), will be crowned The Messiah, (The Hebrew Idiom) and He will rule and reign on this earth from Jerusalem for 1000 years as the King of Kings. All Messianic prophecies will be fulfilled, the lamb will lie down with the lion, the children will play with poisonous snakes, all of Israel will be saved, and the world will be at peace.

OUR TWO QUESTIONS

"Who would concoct such a lie?" and *"Why would they?"*

Who and What Yeshua is happens to be two of the most critical questions in the world. If the Rabbis have it wrong and He is the Lamb, are they rejecting the salvation YHWH has provided for them and creating their own god and their own salvation? If the Christians also have it wrong and He's not the Messiah (yet), are we dealing with "another Christ"? We'll look at this more closely in Parts 4, 5 and 8.

THE TIMETABLE OF GOD — *His Feasts*

To understand the Messiah and His purpose, you must first understand that YHWH's timetable is the Feast system. The first three feasts were held in the spring.

The Passover was established in Egypt as a memorial looking forward to the anointed Lamb of God Who would redeem us all. Today the Passover is a memorial looking back at the incredible price paid for our transgressions. Yeshua became the Passover lamb to redeem mankind from his sins, and He remains the centerpiece of time.

The second feast is *Unleavened Bread*, which symbolizes purity, humility and absolute truth.

The third feast incorporated into the spring system was The *Feast of First-fruits*, which was the first offering of the new year. It represents the resurrection and offering of *Yeshua* (Jesus) as the firstfruits for mankind. It has so many symbolic and spiritual meanings. It is one of the keys, one of the mysteries of God, that most don't even know exist. We will cover the Feasts of the Lord in greater detail later.

Yeshua (Jesus) came to (1) fulfill the spring feasts, (2) be the Passover Lamb, (3) establish the covenant that YHWH wanted to have with the children of Israel, (4) offer himself as the atoning Lamb of God, replacing the Levitical system, (5) establish the Kingdom of God, and (6) become the First-fruits from the dead.

The Feast of Weeks (Pentecost) is symbolic of the type of journey the people will have. The first Feast of Pentecost was on Mt. Sinai where the Mosaic Covenant was given to show man how to obey God and what pleased God. The Second Pentecost was at Jerusalem where the individual was empowered by the Spirit of God to obey and please

God. By *Yeshua* (Jesus) offering His blood for our sin, our hearts could be regenerated by the Holy Spirit, and we could become a holy priest and individually approach YHWH. Just as He wanted us to do at Mt. Sinai.

All the prophecies about *The Ruling, Reigning Messiah* are connected with the fall feasts. The first of the final three is the Feast of Trumpets, which represents the Tribulation period (7 Trumpets). The second is the Day of Atonement, when Messiah will come and save Israel in the valley of Armageddon (actually har Megiddo, Hebrew for "mountain of Megiddo"). The Feast of Tabernacles, the final and greatest of the fall feasts, represents the 1000-year reign of *The* Messiah King. When *Yeshua* (Jesus) comes in the clouds to save His people, *then* He will be *The* Messiah King.

They were all Looking for the "Wrong" Kind of Messiah

Not only were the Scribes and Pharisees looking for the wrong kind of Messiah, *Yeshua's* (Jesus') disciples were, too! Over and over again Yeshua's own disciples asked him when his kingdom was going to be set up. They didn't get it, either. He was continually rebuking them, especially Peter, trying to get them to see that He had come to be the *Messiah Lamb*, NOT the *Messiah King*. It's what everyone wanted and expected—a *Messiah King* to deliver them out from under the pagan Roman rule. They did not recognize their spiritual condition, thus the need for an individual Messiah Lamb to redeem them from a far greater bondage than the Roman oppression. Just like on Mt. Sinai, they were blinded by the infection. Everyone wanted a *Messiah King* to come and set them free—and in one event, not two!

This infection even moved into the new covenant, and soon Messiah-ism, which became *Christianity*, was the "buzzword" for the movement. The problem with this is two-fold. First, the confusion and misunderstanding over Yeshua being the Messiah Lamb, (not the *Messiah King),* began to take root with the growth of the movement. The more anti-Semitic the movement became, the more The *Messiah King* was emphasized for a point of contention. Second, it put a name on what God did not name.

The problem was initially one of semantics, but eventually became one of incorrect doctrine. Once an individual accepted Yeshua (Jesus) as their own lamb, slain for their sins with His blood becoming the acceptable redemption of their soul, the individual was "born again and in-dwelt with the Holy Spirit of God. This led to the revelation (born of the spirit not flesh) that *Yeshua* (Jesus) would be (future tense) the *Messiah King* even though the individual instantly accepts *Yeshua* (Jesus) as his or her own Messiah King over their own life and heart. Individual Messiah King now! National Messiah King later!

Thus, the confusion and battle rage on to this day.

- **Did Yeshua (Jesus) fulfill the Spring Feasts?** *YES!*
- **Is Yeshua (Jesus) the Reigning Lamb of God?** *YES!*
- **So, is Yeshua (Jesus)** *The Reigning Messiah King*? *NO!*

The Myth of Messiah-ism Spreads

Messiah-ism, which later evolved into Christianity, was birthed in Jerusalem after the resurrection and ascension of *Yeshua* (Jesus). If you search the New Testament gospels, you will find no deviation from the teachings of Moses on the nature and existence of God, but many new teachings on how to worship, serve, and obey the God of Israel. Through becoming a disciple of *Yeshua* (Jesus), men could become *kingly priests*!

Isn't it interesting that one of the terms for those who accepted *Yeshua* (Jesus) as their individual Messiah and Redeemer was "believers"? Adherents proclaimed, "I'm a believer!" What they "believed in" had changed their lives. Disciple and Follower were the other common terms used. These are the only titles used by *Yeshua* (Jesus) or the apostles.

Following the resurrection of *Yeshua* (Jesus), as was the custom of the time innumerable thousands from all over the known world filled Jerusalem for the Feast of Weeks (Pentecost). Thousands of Jews became "believers" at the Feast of Pentecost, and the new movement spread quickly across the land. Jews returned to their home synagogues, sharing the news of *Yeshua* (Jesus), Who had risen from the dead. Many gathered more disciples while others were ostracized. The number of believing Jews in Jerusalem grew quickly, with estimates reaching as high as 60,000.

It is important to realize that these were not "converts," but *believers* and *disciples*. They were not converting to another religion. The concept of conversion applied to a gentile who wished to become a Jew, then later to pagans who were "converted" to Christianity. Remember the question that Paul asked in Acts 19:2: *Have you received the Holy Ghost since you believed?* He didn't ask, *Have ye received since you converted?* because they weren't converting to a new religion with a new God and a new set of customs; they were **believing in** *Yeshua* (Jesus) as their personal redeemer and *Sacrificed Lamb*. This was the permanent and eternal version of the sacrifices they had been making all along. The word "convert" is used once in the New Testament:

*Brethren, if any of you do err from the truth, and one **convert** him… (James 5:19);*

This passage is talking about turning a brother back from sin, not to another religion. The word "converted" is used four times by *Yeshua* (Jesus):

*For this people's heart is waxed gross, and their ears are dull of hearing, and their eyes they have closed; lest at any time they should see with their eyes, and hear with their ears, and should understand with their heart, and should be **converted**, and I should heal them (Mat 13:15).*

*And said, Verily I say unto you, Except ye be **converted**, and become as little children, ye shall not enter into the kingdom of heaven (Mat 18:3).*

*That seeing they may see, and not perceive; and hearing they may hear, and not understand; lest at any time they should be **converted**, and their sins should be forgiven them (Mark 4:12).*

*But I have prayed for thee, that thy faith fail not: and when thou art **converted**, strengthen thy brethren (Luke 22:32).*

CRUCIAL POINT: Yeshua (Jesus) did not establish, create, or endorse Christianity as a new religion for the conversion of the Jews. He came to enable the Hebrew people—as well as all who served the God of Abraham—with a system of mercy and redemption (which he modeled perfectly) to empower them to live by the Torah; hence...a New Covenant.

Peter used the term once in Acts:

> *Repent ye therefore, and be **converted**, that your sins may be blotted out, when the times of refreshing shall come from the presence of the Lord (Acts 3:19);*

None of these uses even hint of converting from one religion to another, but rather turning from one's sins. Why, then, all the fuss over the term *convert*?

Convert, or Revert?

He came to establish "The New Covenant," which was actually the same covenant that the children of Israel refused on Mount Sinai. He came to complete the covenant that the Father had made with Abraham, to make kingly priests of individuals who realize their inability to redeem themselves from their own sins, who call out to God, and accept His Son's blood as an acceptable sacrifice. He came as *the injection for the infection. Yeshua* (Jesus) replaced the entire Levitical system, became the Passover Lamb, and fulfilled the spring feasts. He made it possible for redeemed man (Jew or gentile) to walk in the cool of the evening with God once again, just as it was in the Garden of Eden, thus establishing The Kingdom of God. Rather than converting anyone to anything new, this is a picture of having the people revert back to the original design.

The new movement spread first throughout the Mediterranean world and then beyond, impacting Hebrew settlements and then the surrounding gentile communities. It was customary for each synagogue to have a number of gentile converts. These gentiles heard the story of *Yeshua* (Jesus) and many of them became believers. In the earliest days, all of these believers were members of local synagogues keeping Hebrew traditions. That is why the entire movement was originally known as a Jewish sect, which, in fact, it was.

The apostles constituted the only organizational entity of the new movement. Their visits and letters to different believing groups contained the only new decrees or doctrines of the infant community. These letters were not collected and distributed for universal consumption until the second century. *Believers* or *Disciples* still read the Torah, kept the feasts and observed the Sabbath in those countries where they were allowed. All epistles, except for the Epistle to the Philippians, were written to the Hebrew-led Believers at the synagogues, or the splinter groups that left the synagogues, and, in this writer's strong opinion, were originally written in either Hebrew or Aramaic. Hebrew was the language in which all believers and non-believing Jews studied. It would have been very unusual to receive spiritual instruction in Greek for which the original Hebrew was being quoted as reference and instruction. Greek was used only as a trade language between international traders; it was never the daily language of the average Hebrew living in Israel in the first century. Further, classical Greek scholars cite innumerable problems with transliterations and complete lack of idea flow (which would only show up in a translated language).

Why did the Roman Catholic Church propagate the idea that the original letters were written in Greek, instead of Hebrew or Aramaic? We'll cover this papal deception in Part 5.

Some of the Greek-speaking peoples who knew the believers in the first century began to call them by the word "Christian," which is the translation of a Greek word which, in turn, was translated from a Hebrew word for *Messiah*, or *Anointed one*. Many scholars believe it began as a derogatory term. However, adherents of *Yeshua* (Jesus) were still called *disciples*, or *believers*, by the early church.

> *And when he had found him, he brought him unto Antioch. And it came to pass, that a whole year they assembled themselves with the church, and taught much people. And the disciples were called Christians first in Antioch (Acts 11:26).*

Until the third century, the movement was considered by most to be a Hebrew/Jewish sect. Every time an emperor or local magistrate persecuted Jews, he persecuted believers, as well.

The gentile believers eventually began to far outnumber the Hebrews, and many gentile groups either left the synagogues or were asked to do so. As early as the first century, congregations existed in which all or most of the members were gentiles. Some of these congregations moved into homes or any other place they could meet. Many sects evolved with mixtures of Hebrew, Jewish and gentile beliefs. Many different views were created as men tried to blend their historic customs into their newly found religion. This resulted in a competitive spirit, with gentiles becoming more pagan and Hebrews trying to become more Jewish. The Christian, or Messianic, movement was taking shape.

While the infant *"Messianic"* movement was spreading across the known world, you may recall a highly emotional battle was raging in Jerusalem between the Pharisees and the Sadducees. It was the focus of the religious zealots. Individual synagogues usually experienced the same religious clash along with their own "sect of believers." While the Pharisee-Sadducee battle was generating much energy and controversy in each synagogue, a wave of false emotionalism began to sweep across believers regarding the issues as well. The infection took on a passionate role. They chose sides in this frivolous conflict, as do most believers today. The epistles to the Romans and Galatians both address these specific battles. As an exercise in understanding, read these two books as though you were a believing Hebrew in your local synagogue or splinter group with a mixture of Hebrews and gentiles trying to serve God as this new movement developed. Act as if you received these letters in the midst of a heated debate over whether you should live as a Sadducee or as a Pharisee. The epistles will come to life for you, and you will get a clearer picture of the infant church as it existed before the destruction of the Temple in AD 70.

The infant Church was Hebrew in custom and New Covenant in faith. But the bigger question and battle of the day was: *"are we Pharisees or Sadducees?"*

CRUCIAL POINT: *It is hard for modern Christians and Jews to realize that the New Covenant movement was purely a Hebrew/Jewish sect until approximately AD 150, and a splintered Gentile/Hebrew/Jewish sect until AD 325!*

The battle between the Sadducees and Pharisees was so intense that they almost ignored the man *Yeshua* (Jesus). Although they sought a messiah who would drive the Romans out of Israel, the Sadducees wanted a Sadducee Messiah and the Pharisees wanted a Pharisee Messiah, not a messiah who had no loyalty to either camp. Both factions checked Him out, and when they realized that He wasn't going to be "on their side," they wrote Him off as just another troublemaker. They were like a husband and wife having a heated debate because they are broke. They are shouting so loudly, blaming each other for their financial demise, that they are not able to hear one of their children crying out, "Hey, look—I found a sack of gold coins!"

So how did *Yeshua* (Jesus) respond to the Sadducee/ Pharisee conflict? Read Matthew's narrative of *Yeshua's* (Jesus') last visit to the Temple. I have highlighted a few key verses:

> *Then spake Jesus to the multitude, and to his disciples, 2 Saying, The scribes and the Pharisees sit in Moses' seat:...5 But all their works they do for to be seen of men: they make broad their phylacteries, and enlarge the borders of their garments, 6 And love the uppermost rooms at feasts, and the chief seats in the synagogues, 7 And greetings in the markets, and* **to be called of men, Rabbi, Rabbi. 8 But be not ye called Rabbi:** *for one is your Master, even Christ; and all ye are brethren. 9 And* **call no man your father** *upon the earth: for one is your Father, which is in heaven. 10* **Neither be ye called masters:** *for one is your Master, even Christ....13 But* <u>**woe unto you, scribes and Pharisees,**</u> <u>**hypocrites!**</u> *For ye* **shut up the kingdom of heaven against** *men: for ye neither go in* yourselves, *neither suffer ye them that are entering to go in. 14* <u>**Woe unto you, scribes**</u> <u>**and Pharisees, hypocrites!**</u> *For ye* **devour widows' houses,** *and for a pretence make long prayer: therefore ye shall receive the greater damnation. 15* <u>**Woe unto you, scribes**</u> <u>**and Pharisees, hypocrites**</u>*! for ye* **compass sea and land** *to make one proselyte, and when he is made, ye make him* **twofold more the child of hell than yourselves**...*24* <u>**Ye**</u> <u>**blind guides**</u>*, which* **strain at a gnat, and swallow a camel**...*33* **Ye serpents, ye generation of vipers, how can ye escape the damnation of hell** *(Mat 23:1-39)?*

It is clear that neither side was right—the Pharisees with their Babylonian oral law, or the Sadducees with their corrupt temple system.

Who do you think made the argument that *Yeshua* (Jesus) is or is not *The Messiah* (King)? It is the only argument the Rabbinical Jews could win. If they had made the argument as to whether He was the prophesied Lamb, they would never be able to win that one. Unfortunately, Christians have fallen into the trap of arguing with the masters over the wrong subject. Focusing on this argument contributed to the blinding of Israel and the ignorance of Christianity.

It has worked out to be "the doctrine of contention" on both sides. The Rabbinical Jews said you couldn't be Jewish if you *did* accept *Yeshua* (Jesus) as *The Messiah* and the Christians said you couldn't go to heaven or be saved unless you believed He was *The Messiah*. Isn't it ironic that they are both wrong! More infected thinking. More religious error.

The Messianic Myth, Messiah-ism, Christianity, Messianic Judaism; are all built on a false premise: that *Yeshua* (Jesus) is *The Reigning Messiah King*. He is not! He is the seated Lamb of God, the only Begotten Son of the Almighty, YHWH! Stop the myth!

THE BLINDING OF ISRAEL: *The Infection at Work*

All who want to please the God of Abraham, Isaac, and Jacob must realize that God Himself had a plan to *"blind in part"* the Jews so that the gentiles might be made partakers of the covenant of Abraham as seen in Romans 11.

> *For I would not, brethren, that ye should be ignorant of this mystery, lest ye should be wise in your own conceits; that **blindness in part is happened to Israel, until the fullness of the Gentiles be come in.** 26 And so **all Israel shall be saved: as it is written, There shall come out of Sion the Deliverer, and shall turn away ungodliness from Jacob:** 27 For this is my covenant unto them, when I shall take away their sins. 28 **As concerning the gospel,** they are **enemies for your sakes: but as touching the election,** they are **beloved for the fathers' sakes.** 29 **For the gifts and calling of God** are **without repentance** (Rom 11:25-29).*

One of the most remarkable examples of the blinding of Israel is in their own record; their own "holy book," the Talmud. The book of Yoma, part of the Talmud, focuses on the historic interpretation of Yom Kippur, the Day of Atonement. The section containing the record of the last forty years before the destruction of the temple is shown below. The Mishnah (in all caps) represents the preliminary records; the Gemara represents the secondary records; together, they comprise the majority of the Talmud.

YOMA 39 b

'*MISHNAH*. HE SHOOK THE URN AND BROUGHT UP THE TWO LOTS. ON ONE WAS INSCRIBED: 'FOR THE LORD'. AND ON THE OTHER: "FOR AZAZEL.'. THE DEPUTY HIGH PRIEST WAS AT HIS RIGHT HAND, THE HEAD OF THE [MINISTERING] FAMILY AT HIS LEFT. IF THE LOT [HAVING] 'FOR THE LORD' [INSCRIBED THEREON] CAME UP IN HIS

RIGHT HAND, THE DEPUTY HIGH PRIEST WOULD SAY TO HIM: SIR HIGH PRIEST, RAISE THY RIGHT HAND' AND IF THE LOT [WITH THE INSCRIPTION] 'FOR THE LORD' CAME UP IN HIS LEFT HAND, THE HEAD OF THE FAMILY WOULD SAY: SIR HIGH PRIEST, RAISE THY LEFT HAND' THEN HE PLACED THEM ON THE TWO HE-GOATS AND SAID: "A SIN-OFFERING UNTO THE LORD" R. ISHMAEI. SAID: HE DID NOT NEED TO SAY: A SIN-OFFERING. BUT 'UNTO THE LORD'. AND THEY ANSWERED AFTER HIM: BLESSED BE THE NAME OF HIS GLORIOUS KINGDOM FOREVER AND EVER"

b (i) Continuing the account of Mishnah (supru)7a): or 'shook hastily' (because of eagerness, anxiety), (2) The |.T. states that when the high priest pronounced the Ineffable Name those near prostrated themselves, those afar responding with 'Blessed be the name of His glorious kingdom for ever and ever'. ()) It was considered a happy omen when it came up in the right hand, and the temptation was as great as near to improve upon chance by dexterous manipulation.

GEMARA. Why was it necessary to shake the urn?—Lest he take one intentionally.' Raba said: The urn was of wood and profane and could hold no more than the two hands (at its mouth]. —Rabina demurred to this: It is quite right that (its mouth] could contain no more than his two hands, i.e., to prevent his…..

Our Rabbis taught: Throughout the forty years that Simeon the Righteous ministered, the lot ['For the Lord'] would always come up in the right hand: from that time on, it would come up now in the right hand, now in the left. And (during the same time] the crimson-colored strap* would become white. From that time on it would at times become white, at others not. Also: Throughout those forty years the westernmost light 7 was shining, from that time on, it was now shining, now tailing: also the lire d of the pile of wood kept burning strong.' so that the priests did not have to bring to the pile any other wood besides the two logs.' in order to fulfill the command about providing the wood unintermittently: from that time on. It would occasionally keep burning strongly, at other times not, so that the priests could not do without bringing throughout the day wood for the pile [on the altar.]….

Our Rabbis taught: In the year in which Simeon the Righteous died, he foretold them that he would die. They said: Whence do you know that? He replied: On every Day of Atonement an old man, dressed in white, wrapped in white, would join me. Entering [the Holy of Holies] and leaving [it] with me, but to-day I was joined by an old man. dressed in black, wrapped in black. who entered, but did not leave, with roe. After the festival [of Sukkoth] he was sick for seven days and [then] died. His brethren [that year] the priests forbore to mention the Ineffable Name in pronouncing the [priestly] blessing.'…

Our Rabbis taught: During the last forty years before the destruction of the Temple the lot ['For the Lord'] did not come up in the right hand; nor did the crimson-colored strap become white; nor did the westernmost light shine: and the doors of the *Helcal* would open by themselves.

Approximately 40 years before the destruction of the temple, they crucified *Yeshua* (Jesus). A coincidence?

1. *The lot ['For the Lord'] did not come up in the right hand*
   This was a direct sign that the Lord was displeased with Israel as a nation. It was a direct rebuke! It should have drawn the people's attention to the state of their nation and caused a national outcry and demand to discover what was wrong.

2. *Nor did the crimson-colored strap become white*
   This was a direct statement that God was no longer forgiving their sins. This should have brought Israel to its knees, calling on the Lord in fasting and prayer. But it didn't.

3. *Nor did the westernmost light shine*
   Revelation—the ability to see in the darkness, the instruction of Holiness, the ability to comprehend God—were all taken from the Jewish nation.

4. *And the doors of the Helcal [temple] would open by themselves*
   This was a powerful demonstration that the Spirit of the Lord was no longer in the Holy Place, and a proclamation that God had opened the temple to the world.

There is a second record in the Talmud of the "Scarlet Thread."

> 'Rabbi. Nahman Ben. Isaac said it was the tongue of scarlet', as it has been taught: 'Originally they used to fasten the thread of scarlet on the door of the [Temple] court on the outside.**28** If it turned white the people used to rejoice,**29** and if it did not turn white they were sad. They therefore made a rule that it should be fastened to the door of the court on the inside. People, however, still peeped in and saw, and if it turned white they rejoiced and if it did not turn white they were sad. They therefore made a rule that half of it should be fastened to the rock and half between the horns of the goat that was sent [to the wilderness]'.... and it has further been taught: 'For forty years before the destruction of the Temple the thread of scarlet never turned white but it remained red'.
>   (**28**) After the High Priest had performed the service on the Day of Atonement. V. Yoma, 67a.
>   (**29**) This being a sign that their sins had been forgiven.

All of these signs were clear, but Israel just could not, or would not see! *The infection blinded them.* Isn't it ironic that these records exist, not in a Christian historic record, but in the Talmud; the Jewish document read by Jews around the world, *The Oral Law*?

God is always faithful and always merciful. Even *Yeshua* (Jesus) gave warning of what was to come:

> *And Jesus went out, and departed from the temple: and his disciples came to* him *for to show him the buildings of the temple. 2 And Jesus said unto them, See ye not all these things? verily I say unto you,* **There shall not be left here one stone upon another, that shall not be thrown down***...34 Verily I say unto you,* **This generation shall not pass, till all these things be fulfilled (Mat 24:1).**

How long is a generation? Forty years. *Yeshua* (Jesus) prophesied that the temple would be destroyed within that generation; thus within forty years. Was it destroyed? It was! Within forty years of His Son's ascension, God not only sent the New Covenant, sealed in the blood of His Son, but He also made it impossible to continue in the Old Covenant with the destruction of the temple.

Another interesting point at this juncture in Jewish history is that the masses again rejected God's offer. Just as on Mount Sinai where the children of Israel reject the first offer, now they reject the second offer. They rejected the Father on Mount Sinai, then His Son in Jerusalem. God however, takes His Covenant to the world fulfilling the promise He made to Abraham to make his descendants like the stars in heaven or the sands of the sea. Infusing (adopting) the gentiles into the seed of Abraham is the only way this could be accomplished. There are many prophecies concerning Ephraim that become clearer when you realize that Ephraim *could be* mixed into the gentile church brought in by salvation.

HISTORICAL NOTE: When Jacob crossed his hands, he split the blessing for the first time, separating the priesthood and the kingdom. While this has many symbolic meanings, it's also a picture of the gentiles coming into the kingdom because these two boys' mother was a gentile…..an Egyptian!

Israel's 2000 Year Exile

Behold, the days come, saith the LORD, that I will make a new covenant with the house of Israel, and with the house of Judah (Jer 31:31):

That in blessing I will bless thee, and in multiplying I will multiply thy seed as the stars of the heaven, and as the sand which is upon the sea shore; and thy seed shall possess the gate of his enemies; 18 And in thy seed shall all the nations of the earth be blessed; because thou hast obeyed my voice (Gen 22:17).

God does not go back on His word, and His promises are forever. Israel had totally abandoned the teachings of the Torah and God.

CRUCIAL POINT: Yeshua (Jesus) offered the New Covenant ONLY to the House of Judah and the House of Israel, NOT to the gentiles.

*And now, O ye priests, this commandment is for you. 2 If ye will not hear, and if ye will not lay it to heart, to give glory unto my name, saith the LORD of hosts, I will even send a curse upon you, and I will curse your blessings: yea, I have cursed them already, because ye do not lay it to heart. 3 Behold, **I will corrupt your seed, and spread dung upon your faces,** even <u>the dung of your solemn feasts</u>; and one shall take you away with it (Mal 2:1-3).*

So, do you think God honors you when you keep the feasts but reject Him, His Word and His Torah? Haven't the rabbis who created Rabbinic Judaism twisted the teachings of God at least as much as when Israel split from Judah and created their own feast days, sacrificial system and priesthood?

> *Bring no more vain oblations; incense is an abomination unto me; the new moons and sabbaths, the calling of assemblies,* **I cannot away with; it is iniquity, even the solemn meeting.** [14]***Your new moons and your appointed feasts my soul hateth: they are a trouble unto me; I am weary to bear them.*** [15]*And when ye spread forth your hands, I will hide mine eyes from you: yea, when ye make many prayers, I will not hear: your hands are full of blood. (Isa 1:13)*

Do you believe God honors your Sabbaths, feasts, prayers and traditions when you have rejected His Covenant, His sacrifice and His Word?

> *And he hath violently taken away his tabernacle, as if it were of a garden: he hath destroyed his places of the assembly:* **the LORD hath caused the solemn feasts and sabbaths to be forgotten in Zion,** *and hath despised in the indignation of his anger the king and the priest.* [7]*The Lord hath cast off his altar, he hath abhorred his sanctuary, he hath given up into the hand of the enemy the walls of her palaces; they have made a noise in the house of the LORD, as in the day of a solemn feast.* [8]*The LORD hath purposed to destroy the wall of the daughter of Zion: he hath stretched out a line, he hath not withdrawn his hand from destroying: therefore he made the rampart and the wall to lament; they languished together.* [9]*Her gates are sunk into the ground; he hath destroyed and broken her bars:* **her king and her princes are among the Gentiles: the law is no more; her prophets also find no vision from the LORD** *(Lam 2:6).*

It wasn't Assyria, Babylon or Rome that scattered the Jewish people, it was God. It wasn't the pagans who were to blame; it was the teachers of Israel: the rabbis, the scribes, the sages, the Sadducees and the false prophets.

> *I have sent among you the pestilence after the manner of Egypt: your young men have I slain with the sword, and have taken away your horses; and **I have made the stink of your camps to come up unto your nostrils: yet have ye not returned unto me**, saith the LORD (Amos 4:10).*

It is clearly God who is punishing Israel for her wicked ways. But the saddest part of all this is that they are not repenting. What will it take to make these rebellious Hebrews repent? Is there any hope? Can their infection ever be cured?

There *is* hope! Hosea 3 clearly points out the finite number of years without the Levitical Priesthood or earthly king.

> *And I said unto her, Thou shalt abide for me many days; thou shalt not play the harlot, and thou shalt not be for another man: so will I also be for thee. ⁴For the children of Israel shall abide many days without a king, and without a prince, and without a sacrifice, and without an image, and without an ephod, and without teraphim: ⁵Afterward shall the children of Israel return, and seek the LORD their God, and David their king; and shall fear the LORD and his goodness in the latter days (Hos 3:3).*

The book of Hosea contains a note about the nation of Israel and their final exile. While the Israelites were removed from their land several times either partially or completely during their history, their exile never lasted more than two generations. In the sixth chapter of his prophecy, however, Hosea foresees an exile of 2,000 years.

*Come, and let us return unto the LORD... 2 **After two days will he revive us: in the third day he will raise us up, and we shall live in his sight** (Hos 6:1)...*

Since a day is as a thousand years to the Lord, this scripture can be interpreted as follows: **After being exiled for two thousand years, God will bring us back; He will raise us up for the next thousand years and we will live in His sight.**

Hosea's prophecy clearly states the specific timeframe for the final exile for the Jews. We are seeing the fulfillment of this prophecy in our own time.

The exile took place in stages, as did the final development of Rabbinic Judaism. Major events were the destruction of the second temple in AD 70, and the end of the Bar Kokhba revolt in AD 135. It is interesting to note that these events, the destruction of both of the temples and the crushing of the Bar Kokhba revolt, all occurred on the same day of the year, the ninth of the Hebrew month of AV.

A Warning for Gentiles and Christians

Then answered all the people, and said, His blood be on us, and on our children (Mat 27: 25)...

Many quote this verse to justify their belief that this is the cause of all the Jewish woes and persecution around the world. Their vision is very shortsighted. God's plan was put into place before Abraham was born. He had His plan even before this world was created, before its foundation was laid! His plan was and is for every individual to realize his own sinful nature and the inability to redeem himself. He planned for us to need Him and to desire His cleansing in our lives, thus allowing Him to provide our salvation and redemption. Whatever you do, don't fall into the anti-Semitic trap of cursing and abandoning the Jewish people. It has been devastating to everyone who has ever done so! Just check history.

It is also critical to understand the anti-Semitic teaching of Replacement Theology which, in short, teaches that the physical descendants of Abraham, referred to as the Hebrew or Jewish people, were permanently cut off for rejecting *Yeshua* (Jesus) and replaced by the New Testament Church. (Interestingly, Islam is also built on Replacement Theology—Muslims believe that the Jews did not get the "world evangelization" job done so it was handed off to the Christians, who also failed, so now it is their turn to complete man's assignment of bringing all things under subjection to divine rule. The biggest problem with their theory, of course, is that our God of Abraham, Isaac and Jacob is not related in any way to their Allah of Islam, whom they desire to receive the world's worship.) Christian Replacement Theology originated in the Roman Catholic Church and continues to this very day. It's a sure sign of the infection. The Apostle Paul's disagreement with this grievous error is expressed in the Epistle to the Romans:

> For **I speak to you Gentiles**, *inasmuch as I am the apostle of the Gentiles, I magnify mine office: 14 If by any means I may provoke to emulation* them which are *my flesh, and might save some of them. 15* **For if the casting away of them** be **the reconciling of the world, what** shall **the receiving** of **them** be, **but life from the dead?** *16 For if the firstfruit be holy, the lump* is *also* holy: *and if the root* be *holy, so* are *the branches. 17 And* **if some of the branches be broken off, and thou, being a wild olive tree, wert grafted in among them,** *and with them partakest of the root and fatness of the olive tree; 18* **Boast not against the branches**. *But if thou*

boast, thou bearest not the root, but the root thee. 19 Thou wilt say then, The branches were broken off, that I might be grafted in. 20 Well; because of unbelief they were broken off, and thou standest by faith. **Be not highminded, but fear: 21 For if God spared not the natural branches, take heed lest he also spare not thee** *(Rom 11:13-21).*

Paul's statement is a clear and direct refutation of Replacement theology. Further, it is a warning to the new believers not to find themselves on the wrong side concerning the Hebrew/Jewish people. We will explore this topic further in Part 2 where Constantine creates world-wide anti-Semitism.

THE FINAL INCUBATION — THE YAVNEH PERIOD

The episode of Jewish history referred to as "Yavneh" dates from AD 70 to 158. At various times during the nation's persecutions, the sages were forced into hiding. Yet, at times, they managed to reconvene in different places. Two of these were Usha (AD 122) and Yavneh (AD 158).

The Temple's destruction in AD 70 not only created a huge void in Hebrew life, but also left serious dilemmas. Where would the Sanhedrin, the ruling authority for all Jews, convene? How can one receive atonement for sin without the temple? Yochanon Ben Zakkai, a leading Pharisaical teacher of the day, had a ready answer for that question.

"God has provided another means of atonement, for the Scripture says, 'I desire charity and not sacrifice.'" Ben Zakkai interpreted charity to be a *mitzvah*, or commandment. "One receives atonement for sin through good works." In other words, according to Pharasaical authority, the system has changed. Now, one can save *oneself* — the infection moves to the next level. The Pharisees operated for almost 200 years with this very system. Remember, this infection came from Babylon where they didn't have a Temple.

The Pharisaical term *Halachah*, meaning *the way to go* or *the way to walk*, is a legal decision as to what God's will is for any given situation (it also originally covered criminal and civil matters which have since been turned over to the state). *Halachah* is determined through logic and debate based upon prior rulings of the rabbis for over two thousand years.

The Pharisaic leadership invented a system where they did not need a Temple; their authority was the *Halachah* and a growing body of rules which they controlled and adapted as needed. They took all the scriptures where YHWH was sick of all the hypocrisy of the Jews, put a spin on those scriptures and came up with a "works based" salvation so they didn't need the Levitical system, the priests, the temple, *or God*. They called it "Rabbinic Judaism".

Creation of a Religion

Control and manipulation of the people is the primary focus of religion. Telling you what is and is not acceptable and having some kind of "key into eternity" are essential to religions. Requirements for obeying God (unspoken church rules), building programs, and financial control are the primary tools of manipulation used to spread the infection. Acquiring wealth is often a secondary objective of religion.

Pharisaic contributions during the Yavneh period included:

1)   The Jewish prayer book, known as the Siddur, which establishes the order of religious services. Modern Siddurs use much the same order of service and other material compiled during this period.

2)   The establishment of the Passover Seder, which is used to this day.

3)   The adoption of the standard Jewish calendar. This was necessary since the idea that "Twelve New Moons equaled twelve months making one complete year" no longer worked.

The Jews had to change their calendar because a year now contained more than twelve new moons. They had to add a leap month every few years to make their new calendar work. What a miracle! God actually changed time and yet no one even talks about it.

CRUCIAL POINT: God changed TIME! After the events surrounding the crucifixion of the man Yeshua (Jesus) and the destruction of the second temple, THE CALENDAR GOD GAVE TO THE JEWISH NATION ON MOUNT SINAI NO LONGER FUNCTIONED.

Ref: Talmud — Mas. Rosh HaShana 20b

Avodah Zarah 3a Footnote

The cycle of Tammuz' which lasts from 21st June to 22nd September. The Jewish Calendar, while being lunar, takes cognisance of the solar system, to which it is adjusted at the end of every cycle of nineteen years. For ritual purposes, the four Tekufoth are calculated according to the solar system, each being equal to one fourth of 365 days, viz. 91 days, 7 1/2 hours. T. of Nisan, (vernal Equinox) begins March 21; T. of Tammuz (Summer Solstice), June 21; T. of Tishri (Autumnal Equinox). Sept. 23; T. of Tebeth (Winter Solstice) Dec. 22.(19) Ps. II, 3.

4) A method of determining the beginning and ending of Sabbath.
5) The dates on which holidays started and ended and what to do on these holidays.
6) The official canonization of the Tenach, the Jewish Scriptures (Old Testament).
7) The Bihrkat HaMinim—The prayer known as the Shmoneh Esreh, the eighteen benedictions; the Amidah, which is said on the Sabbath and constitutes some of the essentials of the Jewish faith; a nineteenth benediction, known as the Birkhat HaMinim, the curse against the heretics (those Jews who do not follow the beliefs and practices of the rabbis; to be applied to the Messianic Jews of that day).

Are these eighteen really nineteen? — R. Levi said: The benediction relating to the Minim18 was instituted in Jabneh.19 To what was it meant to correspond? — R. Levi said: On the view of R. Hillel the son of R. Samuel b. Nahmani,20 to The God of Glory thundereth;21 on the view of R. Joseph, to the word 'One'22 in the Shema'; on the view of R. Tanhum quoting R. Joshua b. Levi, to the little vertebrae in the spinal column.

The Birkhat HaMinim was originally composed around AD 90. Hebrews who believed in *Yeshua* were considered to be under a curse and had to be removed from the community. With this new proclamation, the New Covenant faith shared by both Hebrews and gentiles was now diametrically opposed to the new Rabbinic Judaism that was adopted at Yavneh, AD 158. What stage of infection would you think these people were in?

After the Bar Kokhba revolt against Rome failed in AD 135, Jews were banned from living in Judea. The traditions of the oral law completely overshadowed the teaching of Moses, including the meanings and purposes of the feasts. The "Yavneh rewrite" went as far as to create a completely different Day of Atonement, the most holy of all days and a new date for the New Year. The Pharisees moved Rosh Hashanah (the New Year) from the first month to the seventh month because one of their rabbis had a "revelation from God." The infection is in total control of the brain and the religion.

Here is another record from the Talmud showing the Rabbinical Jews' refusal to listen to any view outside their own, referred to as *The Oven of Aknai*:

...and this was the oven of 'Aknai.1 Why [the oven of] 'Aknai? — Said Rab Judah in Samuel's name: [It means] that they encompassed it with arguments as a snake, and proved it unclean. It has been taught: On that day R. Eliezer brought forward every imaginable argument , but they did not accept them. Said he to them: 'If the halachah agrees with me, let this carob-tree prove it!' Thereupon the carob-tree was torn a hundred cubits out of its place — others affirm, four hundred cubits. 'No proof can be brought from a carob-tree,' they retorted. Again he said to them: 'If the halachah agrees with me, let the stream of water prove it!' Whereupon the stream of water flowed backwards — 'No proof can be brought from a stream of water,' they rejoined. Again he urged: 'If the halachah agrees with me, let the walls of the schoolhouse prove it,' whereupon the walls inclined to fall. But R. Joshua rebuked them, saying: 'When scholars are engaged in a halachic dispute, what have ye to interfere?' Hence they did not fall, in honour of R. Joshua, nor did they resume the upright, in honour of R. Eliezer; and they are still standing thus inclined. Again he said to them: 'If the halachah agrees with me, let it be proved from Heaven!' Whereupon a Heavenly Voice cried out: 'Why do ye dispute with R. Eliezer, seeing that in all matters the halachah agrees with him!' But R. Joshua arose and exclaimed: '**It is not in heaven**.' What did he mean by this? — Said R. Jeremiah: That the Torah had already been given at Mount Sinai; **we pay no attention to a Heavenly Voice, because Thou hast long since written in the Torah at Mount Sinai, After the majority must one incline.**

R. Nathan met Elijah and asked him: **What did the Holy One, Blessed be He, do in that hour? — He laughed [with joy], he replied, saying, 'My sons have defeated Me, My sons have defeated Me.**' It was said: On that day all objects which R. Eliezer had declared clean were brought and burnt in fire. Then they took a vote and excommunicated him. ....The world was then smitten: a third of the olive crop, a third of the wheat, and a third of the barley crop. Some say, the dough in women's hands swelled up. Baba Metzia 59a

Even the miracles that God performed had no effect on them. Can you feel the pain in God's heart as His children refuse to hearken to His word and even His miracles? What kind of blindness and arrogance can cause a man to fight against God, claiming he is working for God? How the infection must have blinded their minds!

This next scripture, found in Amos 8:13, is terrifying:

In that day shall the fair virgins and young men faint for thirst. 14 They that swear by the sin of Samaria, and say, Thy god, O Dan, liveth; and, The manner of Beersheba liveth; even they shall fall, and never rise up again....even they shall fall, and never rise again!

Do you realize the eternal nature of such punishment? We should pray for mercy on all who have believed and taught a lie as the truth. I believe this would include us all! Haven't we all been infected at one time or another?

The extremes the Rabbinical Jews are willing to go to is portrayed in this next quote from the book, *The Hebrew Yeshua vs. The Greek Jesus* by Nehemia Gordon, the current leader of the Karaite Movement. Below is the quote, in Hebrew, from the Talmud.

לו אמר התורה מן ואינם הואיל זקינים מצות מקיים איני אדם יאמר לא
פי על שנאמר קיים עליך גוזרים שהם מה כל אלא בני לאו ה"הקב
שנאמר גוזרין הן עלי שאף למה (א"י ז"י דברים) יורוך אשר התורה
(ג, (שלום איש) רבתי פסיקתא) (ח"כ ב"כ איוב) לך ויקם אומר ותגזור

Here is the English translation:
"No man should say: In matters such as these I will not obey the elders' commands, since such commands are not to be found in the Torah. To a man who does say such a thing, the Holy One, blessed be He, replies: No, My son! Whatever laws the elders decree for you, obey, for it is said that you are to act *According to the law which they shall teach thee* (Deut. 17:11). Even for Me they decree things, as is said *Whenever thou decreest a thing, He shall obey thee. (Job22:28).*" (*Pesikta Rabbati: Discourses for Feasts, Fasts, and Special Sabbaths*, translated from the Hebrew by William G. Braude, New Haven: Yale University Press, 1968, p.60

Literal translation of last sentence (Nehemia Gordon):
"Why? Because they even impose decrees upon Me, [which I must obey], as it is written, 'You decree a command and He must obey you.' (Job 22:28)"

Contextual translation of last sentence (Nehemia Gordon): "Even I must obey their decrees, as it is written, 'You decree a command and He must obey you.' (Job 22:28)"

It is written as if God himself is saying that He must obey the rabbis! What a tragedy. How did they get to this place of such blatant abominations and heresy? Do you see how the infection works? How it affects the brain, the sight and the hearing?

To this day, all forms of modern Judaism, including Messianic Judaism, are offshoots of the Yavneh experience. Some of my Messianic brothers debate this, but while Messianic Judaism is evolving, it is still an offshoot of Rabbinic Judaism. Let me clarify this point even further. While each congregation and its leadership determines how much or how little of the rabbinic system, customs and tools it incorporates into their lives, services and traditions, the movement is evolving from Rabbinic Judaism and the Yavneh doctrines.

So, is Rabbinic Judaism the biblical religion that God put in place? Absolutely not! No matter which sect or branch of Rabbinic Judaism you choose—Orthodox, Conservative, or Reform— none reflect or contain enough biblical tradition to be called biblical. It is a full-blown religious epidemic.

CRUCIAL POINT: *Karaite Jews, claiming the Sadducee lineage, (they may be rabbinical in origin) are the closest Jewish sect to practice what could be called "Biblical Judaism."*

HISTORICAL FACT: Rabbinic Judaism is not now, nor will ever be, "the religion" of the Jewish people or of the State of Israel. While the majority of Rabbinic Judaism's adherents are ethnically Hebrew, the vast majority of Jewish (Hebrew) people are referred to as secular Jews, having no religious affiliation at all.

REVIEW:
Changes Instituted by Rabbinic Judaism

In Nehemia Gordon's book *The Hebrew Yeshua vs. The Greek Jesus*, Gordon summarizes the five major points of Rabbinic Judaism as **The Five Iniquities:**

> 1. The Two Torahs (Written & Oral)
> 2. The Authority of the Rabbi
> 3. The Irrational Interpretation
> 4. The Traditions of Men
> 5. Man-Made Laws

The following are the most blatant examples of rabbinical revisionism that I see. I call them, **The Seven Steps Away From God.**

1. Rabbinic Judaism created and esteemed the oral law as though given by God, claiming that:
    A. The oral law preceded the written law.
    B. The oral law gives the true interpretation of the written law when in fact Rabbinic Judaism violated Torah by adding to it.

> Consider the following passage in Deuteronomy 4:2: *Ye shall not add unto the word which I command you, neither shall ye diminish* aught *from it, that ye may keep the commandments of the LORD your God which I command you.*

2. The infected Pharisees created a new sect and then a new religion, calling it Rabbinic Judaism.

> Awhile back, I asked a Bible class the question, "What name did God give the religion that He created on Mount Sinai?" After a few wrong answers, including Judaism, I finally told them,

"Nothing! He did not give it a name!" Then I asked, "When *Yeshua* (Jesus) told His disciples to go into all the world and preach the gospel, what name did He tell them to do all of this under? What were they to call this new religion?" The answer again: *Nothing!*

Isn't that just like God?

Judaism was created by Jews without a temple. Christianity was created by a group of gentiles looking for acceptance outside the Jewish constraints and stigma of their time. Even though they didn't technically name themselves, that's what the religious infection became known by.

Now, I realize that everyone wants to be called something so that others will know how to relate to them and vice versa, but my point is there is no "authorized version" of God's true religion on the planet. There never has been, from the Garden of Eden until today. Why? Because God doesn't need or want a religion to represent Him. He wants a personal relationship with you!

When men get involved in religion, they invariably do the same things with it: they use it as a more predictable, formulaic replacement for actual communication with God (which can be kind of messy and inconvenient) or they end up corrupting it or using it to manipulate people. To this author, it seems pretty clear that every man is required to have that personal relationship with God. The only *membership* that will count for eternity will be membership in His body.

3. **Rabbinic Judaism compiled the writings of various rabbis, creating the traditions and teachings of men we see condemned in the New Testament:**
   A. Rabbinical traditions which replace Biblical ones.
   B. The "Kosher Rules" from their own imaginations.
   C. New additions to the oral law which continue to this very day.
   > *Whatsoever thing I command you, observe to do it: thou shalt not add thereto, nor diminish from it (Is God repeating Himself?) Deu. 12:32.*

4. **Rabbinic Judaism redefined the role of the teachers, or *rabbis*, and gave them total authority to control everything—including God. In essence, the rabbis replaced the priesthood.**

5. **Rabbinic Judaism redefined <u>sin</u> and <u>atonement</u>.** They set the standards and they substituted the blood sacrifices for good deeds. This allowed additional control and manipulation of the people. The infection is now an epidemic!

CRUCIAL POINT: *Rabbinic, Messianic, and even Karaite Jews, all over the world continually transgress the Torah and celebrate a pagan, rabbinic Passover Seder—without a lamb. There are wonderful stories and even some good traditions involved, but it's still not a biblical Passover.*

---

6. **With this new authority, Rabbinic Judaism changed the Feasts of the Lord into rabbinical heresy by:**
   A. Adding their own rules to everything, including the Sabbath, where now it's a sin to push an elevator button or answer a phone.

    B. Removing the Lamb from Passover and adding an egg.

    C. Changing Rosh Hashanah (New Year) from the first day of Nisan to the first of Tishri, completely ignoring the biblical date. They celebrate Rosh Hashanah on the Feast of Trumpets. (Jews now have a *Civil* and *Religious* New Year but rarely celebrate the biblical one.)

    D. Changing the Day of Atonement into Babylon heresy. They created the Ten Days of Awe, the "Three Books" and the works one must perform to be kept out of the "Book of Death." They also created the concept of purgatory, which Roman Catholics have since refined.

7. Rabbinic Judaism redefined God. With all the corrupt changes that were made in direct conflict with biblical mandates and precedents, to me the worst thing of all was **the redefining of GOD HIMSELF**. Rabbinic Judaism *changed the Lord and Creator of the Universe into a rabbinical puppet who must now do whatever the rabbis agree on.* What stage of infection do you have to be in to do this? What have they done here? Did they, in essence, murder God by re-creating Him? How does it compare to the murder of mankind? This represents the tip of the iceberg of all the rabbinical changes made.

So Where Did Rabbinic Judaism Come From?

The Pharisees of the Babylon captivity had rejected the Covenant of YHWH as presented by Moses. Having had their system uprooted once, they decided to create a more secure religious system that didn't need the Temple, the Levitical system or even God himself.

This Babylonian Religion began its movement toward Israel in the two centuries preceding the ministry of *Yeshua* (Jesus). The infected Israelites rejected both the New Covenant of YHWH and the Lamb that could take away their sins. After Jerusalem and the temple were leveled in the midst of the failed Bar Kokhba revolt, a group of frightened, persecuted Jewish leaders had had enough of the crazy Messianic movement going on in their synagogues. Blinded by YHWH and infected with confusion, fear, and hate, they gathered in secret place called Yavneh.

The Sadducees, displaced without the Temple, succumbed to the arguments of the Babylonian Pharisees. These men created and formalized a structure for the teachings from Babylon. This Babylonian teaching stated that the Oral Law, or "Oral Torah," known as the Mishnah (which they created), superseded and interpreted the written Torah of Moses. In doing so they decreed themselves to be superior to God Himself. (They did not have to obey God. God had to obey them and their new rules.) In essence, they decreed themselves to be anti-The God of Abraham and anti-The Covenant issued to them through Moses and *Yeshua* (Jesus). They have rejected all of YHWH's Covenants, and therefore are a manufactured religion without the authority of a divine covenant.

They called themselves Rabbinic Judaism.

With just this list of sacrilege, I think it is easy to see why I said in the introduction: ***"Rabbinic Judaism is not a Biblical religion in an apostate condition, it is a man-made religion from Babylon."*** It is only passing itself off as the "evolved" religion of the descendants of Abraham, Isaac, and Jacob.

A Thought and Question for Rabbinic Jews

With the many issues that have been laid out, you might wonder if I have a personal axe to grind. Am I angry with my rabbinic brothers and sisters? Not at all! I live in a small town with less than ten known Jewish people. Except for one lady, they are mostly widows in their seventies and eighties. After their rabbi, the aforementioned Rabbi Joseph, died, there was no one else to conduct services. (By the way, Rabbi Joseph's funeral was conducted by his son, himself a rabbi, and three pastors from the largest Baptist and Church of Christ churches in our town. He was the most widely respected rabbi I've ever met.) I wanted to be a blessing to these sweet ladies in some way and thus honor the memory of Rabbi Joseph. Therefore I began to conduct the traditional Rabbinical Jewish services in the same synagogue in which Rabbi Joseph taught me and I continued to help there for years.

I am no man's judge, and will not allow myself to condemn anyone for what they have been taught, or for the way in which they perceive and worship God. I love my Jewish brothers and sisters and consider it *my blessing* to fellowship and worship with them. While they know what I believe, I neither debate nor try to convince anyone of anything; that I leave to the Holy Spirit. They have all asked me questions privately, questions which I answer unashamedly.

But where is the Hebrew outcry at the hijacking of their faith?

While the religious Epidemic has robbed us all, I believe that the Hebrew people have been robbed of more godly heritage than any other people, or religion. The Creator of heaven and earth chose *them* as a people to be the liaison between Himself and the rest of the world. Unto *them* were the covenants and oracles of God given, that all men might be able to become the "Children of God!" Unto *them* God revealed Himself, reaching out with open arms to embrace them and offering to make *them* a Holy Nation.

While the Hebrews of old were guilty of all types of sin and affronts to God, it is the rabbinical religious system that continues to rob the Hebrew children of their relationship with their godly heritage.

There are many Hebrews today who love God and are seeking to please and obey the God of Abraham, like Rabbi Ernest Joseph. Yet they have so much more to sift through and overcome because of the deceptions of the rabbinical system. The rabbinical religious system is still doing all it can to keep the chosen people blinded.

Rabbi Meir Kahane is another great example of those who want to please God. In his book, *Forty Years*, Rabbi Kahane forcefully and clearly admonishes the Hebrew people to a true faith in their God and blows the trumpet of righteousness, calling the people back to obeying the commandments of the Almighty. He points the finger of responsibility for the Jewish persecutions back at the Hebrews who have abandoned their God and His ways.

Here's a quote from his book, which I highly recommend to all:

[Forty Years, pg. 18]:

How the Almighty pleads with us, His children, to accept all that He
so desires to give us! How the Messiah beats on the doors, how his
footsteps pound on the street! How the Almighty's voice cries
out: "Return unto Me, saith the L-rd of Hosts, and I will
return unto you." (Zechariah 1). Swiftly, gloriously, today,
this very moment!

   "Today, if you but hearken to My voice." (Psalms 95).

   Dear Jew, the Almighty gives us this day life or death. Will
we not choose life?

   Will we have the wisdom to understand, the eyes to see, the
desire to *wish* to see? Will we understand that only the embracing
of total faith and trust in the Almighty will bring the redemption, a
faith that is symbolized by the Manna He once again will feed us?
Will we see the Messiah and act and not allow him to be concealed
again? Will we manifest and prove our faith in the only possible
way - actions, terribly difficult, sometimes terribly dangerous?
Actions that stand up to the gentile without the slightest fear for his
irrelevance; actions that hold onto the Land of Israel, that drive
out the Arab, that cleanse the Temple Mount, that leave the impurity
and curse of the Exile and return home. These are the stuff of which
Jewish faith is made. This is what the Almighty seeks as the forty
years tick away.

Final paragraph in the book:

Will we move forward to greet Moshiach [Messiah] or run
backwards into another vicious cycle of Exile which might over
surpass the former Exiles in its fury and intensity? G-d has given
us free choice. It is in our hands whether we choose death or life
- to continue to mock His name or to follow His commandments and
to bring true peace and security to The Land, ushering in The
Final Redemption that He promised to deliver if we follow in His
commandments.

While Rabbi Kahane's premise is not the same as mine, I
believe the intent is. His heart is broken because his beloved
people are not serving the God of their fathers. (Rabbi
Kahane has not been given this manuscript and I am not
implying that he has in any way approved of the teaching(s)
in this book. I am simply sharing an example of others who
are calling for a return to the faith and teachings of God.)

Can you see the difference? While there are many wonderful Hebrew men, women and even rabbis, the rabbinical religious system and its teachings are completely infected and corrupt. Please pray for the restored sight of the precious Hebrew people so that the examination of all unbiblical traditions would result in a return to God's ways.

Finally, I am aware of how completely unworthy I am of any revealed truth that the Holy Spirit would choose to so graciously bestow upon me. I am unable to elevate my position over anyone else. *Romans 14:4: Who art thou that judgest another man's servant?* Without the light and the mercy of God, I too, am subject to the same infections.

CRUCIAL POINT: *Adam, Cain, Noah, Abraham, Isaac, Jacob, Moses, David and most of the Prophets walked with God. How many rabbis are recorded to have walked with God? From Babylon to Israel, from Hillel to today, where is it recorded that even ONE rabbi walked with God? Where do they teach that we can walk with God?*

If you are a Rabbinic Jew, may I suggest a simple quest? Reread the section *Review: What did Rabbinic Judaism Change?* Take it to the Almighty and ask Him to reveal His truth to you. Ask Him if what I have written is a pack of malicious lies designed to lead you astray, or if it could possibly be the truth that can set you free. The Spirit of the Almighty is as powerful today as it was when the Red Sea was parted. Let the Spirit of the living G-D speak to your heart, and then do whatever He tells you to do. Ultimately, it is Him you will stand before and give account. It is Him alone you must please and obey.

A Thought and Question for Agnostic Jews

Many of my Jewish brothers and sisters have a hard time believing in the existence of God at all. Some were either survivors of the holocaust or are descendants of survivors. I've heard statements like, "If there was a God, He hates us! If there was a God, He couldn't, or wouldn't, let this happen to us." There is another group of Jews that came to a different conclusion stated this way: "God either could have saved us and didn't, or we've overestimated His ability. He knew about the holocaust but didn't have the power to help us." In this, they redefined how God exists *again* and reduced Him to a powerless and helpless entity. What they did not examine was their own lives, the infection they were still spreading and the path they had taken.

As concerning the holocaust, let me share something that is not widely taught today. There were *many* from Europe to Russia who told the Jews not to leave but to stay. It is well documented and many of the older Jews know it's true. But, you don't hear these older Jews out shouting, "It was our rabbis who got many of us killed!" No, that wouldn't be acceptable or popular, but, sadly, it is true. It certainly doesn't begin to absolve the Nazis for what they did, nor make it any less inhumane, but *ALL* the facts should be taught for a complete and balanced history lesson.

Let me ask you to review the entire Holy Scriptures from the Torah to the Prophets. You will notice a repetitive theme throughout. Every time the Jews disobeyed God the same scenario took place: in comes a conquering army, the children of Israel are slaughtered and the survivors are dragged off as slaves. This is the same thing that happened in AD 70 but it was the last time the nation was dealt with until the twentieth century. Remember the prophecy in Hosea 6:1: *Come, and let us return unto the LORD... 2 After two days will he revive us: in the third day he will raise us up, and we shall live in his sight...* Despite the predictable patterns of ancient Israel, we see God being ever faithful to His Holy Word and to His chosen people.

The reality is God is restoring the nation of Israel and He is restoring the seed of Abraham. His promises are to a thousand generations and they will be fulfilled. You are living in a day where you don't have to cry out *Show me a sign!* – they are all around you. There is a reason why 300 million Arabs that live in the region can't drive out 6 million Jews. God loves you and wants to hold you in His arms and restore your faith in Him. If you will reach out to Him, He will reach out to you. Get alone and call out to Him. Ask Him to reveal Himself and His purposes personally to you. He will! Relationships take time to build, so be patient and you will be rewarded beyond your dreams.

A Thought and Question for Christians

So, what should the Christian response to Rabbinic Judaism be?

> *For thus saith the LORD of hosts; After the glory hath he sent me unto the nations which spoiled you:* **for he that toucheth you toucheth the apple of his eye.** *9 For, behold, I will shake mine hand upon them, and they shall be a spoil to their servants: and ye shall know that the LORD of hosts hath sent me. 10 Sing and rejoice, O daughter of Zion: for, lo, I come, and I will dwell in the midst of thee, saith the LORD. 11 And many nations shall be joined to the LORD in that day, and shall be my people: and* **I will dwell in the midst of thee,** *and thou shalt know that the LORD of hosts hath sent me unto thee. 12 And* **the LORD shall inherit Judah his**

portion in the holy land, and shall choose Jerusalem again (Zec 2:8-12).

The physical descendants of Abraham are the "apple of His eye." It is a dangerous thing to lift a hand against them. We are commanded to pray for the peace of Jerusalem, and there is a blessing of prosperity for those who love Israel.

Pray for the peace of Jerusalem: they shall prosper that love thee (Psa 122:6).

For if the casting away of them be the reconciling of the world, what shall the receiving of them be, but life from the dead (Rom 11:15)?

*For I would not, brethren, that ye should be ignorant of this mystery, lest ye should be wise in your own conceits; that blindness in part is happened to Israel, until the fulness of the Gentiles be come in. 26 And so all Israel shall be saved: as it is written, There shall come out of Sion the Deliverer, and shall turn away ungodliness from Jacob: 27 For this is my covenant unto them, when I shall take away their sins. 28 As concerning the gospel, they are enemies for your sakes: but as touching the election, **they are beloved for the fathers' sakes**. 29 For the gifts and calling of God are without repentance (Rom 11:25-29).*

CRUCIAL POINT: The majority of men and women who are raised in Judaism are sincere, passionate, wonderful people and are far removed from the devious plot that created this religion 2,000 years ago. Even then, it was the enemy using people blinded by the infection to deceive the world.

Some Final Thoughts

It is painful to see all the sects of Judaism — the blinded, infected people and the horrible bondage each group goes through trying to be better than the other. The rabbis of their time create new traditions for each sect and then lock that group into time warps. Their hats, and each piece of clothing becomes a ritual with more and more bondage attached. To this day, many Orthodox Jewish women are still required to shave their heads and wear wigs. Many sects are forced to intermarry, causing the health of the overall community to suffer. The epidemic spreads. The infection takes its toll. It is a heartbreaking situation.

Ironically, in spite of these facts, Rabbinic Judaism is the tool that God has clearly used to keep the Jews together for the last two thousand years. Without Rabbinic Judaism, there would have been no Jewish culture or Hebrew language with which to rebuild Israel. While I don't understand why, God knew!

How Do We Respond To All This Information?

All of the historic information supplied in this work is compiled not in anger, hate, or arrogance, but in love. It especially is not intended to be used in a condescending manner towards anyone.

For we wrestle not against flesh and blood, but against the principalities, against powers, against the rulers of the darkness of this world, against spiritual wickedness in high places (Eph 6:12).

In other words, the Devil. The Devil is our only real enemy. This information is given as an injection of truth that should set you free. Should it cause you to feel smarter or better than anyone else, then you have made it a yoke of pride and arrogance around your neck, which is only another type of infection. The Lord despises the haughty. When we receive any truth, it should render us humble, not arrogant. Should we become arrogant, it will be the last truth we receive until we repent. Make sure your heart is clean before the Lord; let no seed of the enemy be planted, or religious infections spread into your mind!

A PRAYER FOR US ALL TO PRAY

Father in heaven, help us to love your children, Israel. We pray for the peace of Jerusalem and for the salvation of the house of Israel and the house of Judah. If my lips have spoken against her, forgive me. If my deeds have been against the seed of Abraham, forgive me. I pray for mercy for Israel and myself. Help me to be a light and a beacon to Israel. Lord, please have mercy and open their eyes to Your Deliverer, Your truths, and Your ways. Lord, wipe out the infection that so easily blinds us, even today. Help me to be a blessing to Israel and not a curse. Amen!

PART 4

CHRISTIAN INCUBATION ERA I
AD 33 - 320

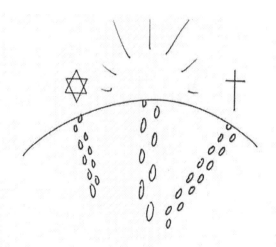

CHRISTIANITY INFECTION

THE GENTILE OUTBREAK: AD 33—320

Note on References: Parts 4 & 5 will no doubt be counted among the most controversial parts to this work, especially to the non-Jewish world. Fortunately, with the internet resources available today, references and statements can be verified immediately. I give several relevant web addresses at the end of this chapter, but please be aware that in time some addresses may change. In the event they do, may I suggest you do an internet search for the specific topic, person, or document you are seeking to verify. Please remember, the "internet highway" is filled with all types of deception and infection, so always use credible sources to do your verifications, such as university and historically established libraries.

All of the creeds, along with the works of Eusebius and Early Church Fathers like Socrates, are available through major university web sites such as Wheaton College and Oxford University, as well as www.earlychristianwritings.com. The sequential timeline can be verified through online encyclopedias and many historical societies.

A Glimpse of the First Three Centuries

After you examine the history and evolution of Judaism and Christianity and are able to get a bird's eye view of the world with a mental timeline, you will see an important pattern emerge. The infection, after incubating awhile, starts shape in an utterly diabolical plot that begins to reveal itself somewhere around 200 BC. From Babylon, a group of exiled Jewish leaders develop a religious paradigm that will become known as the Pharisaical movement, and eventually devolve into Rabbinic Judaism. During the same window of time somewhere among the Greeks, Gnosticism is birthed. Babylon invades Israel (then Judea) from the East while

Gnosticism invades the Believer-Disciples movement from the West. It was a spiritually orchestrated "perfect storm," as though an army general had planned a crisscross attack to destroy them both.

The First Century

The Believer-Disciples, who were part of early Messiah-ism, (soon to be called Christianity), had three major invasions—all in the first century—from the Pharisees, the gentiles and the Gnostics. As the apostles were still living, teaching and writing, the first two invasions were well addressed. The third was barely on the radar. It's almost as if the Gnostics were patiently infiltrating the ranks and building a support base, allowing the apostolic leadership to die off before springing a frontal attack.

Gnostics believed in a secret, esoteric knowledge that elevated those initiates who possessed it to a higher plane. Their "revelations," they taught, were as important as those of the apostles, and since these new teachings were steeped in mysticism and the occult, they presented an extremely cunning type of infection. Mixing their beliefs with early Christianity, they rapidly became a large sect among the believers. What made Gnosticism so dangerous was the timing with which it entered the scene and the methodology it incorporated. It was a masterful tool to spread the infection of syncretism within the growing community.

At the same time Messiah-ism was redefining the religion and religious practices of the believer-disciples, Rabbinic Judaism was redefining their religion for the remaining Hebrew people. Everyone was in the process of rethinking *all* their doctrines. Which parts of the Law were applicable, and which weren't? Which traditions were to be kept and which abandoned? It was during this exact time slot that Gnosticism popped up and said, "Hey, we have a revelation from God!" With Messiah-ism itself based on new revelation, it was an easy sell to many unsuspecting gentile believers. This was the same type of infection that had infiltrated the survivors of the Babylonian captivity.

Actually, you'll find that deceptive "revelations" are a favorite ploy of the evil one in general, as they can be hard to identify upfront, yet wreak a lot of long-term havoc — especially when they look close enough to the real thing to slip in unnoticed. There was a lot of plowing and sowing of new concepts and ideas taking place during this time, and that's when it's easy for tares to be sown in as well — remember, it's our enemy's job, and he's had a lot of years to perfect his strategies.

The methodology of the Gnostics was logic and mysticism. With the supernatural powers of Yeshua (Jesus) and the Jewish apostles, the supernatural was expected to be part of the equation. As the power faded, the mystics ran in and logically explained how the evolution from physical power to mystical power was the preordained, natural progress. A very large sect soon formed, and at one point became so popular that it appeared as if Gnosticism might engulf the entire movement. While many early Church fathers vigorously resisted Gnosticism, it wasn't always easy to tell which teachings were Gnostic in origin.

At the same time the Jewish apostles were proclaiming "the new covenant" in the Jewish religion, the first century saw believer-disciples explode into Eastern Europe and Northern Africa. Pharisaical doctrines and pagan religious customs were the biggest battles. Two of the early hubs for infant Church seemed to be Greece-Turkey to the north of

Israel and Alexandria (a Hellenistic center of that time) in Egypt in the southwest.

The Second Century

By the second century, the infant Church had exploded across the world, becoming less Jewish and more gentile. The Gnostics were moving many of the disciples into mysticism. This period saw the real birth of *Messiah-ism* or *Christianity,* and drastic changes were being made at foundational levels. The infection was spreading and taking on formal characteristics.

Rabbinic Judaism, with a full blown religious epidemic raging, completed its abandonment of biblical traditions, exchanging them for the Oral Law. At Yavneh, a formal proclamation was made, denouncing anyone who accepted *Yeshua* (Jesus) as his or her Messiah. It was officially declared that one could not be Jewish and "Messianic." Consequently, gentile believers and Messianic Jews in synagogues were forced to leave or be silent. This same situation is true today; synagogues of all branches have members who have accepted Yeshua (Jesus) as their personal savior and personal Messiah but must keep it to themselves. What the Yavneh proclamation did was drive the "Christians" or "Messianic believers" as they were being called, further from their Hebrew roots and created even more anti-Semitic feelings. House churches were springing up and rapidly becoming full blown churches.

While the Church was fighting for its very life from the internal infections, the Yavneh proclamation created a new monster to battle. Rabbinic Judaism, as it became known, was not the Biblical religion that Messiah-ism came from; it opposed that old-line religion of the Sadducees. The water becomes very muddy from this point forward. Now, the Christian Church had a different type of infection from the outside. To oppose Rabbinic Judaism, one was seemingly opposing the Jews themselves. I believe this is part of the problem with understanding all the roots of anti-Semitism.

As these early Christian Churches struggled for identity, clarity, truth and unity, it's very easy to judge them for their mistakes. However, in the heat of a battle, decisions must be made and—right or wrong—you have to move forward or face defeat. An attack from the outside, or struggling with a common enemy, has always been a unifying force and I see many of the early church brethren in a battle fighting the Roman Emperors, pagan religions, Gnosticism, and pious Rabbinic Jews along with everything that could be thrown at them. I doubt if we could have done nearly as good a job as they did in trying to bring order to the chaos of the times and of the early church.

It's important to note that all the first century apostles were Jewish. When they passed off the scene, it seemed there were no formal leaders of Jewish descent. Although several early Church fathers emerged, mostly gentile converts, none were giving overall direction in an apostolic fashion. Besides Gnosticism, many differing views and customs and infections from every region were rapidly being mixed into the movement.

The majority of these early church Fathers who were writing were opposing Gnosticism on one hand while trying to find a new "non-Rabbinical Jewish" direction for the vastly gentile Christian Church. Unfortunately, anti-Semitism (Anti-Rabbinic Judaism?) became the driving force of the movement in the second and third centuries. While not so obvious to today's students, nearly every work of the early church Fathers including Ignatius, Justin Martyr,

Tertullian and many others contain anti-Semitic statements and slurs, referring to them as "hypocrites" and "persecutors of our Lord."Some even escalated to encouraging violence against the Jews, allowing the flesh to quench the spirit in the heat of the battle. If your doctrine is based soundly on Scripture, why is it necessary to stir up emotional strife against anyone to sell your side of the argument? And while the early Church Fathers clearly began to focus on Rabbinical Jews, the Gnostic infection continued to creep in everywhere.

Around AD 175, when the Church was overwhelmingly gentile, Irenaeus of Lyons used the term "Catholic Church," meaning "universal" or referring to "the whole body." This was the earliest-known use of the term in reference to the Christian Church. The second century saw Rome join the hubs of Christianity along with Greece/Turkey and Alexandria.

The Third Century

By the third century, most new churches were founded by gentiles with only echoes of its Jewish lineage intact, but Messiah-ism was still considered a Jewish sect. To make matters worse, many Rabbinical Jews arrogantly referred to gentiles as "sons of whores" and "sons of dogs." This aggravated an already intense feeling of animosity toward Jews in many communities. Furthermore, because the Romans (who also considered Christianity a Jewish sect) could never truly conquer the spirit of the Jewish people, a state of unilateral hostility existed between the Jews and Christians. All of these sentiments seemed to come to a head throughout the third century.

Although the Gnostic movement began to formally die out during this time with the early Church defeating its heretical doctrines, the bad news was that Gnosticism had already impregnated the Church with many of its paradigms. When you remove the label of Gnosticism from a teaching, it's not so easy to recognize many of its tenets. Very few today could differentiate between the writings of most of the early Church Fathers and the early Gnostics, except in the obvious cases. Many have missed the Gnostic framework in the Church Fathers' writings coming out of Alexandria which — as an important Hellenistic center — also spread doctrines "under the influence" of philosophy and Hellenism, particularly through Clement of Alexandria and Origen. *The Didache* (an anonymous first or second century work also known as The Teachings of the Twelve Apostles) is one of the most quoted early documents and is laced with Gnosticism. Since so much of present day Church doctrine is based on the *Didache*, I've included the entire document with notes as an appendix to this section.

The third century saw Christianity with nearly all-gentile leadership, splintering three directions and evolving into "a religion" with more and more non-Jewish customs. The Jewishness of Christianity became one of the biggest controversies. Three different schools of thought began emerging: a Roman/Greek paradigm, which wanted to completely sever the Jewishness of Christianity; an Eastern paradigm which wanted to preserve part of it; and the Alexandrian paradigm which was much more Gnostic in philosophy and was trying to re-create it. Alexandria had been the center for mystics for centuries, and its culture embedded in Philo's mysticism and in strong Greek-Hellenistic philosophy. Humanism and Hellenism have much in common. When you start with a foundation so steeped in Gnosticism, it's easy to see where Christianity's paradigms would be rooted, and her early growth influenced.

The seeds of infection were taking root everywhere.

THE RISE OF CONSTANTINE: *The Man who Changed the World*

Was there a conspiracy to destroy the Jews and to abduct Christianity?

With each new Roman emperor, persecution of Jews and Christians came and went. Some emperors tolerated them, others tried to wipe them from the face of the earth. As the fourth century opened, the worst of the persecutions began, coinciding with the entrance of young Constantine.

As you go through this next section, realize that Constantine single-handedly instituted more worldwide changes than any other Roman emperor before or after him. Many were conquering rulers, but no other Roman emperor accomplished social and religious changes that are still practiced to this day. While Constantine was a great warrior and an extremely violent man, his real genius was two-fold—his understanding of human psychology and his ability to take existing conditions and making them work in his favor. He didn't "create" new things as much as he reinterpreted and reinstated others' paradigms, folding cultural norms into his way of thinking. By making a few adjustments at very precise times he was able to make men of passion and character bend to his vision, which always seemed to be good for everyone.

From history's sixth day when man was created until today, individuals who truly changed the entire world have been few and far between. Some of them include Adam, Noah, Abraham, Moses, and *Yeshua* (Jesus). Now, as unlikely as it may seem, we must add Constantine, Emperor of the Roman Empire. Constantine affected history in a way that was every bit as unique and far-reaching as the others;

he changed forever the way the gentile world would look at the God of Abraham.

Chronological History of Constantine

In the years immediately following AD 300, the Church was suffering one of the worst periods of persecution in her history. The Emperor Diocletian — who seemed to have a craving for Christian blood — burned churches, murdered pastors and Christians, burned every text that could be found, and confiscated the properties of churches and anyone known to be a Christian. For believers in that "Jewish Messiah," *Yeshua* (Jesus), it was the darkest day ever.

In 312, the Roman Empire was divided into three parts: western, central and eastern. Constantine inherited the western part when his father died. The central empire, which included Rome, was ruled by Maxentius, Constantine's wife's brother. Maxentius had driven his father, Maximian, off the throne and into exile. The Eastern Empire was ruled by Constantine's sister's husband, Licinius.

Constantine's Youth and Early Reign

Flavius Valerius Constantinus, the son of Constantius Chlorus and Helena, is thought to have been born in Naissus, Serbia, on February 27, AD 272 or 273. When Constantius became Caesar, or emperor, in AD 293, he sent Constantine to the Emperor Galerius as hostage for his own good behavior. Constantine escaped in AD 305, returned to his father, and was at his side in Britain on July 25, AD 306 when his father died. The army then raised Constantine to the throne as ruler of the western empire, and a woman named Minervina bore him a son whom he called Crispus. The period between AD 306 and 324 was a period of continuous civil war.

In AD 307 Constantine married Fausta, daughter of Maximian, who was then Emperor of the central empire. At that time, Constantine was a known worshipper of Apollo, the sun god (also known as Mithra). In AD 310, Constantine gave shelter to his father-in-law Maximian after his son chased him off the central throne. When Constantine learned that Maximian was conspiring to overthrow him, he gave his father-in-law a choice: execution or suicide with his own sword. Falling on one's sword was considered an honorable way to die, and Maximian chose that option.

Constantine then prepared to do battle with his brother-in-law for the central empire. On the evening of October 27, AD 312, while preparing for the battle of Rome, Constantine supposedly saw a vision in the heavens outside the city. Eusebius tells us that Constantine and his army saw a cross of light in the sky with the Greek inscription *en toutō nika (by this, be victorious!)* which was later passed down in the Latin version: *in hoc signo vinces (in this sign you shall conquer).*

A second historian, Lactantius, argues that the emperor had a dream in which he saw the chi-rho symbol, and was directed to have the *signum dei (sign of God)* inscribed on his soldiers' shields. Mort. Pers. F. Heilland ("Die Astronomische Deutung der Vision Kaiser Konstantins," in Sondervortrag im Zeiss-Planatarium-Jena, [Jena, 1948], 1ff), argued that the latter account represents the true course of events because the emperor saw a conjunction of the planets Mars, Saturn, Jupiter, and Venus in the constellations Capricorn and Sagittarius. This astronomic event, which was extremely negative astrologically, would have undermined the morale of Constantine's mainly pagan army. Always the strategist, the emperor decided to convert the sign into a positive force that would be useful to him. (DiMaio, Zeuge, Zotov, Byzantion, 58[1988], 341ff).

Most encyclopedia accounts of Constantine's reign assert that he was the first Christian emperor of Rome. Some theological institutions claim that Constantine became a Christian on the very night when the "divine sign," or Signum Dei, appeared. As a matter of historical record, it was not a cross that Constantine saw; it was a giant "P" formed by the alignment of the planets. Other planets formed a line across the bottom end of the P. Historians tell us that astrologers considered the entire formation a bad omen, but Constantine put a different spin on it. He told his troops that it was a vision, and that he had been told to put the sign on their helmets and shields. He said that doing this would guarantee victory in the morning.

The giant P is in all of the record books for anyone to see. The Roman Catholic Church decided that what he saw was actually the first two letters of "Jesus" in Greek, "P" and "X" *(A pagan Roman sees Greek letters that refer to a Jewish Messiah? Hmmm...).* For the record, subsequent events of Constantine's life radically refute the notion that Constantine converted to Christianity. If he did, it was probably not until a few days before his death when he also was baptized (a common custom of the times).

On October 28, AD 312, the morning after the visionary incident, Constantine's army painted the "P" on their helmets and shields, and went on to a great victory over Constantine's brother-in-law, Emperor Maxentius, at the Battle of Milvian Bridge. Maxentius drowned in the Tiber during the battle, and Constantine, "the newly converted

Christian," ordered the dead emperor's head to be impaled on a pike and carried through the streets of Rome.

Constantine attributed his victory to the sign and refused to sacrifice at the temple of Jupiter, the standard practice of victorious emperors. His adoption of the celestial sign in October AD 312 was initially an act of political expediency. In fact, Constantine never declared which deity gave him the sign. Following his victory, he allowed himself to be called *Pontifex Maximus,* or "Great Father," essentially making himself a god. He immediately had a statue of himself holding the *Labarum* (Chi/Rho symbol) built and placed in a temple. The inscription on the statue read, "By virtue of this salutary sign, which is the true symbol of valor, I have preserved and liberated your city from the yoke of tyranny." Again, no reference to a conversion or praise to the deity who brought his great victory to pass; it was all about what he did. He had coins minted with his image over a blazing sun. Other coins featured the sun god Apollo on one side and "IHS" (In This Sign I conquer) on the other. Does all this sound like he had a conversion experience?

Constantine did immediately stop all persecution of Christians, the right and proper thing for a Christian to do. But it was not about Christianity — he stopped persecution of any and all religions in the western and central empire, which he now ruled.

In February, AD 313, three months after Constantine's "conversion," Constantine and Licinius introduced the historic Edict of Milan. This decree granted all religions, including Christians, the freedom to practice their faith without any interference from the state. Many theologians claim this was a Christian declaration, but in fact it was a declaration of freedom for *all religions,* not just Christianity. Here is part one in its entirety.

EDICT OF MILAN

When I, Constantine Augustus, as well as I, Licinius Augustus, fortunately met near Mediolanurn (Milan), and were considering everything that pertained to the public welfare and security, we thought, among other things which we saw would be for the good of many, those regulations pertaining to the reverence of the Divinity ought certainly to be made first, so that we might grant to the Christians and others full authority to observe that religion which each preferred; whence any Divinity whatsoever in the seat of the heavens may be propitious and kindly disposed to us and all who are placed under our rule. And thus by this wholesome counsel and most upright provision we thought to arrange that no one whatsoever should be denied the opportunity to give his heart to the observance of the Christian religion, of that religion which he should think best for himself, so that the Supreme Deity, to whose worship we freely yield our hearts) may show in all things His usual favor and benevolence. Therefore, your Worship should know that it has pleased us to remove all conditions whatsoever, which were in the prescripts formerly given to you officially, concerning the Christians and now any one of these who wish to observe Christian religion may do so freely and openly, without molestation. We thought it fit to commend these things most fully to your care that you may know that we have given to those Christians free and unrestricted opportunity of religious worship. When you see that this has been granted to them by us, your Worship will know that we have also conceded to other religions the right of open and free observance of their worship for the sake of the peace of our times, that each one may have the free opportunity to worship as he pleases; this regulation is made we that we may not seem to detract from any dignity or any religion.

Part two of the edict gave direction to restore the properties of the Christians that had been confiscated. No other religion had been persecuted like Christianity had been. When you read this edict and know the history it's easy to see the political aspects of Constantine's decisions — he was very careful not to offend any group or any religion.

Yes, it did allow Christians the new-found privilege to freely worship, but it was simply a by-product of a lifting of restrictions for *all* religions and faiths. To call this a "Christian Edict" as if done by and for Christians alone is not accurate. Constantine wouldn't even address God except by vaguely referring to Him as "the Divinity." Diocletion, a particularly brutal emperor who had preceded Constantine, had issued edicts to eradicate all Christians and their properties from the earth. This edict did stop on Constantine's side of the empire, although Licinius ignored the reforms and many atrocities on his side of the empire continued.

No doubt this edict was a good thing, even a great thing, and did create a much better environment for the Christians and the Christian Church. I'm not trying to split hairs, but with all of "slanting of history" and the "politically correct" paradigms that we have to deal with it's imperative that we keep the plumb line in the middle. As you see how Constantine worked, moving the plumb line inch by inch, you will understand why it's important to completely clarify each point. I hope it doesn't come across as "straining at gnats."

If he was a Christian, why did he wait 3 months to stop the persecutions? Why would he allow them to continue at all?

CONSTANTINE STEALS CHRISTIANITY

From the time of Nero onward, life for Christians depended on the mood of the current emperor; it was either horror or peace. Many local governors learned that when Rome required higher taxes, they could take the lands and possessions of Christians and Jews, sell them for taxes, and no one in the Roman government would complain. This practice also came in handy when the locals needed extra funds for their own projects.

With the Edict of Milan, the persecution of Christians ended, Constantine acted friendly toward the Church, and Christian leaders began involving Constantine in their religious disputes. Constantine loved the attention and the feeling of importance that came with being involved in the final rulings of this religion. At the same time, he continued to give large endowments to the temple of his favorite god, Apollo/Mithra.

The empire was fragmented with many different religions and cultures. With each group having its own religious customs, the worship of any god varied greatly from one city to the next. Constantine needed something that would unify and solidify his empire.

As the first anniversary of Constantine's rule approached, bishops from North Africa petitioned him concerning a division that was developing. During past persecutions, church leaders had been ordered to turn over scriptures to the authorities. Many refused and were martyred. Others saved themselves by shrewdly denying having scriptures, or by turning in heretical essays as substitutions. When the persecutions ceased, a controversy arose over accusations against those who had "betrayed" the faith or had not been willing to be martyred. This was called the Donatist Controversy, named after one of the instigators. When the area bishops could not settle the dispute, they appealed to Constantine and met with the Bishop of Rome and eighteen other Italian bishops on October 2, AD 313. Since the meeting had been suggested by Melchiades, the Bishop of Rome, Constantine accepted the premise that councils of bishops should henceforth decide ecclesiastical issues.

At the synod of Aries on August 1, AD 314, 33 bishops met and confirmed the Council of Rome's verdict which stated in part,

> "...And since there are many who seem to fight against the law of the church and think they ought to be admitted...let them not be admitted at all, unless, as we stated above, they prove their case by the public records."

Notice that this edict declares there is a "law of the church". Where did this "law of the church" originate? Where in the New Testament was this action authorized? It was Paul who said in 1 Corinthians 6:1 that all matters of church discipline were to be performed separately from civil authorities. This edict made Church business and disciplines a recorded part of general society and civil law. Thus, soon after Emperor Constantine, supposedly a Christian, was enthroned, the Church allowed itself to be entangled with the state. By calling imperial councils of clergy and enforcing their decisions as legal decrees upon the Church, Constantine was forming a "new kingdom," a celestial Rome, an earthly government with divine power. (Hmmm, can you feel the virus moving through the ranks?)

As the church's new guardian and benefactor, Constantine received the absolute, unquestioning favor and loyalty of the Church. As imperial financial support began to flow, the institutional church appears to have been ready, willing, and able to cut an unspoken deal with the new Emperor.

In AD 314 and 316 Licinius attacked Constantine repeatedly, but was defeated each time. In AD 316, 317 and 320 (or 323), Fausta gave birth to three of Constantine's sons.

One of Constantine's new friends was a bishop named Eusebius of Caesarea. Today, the works of Eusebius are studied extensively as official early church history. While much is taught about Eusebius, there are questions that need to be addressed through this study. No doubt as their friendship evolved, Eusebius made many of the works that he read and trusted available to his friend, Constantine, to study. These probably included *the Acts of Paul, the Shepherd, the Apocalypse of Peter, the Epistle of Barnabas, the Teachings of the 12 Apostles,(the Didache) and the Apocalypse of John*, some of which are known to be Gnostic in origin. However, Eusebius thought so highly of these works that he thought they should be put right up there alongside the scriptures, just as the Rabbinic Jewish Fathers did with the Talmud. (H. E., III, xxv, 4)

Constantine began to act like a Christian, use Christian terms, and organize the fragmented Christian church. Regions were set up and archbishops were delegated. Constantine himself ended up having a bishop, Sylvester. Although he unofficially set up the bishop as the Bishop of Rome and the head bishop of the Church, Constantine was becoming the final authority in all matters.

CONSTANTINE STEALS THE SABBATH:
The Official Day of Rest

In AD 321, Constantine startled his Christian friends when he decreed Sunday to be *Deis Solis* (the day of the Sun). This day had always been an unofficial holiday in the Roman Empire, but it was not called Sunday until Constantine's decree. Constantine ordered all government agencies to be closed on Sunday, and all soldiers were to have the day off. Eusebius writes that he was *"confused about the reason for Constantine's decision; he knew the Sabbath was on Saturday."*

Constantine was supposed to be a Christian! Actually, the decision should have surprised no one. Constantine never recorded a recantation of his worship of the Sun god. He also knew the debate that had been going on in the Christian Church over the Sabbath and the Sunday "Resurrection day."

Why All the Fuss Over the Sabbath?

But this brings us to a pivotal question. *Isn't one day as good as any other?* Can't we worship on Sunday, or on any other day for that matter? And what about Romans 14:5 that speaks of esteeming one day as good as another? This is one of the most controversial and most confused doctrines we have. There are two sides of the fence, and we need to see how we got to the place of confusion to understand what we are to do about it.

To start, let's set the historical and political climate concerning the Sabbath. We have stated and restated the history of animosity between the Jews and gentiles. This also held true among many of the believers. With many of the early churches starting in synagogues and rapidly being thrust into the streets, it should have been expected.

As the debates roared over Law vs. Grace; Judaism vs. Christianity; and Saved vs. Heathen, a new concept arrived on the scene. *The Lord's Day*, historically the Sabbath, would become Sunday, commemorating the resurrection of *Yeshua* (Jesus) thus allowing the gentiles to have their own Holy Day. Without a single scripture to back up their argument, the gentiles made the decision based on logic. It supported their goals to separate themselves from the Jewish contingent. However, it was highly debated and each region of the world had either their Sabbath, or Day of the Lord, depending on the strength and influence of individual leadership of the area.

The *Didache* was at least one of the original Gnostic creators of the Sunday Sabbath and more than likely the creator of the formula used for the Trinity baptism. It was definitely a Gnostic document, was quoted by many of the Gnostic writers and Gnostic Gospels, and is one of the earliest documents from which the early church fathers quoted.

Leaders like Ignatius, Justin Martyr, Clement of Alexandria, Tertullian, Origen and other "Ante-Nicene Fathers" as the Catholic Church refers to them, taught and wrote on their beliefs concerning *The Lord's Day*, and many quoted the *Didache*. This was still being heavily debated as Constantine made his decree.

In the Beginning!

Let's start at the beginning to untangle the issue.

> *Thus the heavens and the earth were finished and all the host of them. 2 And on the seventh day God ended his work which he had made; and he rested on the seventh day from all his*

*work which he had made. 3 **And God blessed the seventh day, and sanctified it: because that in it he had rested from all his work which God created and made** (Gen. 2:1-3).*

The Sabbath was created during the very first week of Creation. It is the first recorded, official religious act and ceremony in all history. It was the way in which God wanted to be honored, as "the Creator" of earth and man. It is a memorial to Him, as Creator.

Understand this truth: **God blessed the seventh day, and sanctified it!** Is there any record anywhere stating that **God blessed and sanctified any other day?** Should this fact, alone, make us cautious about trying to transfer that blessing in our own wisdom?

Moses told the children about the Sabbath *before* they even arrived at Mount Sinai. Again, ***before*** the giving of the Law and before the Covenant of the Law:

*And he said unto them, This is that which the LORD hath said, To-morrow is the rest of the **holy sabbath** unto the LORD: bake that which ye will bake to-day, and seethe that ye will seethe; and that which remaineth over lay up for you to be kept until the morning. 24 And they laid it up till the morning, as Moses bade: and it did not stink, neither was there any worm therein. 25 And Moses said, Eat that to-day; for today is **a sabbath** unto the LORD: today ye shall not find it in the field. 26 Six days ye shall gather it; but on the seventh day, which is **the sabbath**, in it there shall be none. 27 And it came to pass, that there went out some of the people on the seventh day for to gather, and they found none. 28 And the LORD said unto Moses, How long refuse ye to keep my commandments and my laws? 29 See, for that **the LORD hath given you the sabbath**, therefore he giveth you on the* *sixth day the bread of two days; abide ye every man in his place, let no man go out of his place on the seventh day. 30* **So the people rested on the seventh day** *(Exo 16:23-39).*

Later, God adds the keeping of the Sabbath directly to the commandments and makes it a death penalty to break:

Remember the sabbath day, to keep it holy. 9 Six days shalt thou labour, and do all thy work: 10 But **the seventh day** *is* **the sabbath** *of the LORD thy God: in it thou shalt not do any work, thou, nor thy son, nor thy daughter, thy manservant, nor thy maidservant, nor thy cattle, nor thy stranger that is within thy gates: 11 For in six days the LORD made heaven and earth, the sea, and all that in them is, and rested the seventh day:* **wherefore the LORD blessed the sabbath day, and hallowed it** *(Exo 20:8-11).*

CRUCIAL POINT: Why be so severe over this "day of rest"? Because doing so directly honors the One who created the world! By keeping His day, we memorialize YHWH as THE Creator of the universe and the King above all kings.

And the LORD spake unto Moses, saying, 13 Speak thou also unto the children of Israel, saying, **Verily my sabbaths ye shall keep: for it** *is* **a sign between me and you throughout your generations; that** *ye* **may know that I am the LORD that doth sanctify you.** *14 Ye shall keep the sabbath therefore; for it is holy unto you: every one that defileth it shall surely be put to death: for whosoever doeth any work therein, that soul shall be cut off from among his people. 15 Six days may work be done;* **but in the seventh** *is* **the sabbath of rest, holy to the LORD:** *whosoever doeth* any *work in the sabbath day, he shall surely be put to death. 16 Wherefore the children of Israel shall keep the sabbath, to observe the sabbath throughout their generations, for a* **perpetual covenant. 17 It is a sign between me and the children of Israel for ever***: for in six days the LORD made heaven and earth, and on the seventh day he rested, and was refreshed (Exo 31:12-17).*

Can you grasp the power of this statement, or are you asking the usual questions associated with Sabbath-keeping: Is keeping the Sabbath really a "perpetual covenant"? What covenant? Aren't the NT believers shown honoring Sunday as the Sabbath? Is the Saturday Sabbath really a sign forever? Is it just for the Jews? If not, then who?

In answering, I first ask these questions: Are you the seed of Abraham? Have you been made an heir to the promise? Is there any way that these promises *could* apply to you? It might be worth finding out.

Six days shall work be done, but on the seventh day there shall be to you an holy day, a sabbath of rest to the LORD: whosoever doeth work therein shall be put to death. 3 Ye shall kindle no fire throughout your habitations upon the sabbath day (Exo 35:2-3).

Why would God not want any fire in their homes on the Sabbath? One reason He made this stipulation is this: if I could have fire in my house, I would tell my wife or servant to get up and cook some food for me. Someone would not get his or her Sabbath.

I've always been in awe over the reason for the first execution after the Law was given on Mount Sinai. It was only for breaking the Sabbath! Why didn't the Lord just give the culprit a good scolding? It must have been very important *back then*. I sure am glad that God has eased up on us now.

> *And while the children of Israel were in the wilderness, they found a man that gathered sticks upon the sabbath day. 33 And they that found him gathering sticks brought him unto Moses and Aaron, and unto all the congregation. 34 And they put him in ward, because it was not declared what should be done to him. 35 And the LORD said unto Moses, The man shall be surely put to death: all the congregation shall stone him with stones without the camp. 36 And all the congregation brought him without the camp, and stoned him with stones, and he died; as the LORD commanded Moses (Lev 15:32-36).*

The Christian doctrine of the Sunday Sabbath claims that the Lord's Day is Sunday because *Yeshua* (Jesus) was resurrected on Sunday, thus justifying moving the Sabbath from Saturday to Sunday. However, at *Yeshua's* (Jesus') last meeting with His followers, the night before his crucifixion, the subject of the Sabbath came up:

> *And woe unto them that are with child and to them that give suck in those days! 20 but pray ye that your flight be not in the winter, **neither on the Sabbath day** (Mat 24:19-20):*

Now surely, if *Yeshua* (Jesus) was going to change the official Sabbath from Saturday to Sunday in just three days, don't you think He would have mentioned it while He was on the subject? This would have been the ideal place to bring it up. **But, He didn't — not here or anywhere else.**

First Jerusalem Council: *Can Gentiles Be Saved?*

> *And the apostles and brethren that were in Judaea heard that the Gentiles had also received the word of God. 2 And when Peter was come up to Jerusalem, they that were of the circumcision contended with him, 3 Saying, Thou wentest in to men uncircumcised, and didst eat with them. 4 But Peter* rehearsed *the matter from the beginning, and expounded it by order unto them, saying, ...15 And as I began to speak, the Holy Ghost fell on them, as on us at the beginning. 16 Then remembered I the word of the Lord, how that he said, John indeed baptized with water; but ye shall be baptized with the Holy Ghost. 17 ·Forasmuch then as God gave them the like gift as he* did *unto us, who believed on the Lord Jesus Christ; what was I, that I could withstand God? 18 When they heard these things, they held their peace, and glorified God, saying, Then hath God also to the Gentiles granted repentance unto life (Acts 11:1-4, 15-18).*

NOTE: I refer to this meeting as the First Jerusalem Council while others refer to the meeting in Acts 15 as the first. The first Jerusalem council was held to discuss the possibility of, and the scriptural basis for, the salvation of gentiles. The purpose of the second council was completely different: to decide the specific points of the Law with which gentiles had to comply in order to remain in fellowship with believing Jews and vice-versa. Understanding the issues and the council's final response is critical.

Second Jerusalem Council: *Gentile Requirements*

> *And the apostles and elders came together for to consider of this matter. 7a And when there had been much disputing, Peter rose up, and said unto them, Men and brethren,...9*

*And put no difference between us and them, purifying their hearts by faith. 10 Now therefore **why tempt ye God, to put a yoke upon the neck of the disciples, which neither our fathers nor we were able to bear?**...13 And after they had held their peace, James answered, saying, Men and brethren, hearken unto me: 14 Simeon hath declared how God at the first did visit the Gentiles, to take out of them a people for his name.. 19 **Wherefore my sentence is, that we trouble not them, which from among the Gentiles are turned to God**: 20 But that we write unto them, **that they abstain from pollutions of idols, and** from **fornication, and** from **things strangled, and** from **blood. 21 <u>For</u> Moses of old time hath in every city them that preach him, <u>being read in the synagogues every sabbath day</u>** (Acts 15:6,7,9-10,13-14,19-21).*

The *"for"* in this sentence could be translated *"because,"* hence, the reason we only need to deal with these basic, rudimentary elements is because the apostles knew that the new gentile believers would be in the synagogues on the Sabbath learning the Torah! This *critical statement*, especially the last part of verse 21, is one that nearly every scholar ignores: *"...**being read in the synagogues every sabbath day.**"* This part of the verse raises two very important questions:

1) Why are these believing gentiles going to synagogue?
2) Why are they attending services on the biblical Sabbath, if Sunday has been established as the new Sabbath?

Here is evidence the translators did not lose or cover up. It proves that the early church was a Jewish sect that kept the original Sabbath wherever they could. Further proof includes historical records of believers fasting on the Sabbath in the second and third centuries, in countries where they could not keep the Sabbath as a day of rest. Knowing the new believers in *Yeshua* (Jesus) would be in synagogues on the Sabbath, the following was sent to the churches:

> *For it seemed good to the Holy Ghost, and to us, to lay upon you no greater burden than these necessary things; 29 That ye abstain from meats offered to idols, and from blood, and from things strangled, and from fornication: from which if ye keep yourselves, ye shall do well. Fare ye well (Acts 15: 28-29).*

We all know there are many more things than those pointed out that are sin whether committed by a Jew or gentile! No one who seeks to serve God can lie, steal or cheat. Gentile flesh must be put into subjection to the spirit just like saved Jewish flesh. There is a huge list of "thou shalt nots" and to act as if these four things is all there is would be foolish and in direct conflict with the rest of Scripture. Pray through the above scriptures and see what the Lord reveals to you.

Why Were They Counting the Sabbaths?

> *And it came to pass on **the second Sabbath** after the first, that he went through the corn fields; and his disciples plucked the ears of corn, and did eat, rubbing them in their hands. 2 And certain of the Pharisees said unto them, why do ye that which is not lawful to do **on the Sabbath** days? 3 And Jesus answering them said, Have ye not read so much as this, what David did, when himself was an hungered, and they which*

*were with him; 4 How he went into the house of God, and did take and eat the shewbread, and gave also to them that were with him; which it is not lawful to eat but for the priests alone? 5 And he said unto them, that **the Son of man is Lord also of the Sabbath** (Luke 6:1-5).*

This passage (along with Romans 14:5, 6) is used often to teach others to break the Sabbath. Let's look a little closer at the context. First, it was the second Sabbath after the Passover. Second, they didn't grow corn in Israel ("corn" should be translated "grain.") It was spring, so the only thing to eat in the fields was barley. The Pharisees had added many new commandments concerning the Sabbath, and it was a Pharisee who had asked the question. *Yeshua* (Jesus) and His disciples were not breaking *God's* Sabbath laws. They were not working for themselves or for anyone else, and they were not cooking it. As ministers, they were simply doing what all ministers of the Lord were allowed to do, which was to reach out and take enough to feed themselves.

But why were they calling it the second Sabbath? After Passover they were commanded to count seven Sabbaths until the Feast of Weeks (Pentecost) would take place. Everywhere you find a reference to a Sabbath that is counted, it's a Sabbath between Passover and Pentecost. The day after the First Sabbath, after Passover begins, is also the Feast of Firstfruits. It is also a Sabbath. This is a very special feast and the one on which the resurrection is based. More on that later.

Let's continue with the Sabbath cover up. There are several places in the King James Version of the New Testament in which references to the Sabbath were deleted from the translation but still remain in the Greek text. In the scriptures below, where you read *the first day of the week*, you will find that the Greek text reads *the first sabbath*, referring to the first Sabbath after Passover. This was a blatant, deliberate cover-up specifically aimed at hiding, in the majority of translations, the truth concerning the Sabbath. This cover-up makes an interesting study all by itself, and is just one of the problems with translations that we will examine later. Remember, when Paul wrote to Timothy that all Scripture was inspired of God, he was referring to the original manuscripts, not the subsequent translations.

> *In the end of the sabbath, as it began to dawn toward **the first day of the week**, came Mary Magdalene and the other Mary to see the sepulcher (Mat 28:1).*

> *And very early in the morning **the first day of the week**, they came unto the sepulchre at the rising of the sun (Mark 16:2).*

> *Now when Jesus was risen early **the first day of the week**, he appeared first to Mary Magdalene, out of whom he had cast seven devils (Mark 16:9).*

> *Now upon **the first day of the week**, very early in the morning, they came unto the sepulchre, bringing the spices which they had prepared, and certain others with them (Luke 24:1).*

> ***The first day of the week** cometh Mary Magdalene early, when it was yet dark, unto the sepulchre, and seeth the stone taken away from the sepulchre (John 20:1).*

> *Then the same day at evening, being **the first day of the week**, when the doors were shut where the disciples were*

assembled for fear of the Jews, came Jesus and stood in the midst, and saith unto them, Peace be unto you (John 20:19).

*And upon the **first** day of the week, when the disciples came together to break bread, Paul preached unto them, ready to depart on the morrow; and continued his speech until midnight (Acts 20:7).*

Each one of these should read ***"on the first Sabbath"***. Look it up in the Greek and see what is written. Why did they make this erroneous translation?

Acts 20:7 is the scripture most commonly quoted in support of the Sunday Sabbath. However, this next verse states it was on the "first Sabbath," which is the Feast of First-fruits. It proves that the disciples were continuing to keep the feasts, not meeting for Sunday Sabbaths.

*Upon the **first** day of the week let every one of you lay by him in store, as God hath prospered him, that there be no gatherings when I come (1 Cor. 16:2).*

This is the commandment to the church in Corinth, where Paul's message should be read as a charge: "Upon the Feast of First-fruits, prepare an offering." This is required, fulfilling part of the feast. **Once again, evidence that they were *keeping the feasts.***

It's important to realize by the time the translations were appearing that the Church, as a whole, was not keeping the Feasts or the Sabbath. So, the *first Sabbath* was translated for both; the first Saturday after Passover began, as well as for the Feast of First-fruits. That leaves us with two possibilities. The first was they didn't understand the significance of the first Sabbath. The second would be that they knew but didn't want "the common man" to have to deal with this issue. It would appear that the translators did not want the masses to have that information.

Shortly after the Council of Nicea, "the bishops" decided it would be wise to make Sunday the official Sabbath for the Church, severing another tie with the Jews and pleasing Emperor Constantine.

CRUCIAL POINT: *It was Constantine who officially ended the debate, changing the Sabbath from Saturday to Sunday. In addition, there are numerous documents written by Roman Catholic leadership taking responsibility as well. They acknowledged the Bible as unchanging on the issue while declaring they—the Catholic Church—were proving their authority over Protestant sects by the observance of Sunday Sabbath.*

Let's look at a few scriptures that seem, at first glance, to refute our position.

One man esteemeth one day above another: another esteemeth every day alike. Let every man be fully persuaded in his own mind. 6 He that regardeth the day, regardeth it unto the Lord; and he that regardeth not the day, to the Lord he doth not regard it. He that eateth, eateth to the Lord, for he giveth God thanks; and he that eateth not, to the Lord he eateth not, and giveth God thanks. (Rom 14:5,6)

What does this mean? It clearly states, *He that regardeth the day, regardeth it unto the Lord; and he that regardeth not the day, to the Lord he doth not regard it.* Taken in context, what this passage is dealing with is the weaker brethren who are babes in the Lord and just learning God's ways. It is speaking to those who are mature to not condemn our weaker and newer brethren *as they grow*. There are many pieces and parts to understanding the feasts and customs of

God, most of which gentiles don't have a clue, just like counting the Sabbaths. This passage is also telling believers not to condemn themselves over what they believe about this doctrine. This is a learning and growing process. The next scripture is another example of the complexities and what our attitude should be.

> *Let no man therefore judge you in meat, or in drink, or in respect of an holyday, or of the new moon, or **of the sabbath** days:* **17 Which are a shadow of things to come; but the body** *is* **of Christ** *(Col 2:16, 17).*

Colossians 2:16-17 is dealing with the variety of feast details. Do you know how to count the new moons and check for barley before you have your Passover lamb? Do you know how many Sabbaths are in the Feast of Unleavened Bread or Tabernacles? Did you know there were at least two Sundays a year that were Sabbaths? This passage refers to the judgment of one believer by another. Let me sum it up for you: *Stop judging and condemning each other!*

Jewish believers struggled to balance the commandments in the law, the teaching of the Pharisees and the covenant of grace. They also tried to impose their *convictions* on gentile believers. This passage in Colossians instructs us not to allow anyone to condemn us concerning our spiritual walk and understand *all the feast details and Sabbaths*. It is not referring to the weekly Sabbath doctrine. None of us are allowed to condemn anyone, including ourselves, on how we understand and practice the customs of the covenants. This is a lifetime endeavor. While that may seem liberal to some, it clearly reinforces the scriptural mandate, *"every man should work out his own salvation with fear and trembling!"*

However, the Lord never changes! He wanted the Sabbath to be a memorial of His creation the very week He created the world. When did He change His mind? He wants the memorial of His creation to be kept forever. He also knew that believers would be in countries throughout the world, and that it would be impossible for *some* to keep the Sabbath as originally set forth to those in ha Eretz (the Land). Although it is clear that His choice of day has not changed for the Sabbath, how you keep it under the New Covenant is a personal doctrine that you must work out with your Heavenly Father. It is between Him and thee, not thee and me!

Make no mistake. Constantine instituted Sunday observance in honor of his sun god, Apollo (Mithra), whom he celebrated as creator of the world at sunrise on Sunday morning. He decreed Apollo the lord of Sunday, which was a direct affront to the Jews and believers who still kept the Saturday Sabbath.

> **CRUCIAL POINT:** *With this bit of history comes one terrifying point: You can go to church any day you want, and that's okay. You can worship the Lord any day you want and that's okay. But from this point on you cannot in good conscience call Sunday The Lord's Day—unless you consider Apollo your lord. As for the God of Abraham, His day is and always has been and will be from sundown Friday to sundown Saturday. HE never changes! So...why all the fuss over the Sabbath?*

Despite popular opinion, it had nothing to do with *Yeshua* (Jesus) rising from the dead. This was Constantine's precursor to the AD 325 Council of Nicea. It also pleased the majority of the Christian leaders who already had either adapted the Gnostic teaching of Sunday Sabbath, or wanted to. It was win-win: it pleased the worshipers of Apollo, the emperor and the majority of Christian leaders while offending the Jews. What could be better?

If there is confusion in your mind, I encourage you to pray this prayer:

Heavenly Father, I ask for the Spirit of Truth to enlighten my mind as to Your will concerning my life and Your Sabbath. Allow me to know and understand the meanings of the day and how You would have me to observe it. Remove any confusion and any condemnation that may be trying to pry its way into my mind or heart. Help me to please You in all that I do and forgive me of all my failures. Let me see this subject through Your eyes rather than man's traditions and views. Amen.

Constantine Chronology *(continued)*

In AD 324 Constantine once again took arms against his last remaining rival and brother-in-law, the intensely anti-Christian Licinius. As in many other battles, Constantine's son Crispus fought gallantly for his father's cause, and Constantine's army emerged victorious. Licinius was captured, held prisoner, and eventually executed. With Licinius' power broken once and for all, Constantine was the undisputed ruler of the entire Roman world.

The sprawling empire that was now under Constantine's sole control was badly splintered. The eastern part that he had just acquired had many more Christians than the west. To bring about a unified faith, one which would serve as a religious backbone for the empire, he decided to replace paganism with Christianity. Christianity would become the official state religion, a process actually completed during the reign of Theodosius I in AD 391.

Constantine took wide-ranging steps to accomplish his new mission. He passed laws that favored Christianity. He reimbursed churches for their losses, and gave large sums of money to many bishops, making them rich men overnight. New policies favored Christians over pagans in public offices; all the more powerful and prestigious positions were given to Christians. With all of these measures, Constantine set the religious course for the future of Europe, which remains in place to this very day.

Renaming the eastern capital Constantinople after himself, Constantine decided to turn it into a government center that would rival Rome itself. In AD 324, with the help of Licinius' war chest, he undertook an extensive construction program that included churches. Because of Constantine's lavish tastes, the cost to the imperial treasury was extensive. Constantine's subjects groaned each time the emperor levied a new round of high taxes. The sixth century Greek historian Zosimus noted,

> "Constantine's taxes were so excessive that, to pay their debts, fathers were forced to hire out their daughters as prostitutes." **Zonaras** (13.4.29ff), citing Julian (Caes., 335B)

Constantine found that persuasion was not enough to forge a solid, unified faith. Harold Mattingly and B.H. Warmington summarized the religious transformation of the state by noting:

> "While ruler of the West only, where paganism was deeply entrenched, he gave much material to the Church and privileges to the clergy. After he had settled in the east where Christians were more numerous his assertion of the new religion became more emphatic. He openly rejected paganism, without persecuting its adherents, favored Christians as officials, and welcomed bishops at court. His actions in church matters were, however, his own, and designed solely to maintain the unity of the Christian Church as

essential to the unity of the Empire. " OCD,2 s.v."Constantine,"
280).

Constantine was a fox! He was a powerful politician as
well as a master of human psychology. It would obviously
be an assumption on my part, but I can see him requesting
of Eusebius and others around him, the books, scrolls and
debates among the Christian movement. After reviewing
the writings of the early Church Fathers along with the
Gnostics, all Constantine had to do was determine which
doctrines would best suit his cause and agenda and then as
opportunity presented itself, implement them.

After conquering the eastern empire, I believe he
carefully and methodically utilized his office and power to
mold and shape the trembling, unorganized religion into the
unifying factor of the multitudes.

PART 5

CHRISTIAN INCUBATION ERA II
AD 321-333

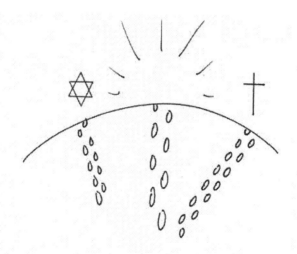

CHRISTIANITY INFECTION

CONSTANTINE STEALS GOD: *The Nicene Council*

How can anyone steal God?

It is easier than you might think, although there are some prerequisites. First, you would need to be the ruler of the entire "civilized" world. Second, you would need to control one of its major religions, especially one that has been horribly persecuted so that everything you did would seem wonderful. It would also help if your religion had evolved from a race of people (the Jews, for instance) whom the majority of the population had learned to disdain.

Once all these things were in place, stealing God would be a piece of cake. You would merely change the way you describe God. You would give Him attributes that were not His. You would change His laws and customs and teach the entire world how great your "new revelation of God" is and how wonderful your new religious customs are. It would also help if you had fits of rage and murdered those who upset you to assure you were taken seriously. And one final thing: you would finance a new Church and never admit that it came complete with a new God and a new religion. You would just convince everyone that your "new revelation" was straight from heaven and that any other view was heretical.

And so it was. *How could such a thing have happened?* you may ask. Wouldn't there be many scholars who knew the truth and would therefore not accept this false religion? Well, one might think so, and when you read *Foxe's Book of Martyrs*, you learn that there actually were many. The Roman Catholic Church, the vehicle for Constantine's religion, has murdered millions of people who refused to bow to its doctrines. This study, however, is not about

Roman Catholics and their specific history, rather it is about the evolution of Christianity as a whole, and its doctrines.

Every great movement must have an identifiable and threatening "bogeyman" to overthrow. Arius, a bishop in Alexandria (the center for mysticism), had learned a new doctrine from his teacher, *Lucian of Antioch*. Known as "the Arian doctrine," or Arianism, it stated that *Yeshua* (Jesus) was created by God; He was above the angels, but below God, thus not truly God. Arianism had been spreading in the eastern provinces of the Roman Empire from around the turn of the fourth century and was causing quite a controversy.

The following excerpts are from *Bernard Lonergran's* book, *The Way to Nicea (pg. 86-88)*. I've placed them in chronological order so you can see the evolution of Arius' doctrine:

The letter of Alexander of Alexandria, written to all the Bishops of the Church, about the year 319:

*"God was not always Father, but there **was** a time when he was not Father. The Word of God did not always exist, but was made out of nothing. For God, who is, brought into existence, out of what was non-existent, one who was non-existent, and so there was a time when he was not. For the Son is something created, something made. He is not similar to the Father in respect of substance (ousia); neither is he the true and •natural Word of the Father, nor is he the Father's true wisdom, but belongs to the things that have been made and created. He is improperly called the Word and wisdom, since he himself was made through the word of God in the proper sense, and through the wisdom that is in God, in which wisdom God made not only all other things, but him as well. Therefore, he is mutable by nature, as all rational creatures are. The Word is outside of God's substance, other than God's substance, apart from God's substance. The Son cannot tell all about the Father; for he cannot see the Father perfectly, and his knowledge of the Father is imperfect and imprecise. Indeed, the Son does not even know his own substance, as it is in itself. For it was for our sakes that he was made, so that*

through his instrumentality, as it were, God might create us; and he would not have existed, if God had not wished to bring us into being. To the question, whether it is possible that the Word of God is such that he could be changed in the way that the devil was changed, they did not draw back from answering that it is indeed possible, because, being made and created, he is by nature changeable".'

In his first letter Arius said that the Son is mutable, or changeable; later he taught that the Son is immutable.

Arius himself had earlier written to Eusebius of Nicomedia, a fellow-student of his at the school of Lucian, in the following vein:

"But what we say, and what we believe, is what we have taught, and still teach: namely that the Son is neither unbegotten nor in any way a part of the unbegotten, and neither was he made from any pre-existing matter; by the decision and counsel (of the Father) he subsisted before all ages. He is fully God, God's only-begotten Son, and he is immutable; but before he was begotten, before he was created, before he was constituted in being by the Father, he did not exist. For he was not unbegotten. They persecute us because we say that the Son has a source and a beginning, but God has not. This is why they abuse us, and also because we use the phrase 'out of nothing'; but we used this phrase because the Son is not a part of the Father, nor, on the other hand, was he made out of any pre-existing matter".

This is the final letter written by Arius in defense of his doctrine.

Arius' letter to Alexander:
"This, blessed father, is the faith that we received from our elders, and also learned from you. We acknowledge one God, who alone is unbegotten, who alone is eternal, who alone is without beginning, who alone is true, who alone is immortal, who alone is wise, who alone is good, who alone is full of power; it is he who judges all, who controls all things, who provides all things; and he is subject to no change or alteration; he is just and good; he is the God of the Law and of the Prophets and of the New Covenant:
"This one God, before all time, begot his only-begotten Son, through

whom he made the ages and the universe. He begot him not just in appearance, but in fact; by his own will he made his son to subsist and he made him unchangeable and unalterable. God's perfect creature, he is unlike any other creature; begotten, yes, but unique in the manner of his begetting:

"This offspring of God is not, as Valentinus taught, an emission of the Father; neither is he, as Mani taught, a part of the Father, consubstantial with him; neither is he the same person as the Father, as Sabellius said, dividing the unity; nor is it, as Hieracas held, as if there were one torch from another or one lamp with two parts. Neither is it true to say that he who previously existed was then begotten, or constituted as son: you yourself, blessed Father, many times, in council and in the midst of the Church, refuted those who held these views:

"But we say that he was created, by God's will, before all ages; from the Father he received being and life, and in creating him the Father conferred his own glory on him. Yet the Father, in giving all things into his possession, did not despoil himself of them: he contains all things in himself in an unbegotten way, for he is the source of all things. Therefore there are three substances (hypostases).

"But God, who is the cause of all things, is absolutely the only one who is without beginning. The son, born of the Father before all time, created and constituted in being before all ages, did not exist before he was begotten: born outside of time, generated before all else, he alone received being from the Father. He is not eternal, coeternal with the Father, nor is he, as the Father is, unbegotten; neither, as some say of things that are related to each other, does he have being simultaneously with the Father. For thus there would be two unbegotten principles. But God, as he is a unity (monas) and source of all things, so he exists before all things. Therefore he also exists before the Son, as we have heard you preach to the whole people. Inasmuch, then, as the Son has being, glory and life from the Father, in so much is God his source. He is his Lord, as being his God and existing before him.

"If some people understand the phrases from him, from the womb and I came forth from the Father and I come as implying that he is a consubstantial part of the Father, or a sort of emission, they make the Father composite, divisible and changeable; indeed God would be a body, if they had their way, and the incorporeal God would be

affected in ways in which only bodies can be affected".

These men were debating the way in which *Yeshua* (Jesus) existed. The controversy was not how the Father existed, but how *Yeshua* (Jesus) came to exist and how He fit into relationship with the Father. They were declaring the *Shema*, "Hear oh Israel, the Lord our God, the Lord is one," while trying to make sense of it rationally. Using reason to figure out spiritual truths should make us cautious. Reason is finite; its logic cannot explain spiritual mysteries.

For over 300 years following *Yeshua's* (Jesus') ascension, no group had attempted to redefine *how* God existed. Now a church-wide debate was raging over the question, "Is *Yeshua* (Jesus) God, or not?" Many important changes took place as God moved from the Old Covenant of the Law to the New Covenant of Grace. It seems strange that neither *Yeshua* (Jesus), nor the apostles who established the New Covenant addressed the questions the Church was now debating if they were important teachings of the Bible. How does God exist? Is He one, two or three? The timing couldn't have been better for the next event, which would be the most profound episode of Constantine's reign for the simple reason that it completely changed both Christianity and history.

It all began when several bishops went to Constantine to tell him that Arianism was destroying the very fabric of the empire's religion, which was Constantine's unifying force. They wanted Constantine to call an official council to stop this horror. If the bishops' intentions were good, their strategy was badly flawed. If Constantine called the council he would absorb the expenses, including royal food and lodging for the all the bishops. Under these conditions, the Church was "selling" its authority for food and lodging.

When Constantine agreed to call and finance the entire meeting, he tacked on a seemingly small item to the agenda: a new Resurrection Day would be chosen. The current Resurrection Day was celebrated on a *Jewish holiday*, the Feast of the First Fruits, the first Sabbath after the Passover. Now, Constantine hated the Jews and all things Jewish, especially their feasts. If he was going to pay for the council, he wanted a new Resurrection Day.

The Nicene Council took place in AD 325, and was attended by 318 very carefully selected delegates. After two months of debate (although the issue actually dated back to Polycarp's time and was known as the "Quartodeciman controversy" based on the Nisan 14 date) and, presumably, many wonderful meals, the council had neither settled the Arian issue nor determined the new Resurrection Day. The only result was a compromise document drafted by Eusebius, Constantine's friend. Finally, Constantine went, in person, to chair the *last* debate.

A RECORD OF CONSTANTINE'S ENTRANCE

Then the whole council, with dignified modesty, became calm, all for the first time preserved silence, awaiting the approach of the Emperor. Presently one of his most intimate friends entered, then another and another. [Then after] a certain signal, by which the arrival of the Emperor was to be announced...that all might rise, at last he came advancing along the midway, as if some celestial messenger of God, by the glittering of the purple robe verily dazzling the eyes of all, and flaming, as it were, gleaming in the sunbeams, being adorned by the utmost splendor of gold and precious stones...His height surpassed that of all who were around him...the symmetry of his form, and its elegance...the robustness being unequalled... To which personal superiority, truly wonderful in itself... proclaimed the excellence of his mind worthy of, and even above, all praise. The Emperor, coming to the head of the seats, at first stood. And a low chair, made of gold, was placed before him...after the Emperor [was seated], all the rest seated themselves."

Quite a grand entrance, wouldn't you say? The council was spellbound and mesmerized by his rock star entry; his charisma was perceived to be nearly divine. After accolades from one of the bishops, he asked if the council had reached conclusions concerning the issues of *Yeshua* (Jesus) or the new Resurrection Day. Constantine was shown the compromise draft by Eusebius, who replied that there had been no final agreement. Constantine then rose and delivered a speech that would have made a Unitarian proud:

CONSTANTINE'S SPEECH *(Excerpt)*

It was once my chief desire, dearest friends, to enjoy the spectacle of your united presence; and now that this desire is fulfilled, I feel myself bound to render thanks to God, the universal King, because, in addition to all His other benefits, He has granted me a blessing higher than all the rest, in permitting me to see you . . . all united in a common harmony of sentiment. I pray therefore that no malignant adversary may henceforth mar our happy state . . . for, in my judgment, intestine strife within the church of God is far more evil and dangerous than any kind of war or conflict; and these our differences appear to me more grievous than any outward trouble. Accordingly . . . as soon as I heard of your dissensions, I judged it to be of no secondary importance, but with the earnest desire that a remedy for this evil also might be found through my means, I immediately sent to require your presence . . . Delay not, then, … you ministers of God . . . to discard the causes of that disunion which has existed among you, and remove the perplexities of controversy by embracing the principles of peace . . ."

Constantine then reworded the decree to match his view of the Godhead. The council voted unanimously in favor, and the historic document known as the Nicene Creed was adopted and sent to all the churches.

THE NICENE CREED

I believe in one God the Father Almighty; Maker of heaven and earth, and of all things visible and invisible. And in one Lord Jesus Christ, the only-begotten Son of God, begotten of the Father before all worlds [God of God], Light of Light, very God of very God, begotten, not made, **being of one substance [essence]** with the Father; by whom all things were made; who, for us men and for our salvation, came down from heaven, and was incarnate by the Holy Ghost of the Virgin Mary, and was made man; and was crucified also for us under Pontius Pilate; He suffered and was buried; and the third day He rose again, according to the Scriptures; and ascended into heaven, and sitteth on the right hand of the Father; and He shall come again, with glory, to judge both the quick and the dead; whose kingdom shall have no end.

(This last paragraph was added in AD 381):

And [I believe] in the Holy Ghost, the Lord and Giver of Life; who proceedeth from the Father [and the Son]; who with the Father and the Son together is worshipped and glorified; who spake by the Prophets. And [I believe] in one Holy Roman Catholic and Apostolic Church. I acknowledge one Baptism for the remission of sins; and I look for the resurrection of the dead, and the life of the world to come. Amen.

Notice that the Council of Nicea did not deal with the person of the Holy Spirit, but the newly formed Roman Catholic Church came back later and added it!

How is it that Constantine—rather than one of the bishops—came up with the formula? Why did the emperor of Rome redefine how God and *Yeshua* (Jesus) exist? What was his motive? What was the intended effect of his doctrine? The answers to these questions, I think you will see, emerge from his Easter Edict. Clearly, his new doctrine of the Godhead was anti-Semitic: Constantine wanted the Jews expelled from *his* religion.

The battle was over *homoousion,* a word that many theologians say means "equaled" or "**being of one substance.**" On the surface, its usage in the Nicene Creed seems harmless enough, but the word has a much deeper meaning, and was heavily debated and contested at councils for many years to come. I will address comments from those councils later.

The true meaning of *homoousion* is "identical." *Yeshua* (Jesus) was/is *identical* to the Father. Ironically, the creed declares the words "begotten by the Father before all worlds," but then denies "begotten" in the notion of co-existence. This means that Constantine redefined not only the way in which *Yeshua* (Jesus) exists, but also stated that the Father and the Son are identical twins. When you are coequal, coeternal, co-everything, you are identical, or "homoousion."

There is not a single scripture verse or quote from *Yeshua* (Jesus) or the apostles claiming that *Yeshua* (Jesus) is "co-" anything with the Father. This is a subtle fabrication of Satan, instituted by Constantine and tolerated by the Church. Later, I will cover in detail all the references to the relationship between *Yeshua* (Jesus) and the Father.

We should realize that we are dealing here with perhaps the biggest hoax ever perpetrated on mankind, worse than all the cults and false religions that have deceitfully stolen the souls of ignorant men and women. Do you recognize the pattern? It is the same spirit that swallowed the religious Jews. Constantine had "a better revelation!"

Yet the so-called "better revelation" was just a repeat of the religion of the Babylonians, a system of rites and practices covered in detail by Alexander Hislop's book *The Two Babylons*. From the priesthood to the confessional, the duplication of religion revealed by the book is so incredible that I considered calling this book *The Three Babylons*. But our subject here is the recurring pattern in the evolution of religion, not the practices that the Roman Catholic Church shares with the religion of ancient Babylon. Again, we are not "bashing" Roman Catholicism, but the similarities are quite remarkable.

So, was Constantine successful in his goal of uniting his empire and creating a deity that the Jews could not tolerate? I would say that Constantine was very successful in both regards. The Nicene Creed established a new doctrine, which, incidentally, matched the Babylonian formula, "the Trinity, three gods in one." This created a new stumbling block for the Jews. Not only did they have to accept Yeshua (Jesus) as their redeemer and messiah, but they also had to accept Him as "identical" or "coequal" with God, their Father who told them there was no other God!

It is worth noting here that by the second and third centuries, Rabbinic Jewish teachers were instructing their followers on how to combat the Christian teaching of TWO GODS, not three. You will note the slander of the gentiles by the rabbis:

> Rabbi Hiyya bar Abba said: "If the Son of the Whore says to you, 'There are two Gods,' tell him, 'I am the one of the sea, I am the one from Sinai...'; if the Son of the Whore says to you, 'There are two Gods', tell him, 'It is not written here (Deu 5,4), the Gods spoke face to face to face (with each other), but, 'The Lord spoke with you face to face'." (Pesiqta rabb. 100b f., ed Friedmann; texts in Strack, l.c./S 10) Similar texts are quoted by Strack (l.c/S 22f and g; Mekh. on Exo 20,2 and Deu 32, 39) in which "two powers" are mentioned. Strack remarks, "I know of no such early rabbinical reference to the Trinity. The old-Rabbinic tradition saw, then, in the Christian teaching of their time "two Gods," "two powers," at work."

These are historic records, not opinions or documents manufactured to prove a point. The Jewish rabbis were teaching that Christians were spreading their doctrine of "Two Gods (The Father and the Son)." While there are several records of the Ante-Nicene Fathers dabbling with a

Trinitarian concept, including the formula for baptism in the *Didache*, there is no early record of the Trinity being taught until after the Council of Nicea.

Constantine and the gentile Christians reinvented both YHWH and Yeshua. Part of the Christian anti-Semitic propaganda is that *Yeshua* (Jesus) is *The* Messiah King! It's a lie that even He refuted. It was easy to sell; even his own disciples were confused about it, as they were waiting on a Messiah King, too. They also created the Trinity doctrine and proclaimed *Yeshua* (Jesus) coequal to YHWH. The gentiles knew this doctrine would drive the Jew even further away from the Church.

Do you remember our critically important question about Yeshua (Jesus)? "Who would concoct such a lie?" and "Why would they?"

We saw the Babylonian based Rabbinic Judaism recast the role of YHWH (God) in the Yavneh period as henceforth subservient to them, and establish the Rabbis as the new "authority on earth."

Now we see Constantine bridling the Christian Church with a completely new, non-scriptural, co-equal "Deity Team" that he fabricated. Why would he do that? What was his motivation? How did the "Church Fathers" abide such blasphemy?

Oh, I remember...only selected bishops were invited. (More as we dig though the annals of history.)

CONSTANTINE STEALS THE FEASTS:

The Easter Edict

At the Council of Nicea, Constantine declared the new Resurrection Day to coincide with the spring feast of Ishtar, the fertility goddess. Unsurprisingly, when his "suggestion" came to a vote, it passed unanimously.

Easter: The New Resurrection Day

In the Easter Edict that followed, the council commanded all churches celebrate Easter instead of the Passover. Death penalties were issued to anyone who celebrated Passover or refused to celebrate Easter. Discipline of the church body was handed over to the State. Indeed, this was a shocking turn of events. (Notice that Constantine refers to the Roman Catholic Church as if it was the only Christian Church in the empire.)

THE EASTER EDICT *(Excerpt)*

"Constantine Augustus, to the churches: Having experienced, in the flourishing state of public affairs, the greatness of divine goodness, I thought it especially incumbent upon me to endeavor that the happy multitudes of the Roman Catholic Church should preserve one faith ... When the question arose concerning the most holy day of Easter, it was decreed by common consent to be expedient, that this festival should be celebrated on the same day by all, in every place. For what can be more beautiful, what more venerable and becoming, than that this festival ... be observed by all in one and the same order, and by a certain rule. And truly, in the first place, it seemed to everyone a most unworthy thing that we should follow the custom of the Jews in the celebration of this most holy solemnity, who, polluted wretches!, having stained their hands with a nefarious crime, are justly blinded in their minds. It is fit therefore, that rejecting the practice of this people, we should perpetuate to all future ages the celebration of this rite, in a more lawful order, which we have kept from the first day of our Lord's passion even to the present times. Let us then have nothing in common with the most hostile rabble of the Jews. We have received another method from the Savior. A more lawful and proper course is open to our most holy religion. In pursuing this course with unanimous consent, let us withdraw ourselves, my much-honored brethren, from that most odious fellowship. It is indeed in the highest degree preposterous, that they should superciliously vaunt themselves, that truly without their instruction, we cannot properly observe this rite. For what can they rightly understand . . . being carried away by an unrestrained impulse wherever their inborn madness may impel them . . . Why then should we follow those who are acknowledged to labor under a grievous error, But if what I have said should not be thought sufficient . . . use every means, that the purity of your mind many not be affected be a conformity in any thing with the customs of the vilest of mankind. Besides, it should be considered that any dissension in a business of such importance, and a religious institution of so great solemnity, would be highly criminal . . . Wherefore, that a suitable reformation should take place in this respect [to keeping Easter instead of Passover] and that one rule should be followed, is the will of divine providence, as all, I think, must perceive. As it is necessary that this fault should be so amended that we have nothing in common with the usage of these parricides and murders of our Lord; and as that order is observed by all the churches of the West, as well as those of the southern and northern parts of the world, and also by some in the East, it was judged therefore to be most equitable and proper, and I pledge myself. . . that the custom which prevails with one consent in the city of Rome . . . would be gladly embraced by your prudence, considering that not only the greatest number of churches [observe Easter] . . . but also that it is most religious and equitable that we all should wish what the strictest reason seems require, and to have no fellowship with the perjury of the Jews . . . that the most holy day of Easter be celebrated on one and the same day . . . Wherefore ... it is your duty to receive and establish the arguments already stated, and the observance of the most holy day . . . and that I may rejoice with you; seeing that the cruelty of the devil is taken away by divine power, through my instrumentality ...May God preserve you, my beloved brethren."

As a footnote to all of this, Constantine even declared that if Easter did perchance fall upon the Passover weekend, it was to be postponed until the *next* weekend, making it officially impossible to celebrate the new Resurrection Day on the Feast of First-fruits, the true Resurrection Day. The practice continued until the 20th century.

Even a cursory reading of the Easter Edict makes Constantine's hatred for the Jews quite obvious. It is no wonder that Constantine didn't want Jews to celebrate the Passover, or Christians to celebrate on the true Resurrection day. But what was behind all of this? Clearly, Constantine was driving another wedge between the Jews he despised and the Church he was cultivating for himself. Let's review a few of his descriptions of Jews in the edict:

> *"It seemed to **everyone** a most **unworthy thing** that we should follow the custom of the Jews in the celebration of this most holy solemnity, who, **polluted wretches**! Having **stained their hands with a nefarious crime**, are **justly blinded in their minds.**"*

In fact, no one but Constantine was complaining about the feasts or the Resurrection day being tied to Passover. It had been discussed and had been a topic of controversy, especially back in the late second and early third Century. The debate centered around when to celebrate — on Nissan 14th or Sunday. It was not however, a hot topic at that time.

> *"Let us then have nothing in common with the **most hostile rabble of the Jews**. We have received another method from the Savior."*

Now he says "we," but it is a historical fact that he was the only one who brought this issue to the table and it was his idea alone for the solution.

> *"It is indeed in the highest degree preposterous**, that they should superciliously vaunt themselves**, that truly without their instruction, **we cannot properly observe this rite.** For what can they rightly understand . . . **being carried away by an unrestrained impulse***

> **_wherever their inborn madness may impel them_** . *Why then should we follow those who are acknowledged to labor under a grievous error?"*

Jews "vaunt themselves" and suffer from "inborn madness," Constantine declares. Surely these statements remind us of those of another era — that of Nazi Germany. Constantine lit the fuse later supported by Luther of anti-Semitism in Christianity that would burn for many centuries and lead to the general state of apathy and lack of response that marked the Church during the Holocaust.

> *"As it is necessary that this fault should be so amended that <u>we have nothing in common with the usage of **those parricides and the murderers of our Lord.**</u>"*

Given that it was a Roman governor in Jerusalem who crucified *Yeshua* (Jesus), which is stated in the Nicene Creed, it is ironic that a Roman emperor blamed the Jews for His death.

It was from this time in history that the Jews were universally branded as "Christ Killers." Yet, weren't our sins the very reason *Yeshua* (Jesus) came to earth and died? Did He not say that He laid down His life and that **no one** took it from Him? In fact, if *Yeshua* (Jesus) was deity, no man could kill Him. God would have to sacrifice His only begotten Son for us, because He was the only one who could kill Him. Now, that's food for thought. Did the Father come to the cross and sacrifice His Son after the pattern of Abraham and Isaac? If this is correct, then the responsibility for *Yeshua's* (Jesus') death belongs to God, not the Jews or the Romans.

> "But also that it is most religious and equitable that we all should wish what the strictest reason seems to require, and <u>to have no fellowship with **the perjury of the Jews."**</u>

By celebrating Resurrection Day on the Feast of First-fruits, do we indeed have fellowship with the "perjury of the Jews"? Or do we have fellowship with the Lord of the Feasts?

". . . and that I may rejoice with you; seeing that the cruelty of the devil is taken away by divine power, through my instrumentality."

History makes it painfully obvious that Constantine was an instrument of spiritual powers—unfortunately, the powers of darkness. To sum up Constantine's feelings:

"The Jews, polluted wretches, having stained their hands with a nefarious crime, are justly blinded in their minds. The most hostile rabble of the Jews, being carried away by an unrestrained impulse wherever their inborn madness may impel them, those parricides and murderers of our Lord."

Clearly, more attention was given in the Easter Edict to the hatred and rejection of the Jews than the new Resurrection Day. Sadly, there was probably no more opportune time for this to occur. It fanned the flames of a vast wave of anti-Semitism that was already sweeping the empire. Can you imagine sending this document to people who didn't despise the Jews? What would their reaction have been? Below, you can read the Nicene Decree that everyone was supposed to proclaim and that anyone "in question" was to read publicly.

THE NICENE DECREE

"I renounce all customs, rights, legalisms, unleavened breads and sacrifice of lambs of the Hebrew, and all other feasts of the Hebrew, sacrifices, prayers, aspersions, purifications, sanctifications, and propitiations, and fasts, and new moons, and Sabbaths, and hymns and a chants and observances and synagogues, and the food and drink of the Hebrew; in one word, <u>I renounce absolutely everything</u> <u>Jewish, every law right and custom</u>...And if afterwards I wish to deny and return to Jewish superstition, or shall be found eating with Jews, or feasting with them, or secretly conversing and condemning the Christian religion instead of openly confuting them and condemning their vain faith, then let the trembling of Cain and the leprosy of Gehazi cleave to me, as well as the anathema in the world to come, and may my soul be set down with Satan and the devils."

Can you feel the hatred Constantine had for the Jews? Can you see how he is manipulating this weak and fragmented thing called "the Church" into his paradigm?

Evolution of Replacement Theology

What I have to say next, I say with respect, but in all honesty. Today, there are many in the Body of Christ who, knowingly or unknowingly, are deceived by Constantine's doctrine which can go by no other name than Replacement Theology.

The following passages from Paul were obviously overlooked or ignored by early Church Fathers and Replacement Theology groups:

> *What advantage then hath the Jew? or what profit* is there *of circumcision? 2 **Much every way**: chiefly, because that unto them were committed the oracles of God. 3 For what if some did not believe? shall their unbelief make the faith of God without effect?...9 What then? **are we better** than* **they? No, in no wise:** *for we have before proved **both Jews and Gentiles, that they are all under sin**; 10 As it is written, There is **none righteous, no, not one*** (Rom 3:1-3,9-10).

I have friends who teach Replacement Theology, claiming that the Church now receives all of the promises made to the Jews and replaces Israel with born-again saints (although I could never understand why they wouldn't take on the curses, too, if they insist on taking the blessings). In the following verses, we are told how gentile believers are **brought into** _the family_. There is no implication that the Jews are being replaced by saved gentiles:

> *Wherefore remember, that ye* being *in time past Gentiles in the flesh, who are called Uncircumcision by that which is called the Circumcision in the flesh made by hands; 12 That at that time* **ye were without** *Christ,* **being aliens from the commonwealth of Israel, and strangers from the covenants of promise, having no hope, and without God in the world: 13 But now in Christ Jesus** *ye who sometimes were far off* **are made nigh** *by the blood of Christ. 14 For he is our peace,* **who hath made both one,** *and hath broken down the middle wall of partition* **between us;** *15 Having abolished in his flesh the enmity, even the law of commandments* contained *in ordinances; for* **to make in himself of twain one new man,** *so making peace; 16 And that he might* **reconcile both unto God in one body by the cross,** *having slain the enmity thereby: 17 And came and preached peace* **to you which were afar off,** *and to them that were nigh. 18* **For through him we both have access by one Spirit unto the Father** *(Eph 2: 11-18)*.

This passage in Romans 11 is as clear as it can get. If you can't see this, then I fear you have a blindness put over your eyes and are in as great a danger as those Jews.

> *For* **I speak to you Gentiles,** *inasmuch as I am the apostle of the Gentiles, I magnify mine office: 14 If by any means I may provoke to emulation* them *which are my flesh, and might save some of them. 15* **For if the casting away of them** be **the reconciling of the world, what shall the** *receiving of*

them *be, but life from the dead?* 16 *For if the firstfruit* be *holy, the lump* is *also* holy: *and if the root* be *holy, so* are *the branches.* 17 *And* **if some of the branches be broken off, and thou, being a wild olive tree, wert grafted in among them**, *and with them partakest of the root and fatness of the olive tree;* 18 **Boast not against the branches**. *But if thou boast, thou bearest not the root, but the root thee.* 19 *Thou wilt say then, The branches were broken off, that I might be grafted in.* 20 *Well; because of unbelief they were broken off, and thou standest by faith.* **Be not highminded, but fear**: 21 **For if God spared not the natural branches, take heed lest he also spare not thee (Rom 11:13-21).**

In the above verses, the instruction is twofold: God chose to "graft in" gentiles, and gentiles are warned not to boast against the natural branches (Jews) or else they too will not be spared. This is a warning from God. Do not use your mouth, or your hand, or your vote against Israel; doing otherwise invites the pruning hand of God in your life.

For I would not, brethren, that ye should be ignorant of this mystery, lest ye should be wise in your own conceits; **that blindness in part is happened to Israel, until the fulness of the Gentiles be come in.** 26 *And so* **all Israel shall be saved**: *as it is written, There shall come out of Sion the Deliverer, and shall turn away ungodliness from Jacob:* 27 *For this is my covenant unto them, when* **I shall take away their sins**. 28 *As concerning the gospel,* **they** are **enemies for your sakes**: *but as touching the election,* <u>**they**</u> <u>are</u> <u>**beloved for the fathers' sakes**</u>. 29 *For the gifts and calling of God* are *without repentance.* 30 *For as ye in times past have not believed God, yet have now* **obtained mercy through their unbelief (Rom 11:25).**

In the above verses, it is clear that the Jews *are "beloved" by the Father.* Whoever blesses them, God will bless. Whoever curses them, God will curse. Why not take a moment right now to ask yourself the question, "Have I, as a believer, been guilty of cursing Israel?" If the answer is yes, you have the privilege right now, through the blood of your Messiah Lamb, of asking God to forgive you and to remove any curses from your life and family.

> **CRUCIAL QUESTION:** What does God think when those who profess to be "His Children" and followers of His son celebrate Pagan Feasts specifically designed to be anti-Jewish, anti-biblical and in reality anti-God? Could it bring a curse on us and our children?

What Is All The Fuss About The Feasts?

"All those feasts of the Jews were under the Old Covenant, not the New Covenant!" Surely this is a statement that most of us have heard at some point, and we all deal with it in one way or another.

It reminds me of the time when a pastor asked me to teach his church about the "Jewish feasts." I remember asking the congregation, "Have you heard of the Jewish feasts?" Many nodded and a few lifted their hands.

"So, you've heard of Purim and Chanukah?" They looked a little puzzled. "Those are the Jewish feasts!" Since I love stimulating the thought process, I added, "the other feasts that you refer to as Jewish are actually the Feasts of the *Lord.*"

This was a new revelation for them, so I asked, "Do you know which feasts were set up by God before the covenant of the law was established?" Now the frowns and grimaces really started filling the faces of these good Baptist folk. Eyes searched to and fro. Shrugs and shaking heads filled the room. Finally, I answered the question for them. "Passover and the Feast of Unleavened Bread were established in the land of Egypt before the covenant of the law on Mt. Sinai." What does all of this mean? In simple terms, it means that the feasts are not part of "the law," they were pre-law. The response and understanding of the covenants of law and grace is quite diverse and interesting to observe when discussing this subject.

"Don't try to put us back under the law!" is another statement most of us have heard before, and it's a valid one. The New Testament makes it clear that going back under the law to earn righteousness is an abomination for all who have "put on" *Yeshua* (Jesus), or the unblemished Messiah Lamb, as their righteousness. Let us therefore examine what the scriptures have to say on the subject of the feasts:

A CALENDAR WITH HOLIDAYS: THE FEASTS

ROSH HASHANAH:

> *And the LORD spake unto Moses and Aaron **in the land of Egypt**, saying, 2 This month shall be unto you **the beginning of months**: it shall be the first month of the year to you (Exo 12: 12:1-2).*

PASSOVER:

> *Speak ye unto all the congregation of Israel, saying, **In the tenth day** of this month they shall take to them every man a lamb . . . 6 And ye shall keep it up until **the fourteenth day** of the same month: and the whole assembly of the congregation of Israel shall kill it in the evening. . . . . **11b it is the***

> LORD'S Passover . . . **14 And this day shall be unto you for a memorial; and ye shall keep it a feast to the LORD throughout your generations; ye shall keep it a feast by an ordinance for ever** (Exo 12: 3a, 6, 11b,14)

UNLEAVENED BREAD:

> **Seven days** shall ye eat unleavened bread . . . **17b: therefore shall ye observe this day in your generations by an ordinance for ever** (Exo 12:15a, 17b).

Significantly, this calendar and combination feast was established in Egypt *before* the exodus and at least a month before the covenant of the law. Most scholars believe the Covenant of the Law was established fifty days later, at Pentecost, the Feast of Weeks. So, *"**Observe this day in your generations by an ordinance for ever,"** is a pre-law commandment.

Later, after the children of Israel refused the original covenant, the Lord included His feasts in the commandments of the law and incorporated the Levitical system with the sacrifices. This begs some interesting questions. If God never changes, were these the feasts of the Lord before Moses? Before Abraham? Again, if God never changes, are they still His feasts today? If they are, who should be keeping them?

FEASTS OF THE LORD

> And the LORD spake unto Moses, saying, 2 Speak unto the children of Israel, and say unto them, **Concerning the feasts of the LORD**, which ye shall proclaim to be holy convocations, even **these are my feasts** (Lev 23:1).

So, whose Feasts are they? Notice how the entire year is laid out for the children of Israel. What you may not realize is the entire plan of YHWH is in His Feast's. Everything from creation to the Millennium, but that's another study.

SPRING

The New Year, which occurred in the spring, was a weeklong celebration that included Passover, Unleavened Bread, and First-fruits. Designed to be a time of focusing on God, the New Year was a weeklong vacation in which parents taught their children about slavery, liberty, deliverance, and holiness. What a way to start the year!

PASSOVER/UNLEAVENED BREAD/FIRST FRUITS

In the fourteenth day of the first month at even is the Lord's Passover. 6 And on the fifteenth day of the same month is the feast of unleavened bread unto the LORD: seven days ye must eat unleavened bread....10 Speak unto the children of Israel, and say unto them, When ye be come into the land which I give unto you, and shall reap the harvest thereof, then ye shall bring a sheaf of the firstfruits of your harvest unto the priest (Lev 23:5,6,10).

SUMMER

In summer, Israel enjoyed a break from heat and work. It was a time, once again, to think about the Lord and the giving of His written word (Torah).

PENTECOST (WEEKS)

*Even unto the morrow after the seventh sabbath shall ye number **fifty days**; and ye shall offer a new <u>meat</u> offering unto the LORD (Lev 23:16).*

FALL

The Blowing of Trumpets, the Day of Atonement, and
Tabernacles. What a way to wrap up the year! Children
learned about God and His great mercy, and the need for
blood atonement for our sins. These were sobering events,
ones that were followed by the biggest "vacation/reunion"
during which everyone camped out for a week and told
stories of God and His great provision.

TRUMPETS

*Speaking unto the children of Israel, saying, In the seventh
month, in the first day of the month, shall ye have a Sabbath,
a memorial of blowing of trumpets, an holy convocation. 25 Ye
shall do no servile work therein: but ye shall offer an offering
made by fire unto the LORD (Lev 23:24).*

ATONEMENT

*Also on the tenth day of this seventh month there shall be a
day of atonement: it shall be an holy convocation unto you;
and ye shall afflict your souls, and offer an offering made by
fire unto the LORD (Lev 23:27).*

TABERNACLES

*Speak unto the children of Israel, saying, The fifteenth day of
this seventh month shall be **the feast of tabernacles** for
seven days unto the LORD . . . 42 Ye shall dwell in booths
seven days; all that are Israelites born shall dwell in booths: . .
44 And Moses declared unto the children of Israel **the feasts
of the LORD** (Lev 23:34).*

In the days of the Old Covenant, God had a system — the
Lord's feasts — to develop Israelite men, women and
children into Godly warriors, strong in faith and grace. Are

we right to assume that He doesn't have any such system for us today?

CRUCIAL POINT: *Yeshua (Jesus) is a completely Hebrew Messiah Lamb, fulfilling the spring feasts that were given to the Hebrew children as commandments. Yeshua becomes the PASSOVER LAMB. He lives a sinless life, therefore He is the UNLEAVENED BREAD. He rises from the dead on the FEAST OF FIRST FRUITS. He sends the Holy Spirit "upon" the disciples at the FEAST OF WEEKS (Pentecost).*

What was it about these feasts that Constantine so feared and hated? The Rabbinical Jews had already polluted their feasts, so what did he hope to gain by removing them from Christianity?

In the light of the fulfillment of the feasts in *Yeshua* (Jesus), it becomes clear that, in the final analysis, "the Jewish" *Yeshua* (Jesus) was the real object of Constantine's hatred. Since all future prophecies are tied to the fall feasts, comprehending them requires a solid understanding of the "Jewish perspective." Did Constantine know this?

Just as he had done with the Sabbath, Constantine did what neither *Yeshua* (Jesus) nor the apostles nor the scriptures called for, the removal of the feasts from the Church. Yet, no outcry was raised, no battle was fought. Constantine simply opened his wallet and bought the Church. Tired of fighting, and aware that the Jews had polluted the real feasts, the Church sold herself just as Esau sold his birthright for a bowl of soup. Thus Constantine severed Christianity from both its Jewish and Biblical roots.

How to Keep the Feasts

We know that the early Church kept the Sabbath and celebrated the feasts wherever possible. Consider this interesting scripture, one that modern theologians tell us concerns communion, not one of the feasts.

> *Your glorying is not good. Know ye not that a little leaven leaveneth the whole lump? 7 Purge out therefore the old leaven, that ye may be a new lump, as ye are unleavened. For even* **Christ our passover is sacrificed for us**: *8 Therefore* **let us keep the feast**, *not with old leaven, neither with the leaven of malice and wickedness; but with the unleavened bread of sincerity and truth* (1 Cor 5:6-8).

Have you been taught how to keep this feast with unleavened bread?

> **CRUCIAL QUESTION:** What would our children and grandchildren be like if they were raised in a true biblical feast environment?

What Happened To The Lamb?

The tragedy is that both the Jews and Christians lost the feasts and the lamb! You cannot observe a *biblical* Passover without a lamb! Rabbinic and Messianic Jews all over the world continually transgress the Torah and celebrate a pagan, rabbinic Passover Seder, without a lamb.

The Passover was established in Egypt as a memorial looking forward to the anointed Lamb of God that would redeem us all. Today the Passover is a memorial looking back at the incredible price paid for our transgressions.

Should it be done without a Lamb? The first thing we need to realize is this is the Lord's Passover and it's His sacrifice, not ours. ...*it is the LORD'S Passover (Exo 14:11b).*
The next thing we realize is that we kill the Passover; we do not sacrifice the Passover.

Then Moses called for all the elders of Israel, and said unto them, Draw out and take you a lamb according to your families, and **kill** the Passover (Exo 12:21).

Then we notice that it was originally set up to be done in the individual homes and that was the directive for the future.

> *And the LORD said unto Moses and Aaron, This is the ordinance of the passover: There shall no stranger eat thereof: 44But every man's servant that is bought for money, when thou hast circumcised him, then shall he eat thereof. 45A foreigner and an hired servant shall not eat thereof. 46In one house shall it be eaten; thou shalt not carry forth ought of the flesh abroad out of the house; neither shall ye break a bone thereof. 47All the congregation of Israel shall keep it (Exo 12:43).*

After the Children of Israel refused the covenant of the individual priesthood, YHWH gave instruction that they could not have the Passover at their homes because they were not priests. They forfeited this right.

> *Thou mayest not sacrifice the passover within any of thy gates, which the LORD thy God giveth thee: 6But at the place which the LORD thy God shall choose to place his name in, there thou shalt sacrifice the passover at even, at the going down of the sun, at the season that thou camest forth out of Egypt. 7And thou shalt roast and eat it in the place which the LORD thy God shall choose: and thou shalt turn in the morning, and go unto thy tents (Deu 16:5).*

The non-believing Jew or Rabbinical Jew can't have the lamb because he doesn't accept the new covenant and is therefore bound to the old covenant which requires a Temple and a priest. Under the new covenant, as individual priests we should keep Passover in our own homes as directed in Exodus 12. This shows we are not living under the covenant the Law.

Who should keep the feasts and how they should be kept is another study and another book. For now, this lesson remains: be aware of who took the feasts (and how) from the followers of *Yeshua* (Jesus). I will address this in the last part of this work.

Constantine Banishes the Arians

Constantine's final act at the Council of Nicea was the banishment of the leaders of the Arian controversy. Arius, Eusebius of Nicomedia, and Theognis were stripped of their respective bishoprics and sent into exile. In The Arian Decree, a letter addressed to all the bishops, Constantine wrote:

THE ARIAN DECREE

> If any treatise composed by Arius should be discovered, let it be consigned to the flames, in order that not only his depraved doctrine may be suppressed, but also, that no memorial of him may be left. This therefore I decree, that if any one shall be detected in concealing a book compiled by Arius, and shall not instantly bring it forward and burn it, the penalty for this offense shall be death. May God preserve you.

Constantine got most everything he wanted. With a few strokes of the pen, he banished the Arians and ordered their books burnt under the penalty of death. Later, he would reverse himself by recalling the Arians and banishing some of the Trinitarians. As you will see in his choice of deathbed baptizer, Constantine's political expediency knew no bounds.

REVIEW: What Did The Council of Nicea Accomplish?

- Produced the Nicene Creed, out of which Trinitarianism was born.
- Replaced the Feasts of the Lord with the pagan celebration of Easter.
- Severed the infant Church from its God-given Hebrew heritage.

- Established the new religion on anti-Semitic foundations.
- Cemented Constantine as the unofficial head of the new Church.

> **CRUCIAL POINT:** *These initial steps of Constantine would be the roots of imported paganism and the virus that would infect the Christian church permanently. By befriending the Church, he was able to do what seemed as if the devil himself was not able to do. When trying to destroy it by massive persecution didn't work, he instead embraced it and changed everything about it.*

The Nicene Council, under Constantine's leadership, changed the course of history. In an act of enormous significance, Constantine officially set up Sylvester as the Bishop of Rome and the *head of the Church*. Thus was established **the first Pope** and the supremacy of the Roman Catholic Church. Indeed, under his leadership, the Council of Nicea set a course that would impact history forever.

CONSTANTINE STEALS THE BIBLE: *The Byzantine Text*

As mentioned, in the centuries leading up to Constantine's reign, the Church suffered varying degrees of persecution under each succeeding emperor. The Church lost people, buildings, and property. Depending on the extent of public rage, entire congregations were wiped out. Yet, perhaps worst of all, every Scripture manuscript that fell into the hands of persecutors was destroyed. Sadly, this wholesale destruction has made it next to impossible to find the manuscripts from which authors wrote the original text.

Today there are Bible scholars who have made it their mission to find an original New Testament manuscript. Should they discover one, they expect it to be written in Greek. Greek, they say, was the perfect tool to spread the

> **CRUCIAL QUESTION:** What would have happened if the majority of the 318 Bishops had been Arian instead of only the six who attended? Since everything pointed to Constantine's need for unity, it is likely that Arianism would have been the politically correct doctrine.

Gospel because it was an international language spoken widely and fluently by all the peoples, including the Jews, in the first century Mediterranean world.

Throughout their history, the Jews — despite being conquered many times by different countries — have shown a remarkable resilience against the influence of foreign languages and customs. Call it a miracle of stubbornness, or credit the sovereignty of God, but somehow, some way, the Jews have survived and flourished as a cohesive people and culture.

The almost universal acceptance of Greek as the language of the original New Testament scriptures is, at best, a general misconception or, much worse, another anti-Semitic fabrication. Greek was only used as a trade language among merchants whose business took them in and out of different countries, including Israel. It's true that most politicians, tribal leaders, and wealthy merchants would have been able to communicate in Greek. But Greek was never a language spoken fluently by the masses in Israel. This was true when the Greeks, and later the Romans, ruled Israel.

The language of Israel has been Hebrew and Aramaic for at least the last 3,200 years. Hebrew has been the official religious language for that same time. All of the books of the Tanach (Old Testament) were written *by* Hebrews, *about* their Hebrew God, *to* their Hebrew countrymen, and *in* Hebrew (except for some Chaldean portions). The same is true for most, if not all, of the New Testament. *Yeshua* (Jesus) taught, and all Jewish writers wrote, in Hebrew and Aramaic. Why then would all the books of the New Testament be written in Greek?

Of all the books in the New Testament, only the epistle to the Philippians was written specifically to gentiles while the Gospel of John had a dual audience. Paul, the apostle to the gentiles, and Luke were likely the only authors who were fluent in Greek. The rest of the books, including Matthew, Mark, Luke, Acts, Romans, I & II, Timothy, Hebrews, James, the epistles of Peter and John, and the Revelation were addressed to Jews who spoke Hebrew and Aramaic. The remaining books could have targeted either gentiles or Jews, but remember that Paul's primary purpose in writing was to encourage believers to stop living under the law and to begin walking and living in the Spirit. Trying to live under the law was mainly a problem for Jews, not gentiles. And again, the Jews spoke Hebrew and Aramaic.

The following are a collection of passages from differing scholars and institutions that seem to agree with my view on the originals being in Hebrew or Aramaic.

ORIGINAL LANGUAGE OF THE NEW TESTAMENT

Language of First Century Israel

A single master from the earliest ages has in fact dominated the Middle East, through all of its political turmoil, until the present day. The Semitic tongue has dominated the Middle East from ancient times, until the modem day. Aramaic dominated the three great Empires, Assyrian, Babylonian. and Persian. It endured until the seventh century, when under the Islamic nation it was displaced by a cognate Semitic language, Arabic. Even today some few Syrians, Assyrians and Chaldeans speak Aramaic as their native tongue, including three villages north of Damascus. The new Covenant Aramaic Peshitta Text with Hebrew Translation, Bible Society of Jerusalem; 1986;p iii

The Babylonian Exile

Some scholars have proposed that the Jews lost their Hebrew language, replacing it with Aramaic during the Babylonian captivity. The final evidence against this line of thinking is the fact that the post-captivity books (Zech., Hag., Mal.. Neh., Ezra, and Ester) are written in Hebrew rather than Aramaic.

Hellenization

Some scholars have also suggested that under the Helene Empire Jews lost their Semitic language and in their rush to Hellenize, began speaking Greek. The books of the Maccabees do record an attempt by Antiochus Epiphanies to forcibly Hellenize the Jewish people. Did anyone read about Judas Maccabee? Did any of the scholars know about the army that defeated the Greeks and eradicated Hellenism? Do they know about or understand Chanukah, the feast of the dedication of the Temple, a holiday that even Yeshua observed in the first century? Those scholars who claim that the Jews were Hellenized and began speaking Greek at this time seem to deny the historical fact of the Maccabean success.

During the first century, Hebrew remained the language of the Jews living in Judah and to a lesser extent in Galilee. Aramaic remained a secondary language and the language of commerce. Jews at this time did not speak Greek; in fact one tradition had it that it was better to feed ones children swine than to teach them the Greek language. The Greek language was inaccessible and undesirable to the vast majority of Jews in Israel in the 1st century. Even though everyone seems to teach to the contrary, the fact is, the majority of the Jews in Israel, in the 1st Century did not know Greek.

The Testimony of Josephus

The first Century Jewish historian, Flavius Josephus (Joseph ben Matthais) son of a priest (AD. 37-c.100.) testifies to the fact that Hebrew was the language of first century Jews. Moreover, he testifies that Hebrew, and not Greek, was the language of his time. Josephus gives the only firsthand witness to the destruction of the Temple in 70 C.E. The Romans had him translate the call to the Jews to surrender into "their own language." *Josephus The War of the Jews Book 5:9:2.*

The next statement made by Josephus should rattle the Greek professors but it seems to go unnoticed.

I have also taken a great deal of pains to obtain the learning of the Greeks, and understanding the elements of the Greek language although I have so long accustomed myself to speak our own tongue, that I cannot pronounce Greek with sufficient exactness: for our nation does not encourage those that learn the languages of many nations. *Josephus The Antiquities Book 20:11:2.*

Is this not a clear historical record? Josephus makes it clear that first century Jews spoke "their own language."

Archaeology

Archaeologists have found confirmation of Josephus's claims. The Bar Kokhba coins are one example. Jews struck these coins during the Bar Kokhba revolt (c. 132 C.E.). All of these coins bear only Hebrew inscriptions. Countless other inscriptions found at excavations of the Temple Mount, Masada and various Jewish tombs, have revealed first century Hebrew inscriptions.

Even more profound evidence that Hebrew was a living language during the first century may be found in ancient Documents from about that time, which have been discovered in Israel. These include the Dead Sea Scrolls, and the Bar Kokhba letters.

The Dead Sea Scrolls consist of over 40,000 fragments of more than 500 scrolls dating from 250 B.C.E. to 70 C.E. Theses Scrolls are primarily in Hebrew and Aramaic. A large number of the "secular scrolls" (those which are not Bible manuscripts) are in Hebrew,

The Bar Kokhba letters are letters between Simon Bar Kokhba and his army, written during the Jewish revolt of 132 C.E.. These letters were discovered by Yigael Yadin in 1961 and are almost all written in Hebrew and Aramaic. Two of the letters are written in Greek, both were written by men with Greek names to Bar Kokhba. One of the two Greek letters actually apologizes for writing to Bar Kokhba in Greek, saying "the letter is written in Greek, as we have no one who knows Hebrew here."

The Dead Sea Scrolls and the Bar Kokhba letters not only include first and second century Hebrew documents, but also give even more significant evidence in the dialect of that Hebrew. The dialect of these documents was not the Biblical Hebrew of the Tenach (Old Testament), nor was it the Mishnaic Hebrew of the Mishna (c. 220 C.E.). The Hebrew of these documents is colloquial; it is a fluid living language in a state of flux somewhere in the evolutionary process from Biblical to Mishnaic Hebrew. Moreover, the Hebrew of the Bar Kokhba letters represents Galilean Hebrew (Bar Kokhba was *a* Galilean), while the Dead Sea Scrolls give us an example of Judaean Hebrew. Comparing the documents shows a living distinction of geographic dialect as well; a sure sign that Hebrew was not a dead language.

Final evidence that first century Jews conversed in Hebrew and Aramaic can be found in other documents of the period, and even later. These include: the "Roll Concerning Fasts" in Aramaic (66-70 C.E.), "The Letter of Gamaliel" in Aramaic (c. 30 -110 C.E.). "Wars of the Jews" by Josephus in Hebrew (c. 75 C.E.), the "Mishna" in Hebrew (c. 220 C.E.) and the "Gemara" in Aramaic (c. 500 C.E.)

Additional reading: *The Semitic Background of the New Testament* by Joseph A. Fitzmyer, Wm. Eerdmans Publishing, 1997, ISBN 0-8028-4344-1 especially from pp. 271-305

If Hebrew and Aramaic were the languages of Jews living in Israel in the first century, wouldn't the New Testament have first been written in these languages? A number of noted scholars have argued that at least portions of the New Testament were originally penned in a Semitic tongue.

Scholars on the Language of the New Testament

Aramaic was one of the great languages of the civilized East. It flourished mainly from the sixth to the third centuries B.C., during the period when oriental empires ruled the civilized world, when it was the international medium of governmental, cultural, and commercial intercourse form the Euphrates to the Nile, even in countries where there was no indigenous Semitic culture. It became the language of the Jews, when exactly is not known, put probably during and after the Exile....

Four languages were to be found in first-century Palestine: Greek was the speech of the educated 'hellenized' classes and the medium of cultural and commercial intercourse between Jew and foreigner; Latin was the language of the arm of occupation and, to judge from Latin borrowings in Aramaic, appears also to some extent to have served the purposes of commerce, as it no doubt also did of Roman law; Hebrew, the sacred tongue of the Jewish Scriptures, continued to provide the lettered Jew with an important means of literary expression and was cultivated as a spoken tongue in the learned coteries of the rabbis; Aramaic was the language of the people of the land and, together, with Hebrew, provided the chief literary medium of the Palestinian Jew of the first century; Josephus wrote his Jewish War in Aramaic and later translated it into Greek: (Preface, I; cf. Antiquities, xxii.w. See also Dalman: *Jesus-Jeshua*, chapter on the three language of 1st century)

If Jesus was a Galilean Rabbi, it is not unlikely that He made use of Hebrew as well as Aramaic, especially, as T.W. Manson has suggested, in His formal disputations with the Pharisees. (*Teaching of Jesus*) M.H. Segal has gone so far as to claim that "Mishnaic"

Hebrew, the kind of Hebrew we find in the Mishnah, was actually a spoken vernacular in Judea in the time of Christ. In the Palestinian Talmud Aramaic and Hebrew are found together, sometimes in the form of a kind of Mischsprache; sentences half Hebrew, half Aramaic, are familiar to the reader of the Talmud, and this artificial language, rabbnical in origin, may well have been in use before as after the fall of Jerusalem.....

At the basis of the Greek Gospels, therefore, there must lay a Palestinian Aramaic tradition, at any rate of the sayings and teaching of Jesus, and this tradition must at one time have been translated form Aramaic into Greek. Some have thought that the Evangelists themselves were the translators of these Aramaic sources of the Gospels; they certainly must have utilized, if they did not themselves translate, early translation sources." *Matthew Black An Aramaic Approach to the Gospel and Acts. p. 13-15.* Additional reading:

Burney, Charles, *The Aramaic Origin of the Fourth Gospel*, Oxford at the Clarendon Press, 1922
Frederic Henry Chase, *The Syro-Latin Test of the Gospels*, London, Macmillan and Co, 1895 and also *The Old Syriac Element in the Text of Codex Bezae*, London, 1893.
J.A. Fitzmyer, "The Aramaic Language and the Study of the New Testament" JBL 99/1 (1980): 5-21.
William Wright, *A Short History of Syriac Literature*, Gorgias press, 2001 (reprint of original, published in London by Adam and Charles Black, 1894.
The Aramaic Sayings of Jesus, Basil Fletcher, Hodder & Stoughton, 1967, Signs of the Cross, Andrew Roth

In addition here are several websites you can research that were in operation at the time of this writing.

www.peshitta.org: under introduction there is a good history of Aramaic.
www.jerusalemperspective.com – they believe that Hebrew was spoken extensively in the 1st century. Good articles!
www.gorgiaspress.com – they have reprinted many of the public domain books on Syriac and Aramaic and different historic items.

On top of all the other evidence there were a number of references by the Early Church Fathers to the Gospel of Matthew originally written in Hebrew. Many of these are collected in the book *The Jewish Roman World of Jesus* by Dr. James Tabor.

Papias - Matthew composed the sayings of the Lord in the Hebrew language, and everyone translated them as best as they could.

Irenaeus - Matthew wrote a gospel in the Hebrew language, while Peter and Paul were preaching the Gospel and founding the church in Rome.

Clement - Matthew was written before Mark and John and at the same time as Luke.

Origen - The first Gospel was that according to Matthew, who was once a toll-collector but later an apostle of Jesus Christ. He published it for those who became believers from Judaism, since it was composed in the Hebrew language.

Jerome – Matthew, who was also (called) Levi, was an apostle and former tax-collector. He first composed the gospel of Christ in Hebrew letters and wrote for the Jews of Judea. It is not known who translated the gospel into Greek. The Hebrew gospel still exists, and Jerome claimed to have read it.

Jerome also asserts that Matthew wrote in the Hebrew language (Epist. 20.5), and he refers to a Hebrew Matthew and a Gospel of the Hebrews-unclear if they are the same. He also quotes from the Gospel used by the Nazoreans and the Ebionites, which he says he has recently translated from Hebrew to Greek (in Matt. 12.13).

So, contrary to popular and scholarly opinion, I believe there is substantial evidence the original New Testament scriptures were written in Hebrew or Aramaic, with the possible exception of the epistle to the Philippians. With that in mind, realize that the scriptures you read today in English or other native tongue went through a minimum of two different sets of customs, paradigms and idioms, rather than the one you have been taught. In other words, you are not reading the works of Jewish believers who were writing to Greek-speaking disciples who would have made all the examples clear between the cultures. Instead, you are reading translations from Greek translations of Jews writing to Jewish believers. Greek and Jewish cultures were so diametrically opposed to each other that many fine points were lost.

Also of importance here is the vast difference in complexity between the two languages. Here is how Jan Mangier, an Aramaic translator, explained it to me:

"I would not say that Hebrew or Aramaic is a 'crude' language compared to Greek. It is a totally different approach to language than western languages such as Greek and even English have. The precision is not in the endings and tenses and forms, but in the word families. Every word belongs to a root family and thus has a continuity in its essential meaning that is not possible in Greek." See Thorleif Boman, *Hebrew Thought Compared with Greek*, pp. 27-28:

"If Israelite thinking is to be characterized, it is obvious first to call it dynamic, vigorous, passionate, and sometimes quite explosive in kind; correspondingly Greek thinking is static, peaceful, moderate, and harmonious in kind...The verbs especially, whose *basic meaning* always expresses a movement or an activity, reveal the dynamic variety of the Hebrews' thinking. When a verb is to express a position like sitting or lying, it is done by a verb which can also designate a movement. An example of this is the name 'Yahweh' which really is from the verb 'being' but it is not a static concept. All the references to Yahweh as 'the eternal one' are active: how he deals with his people. One could translate the name into English perhaps better as 'the effective one'."

I had said that Hebrew was a very simple, even crude, language. She explained, "Because it's so simple, its complexity comes not from the words that are used but in word groupings and word combinations." On the other hand, Greek is very precise and extremely complex. I use this example often to try and explain the difference:

If I said 'red' in Hebrew, it is a single choice. If I said 'red' in Greek there might be seven choices so you would know how much orange was in the red, and how light or dark it was. It is almost like comparing English on elementary school levels with English on advanced college levels; the difference is that great. The question is, would such differences make the process of translation easier or more difficult? To do it well, you would have to be a master of both languages and cultures.

As gentiles gradually became the majority in the Church, the original Hebrew and Aramaic texts were no longer valued as much as Greek or Latin translations. These versions, which were more readable, were translated by gentiles who often harbored prejudice against Jews. Even before Constantine's time, as the Church grew anti-Semitic in many areas, Hebrew names and idioms were purged when the scriptures were translated into Greek. For example, YOCHANAN was changed to IOANNES, (Ee-o-an'-nace) and then to John. YA'AKOV was changed to IAKOBOS, (Ee-ak'-o-bos) and then to James. KEFA became PETROS, (Pet'-ros) and then to Peter. Y'hudah became IOUDAS, (Ee-oo-das') then Jude.

There are so many *variants* between the Greek texts that it's almost laughable that scholars refer to them as inerrant or not containing any errors. So where can we find the inerrant scriptures that we all believe in and teach about? I believe as we uncover more hidden treasures we will find the original Aramaic and Hebrew texts.

"But what about the anointing?" you may be asking. "Don't you believe in the anointing?"

Yes! Absolutely! That's why I still study and teach from the King James Bible. It is important to know the difference between God's Word and man's work. Until we find the originals, we have what God saw fit to allow us to have and there is enough truth to be found in that to keep a scholar busy for a lifetime. **Truth is not God's enemy. Ignorance is.** *My People perish from a lack of knowledge.*

The Byzantine Text

Constantine decided to commission the copying of the text known as the New Testament. He paid for this process, and the resulting Greek text was warmly referred to as the Byzantine Text. Yet somehow, the copying of the text systematically removed even more of its Jewishness. The names of towns and feasts changed, and at times transliterations were used instead of translations.

Although little of this editing affected the context, a few things did. For example, if there is no other name whereby men must be saved, would not the name of the Savior be important? The name is a very Jewish one, *Yeshua.* The translators came up with IESOUS (ee-ay-sooce'), a Greek word that was later translated into Jesus. No one knows the origin of IESOUS; despite many claims to the contrary, it is neither a translation nor a transliteration of *Yeshua.* To their credit, when translating MASHIYACH, (Maw-shee'-akh;) into CHRISTOS, and later into Christ, they came up with terms with the same meaning, "the anointed one."

In addition to mistranslating key terms, the translators apparently deleted and added verses here and there to reinforce their own doctrines. In Matthew 28:19 of the Byzantine text, we read . . . *baptize them in the name of the Father, and of the Son, and of the Holy Spirit.*

This verse does not exist in any manuscript dated earlier than the Byzantine text of Constantine. Strangely, in each of the three existing pre-Constantine manuscripts, the last page is mysteriously missing; they were either lost or stolen. The only reliable source is in Aramaic; it says "baptize them in My name (Yeshua)," not in the name of the Father, and of the Son, and of the Holy Spirit. You may not have gotten that, so I'll repeat it. The last page *in all three* Greek manuscripts which are older than the Byzantine text (AD 325) that contain Matthew 28:19 are missing. **They can't be found!** Who would steal the last page, and why?

Even Eusebius of Caesarea, Constantine's friend, in his most celebrated work *Ecclesiastical History*, quotes Matthew 28:19, "in my name." In Book III of his *History*, Chapter 5, Section 2:

> But the rest of the apostles, who had been incessantly plotted against with a view to their destruction, and had been driven out of the land of Judea, went unto all nations to preach the Gospel, relying upon the power of Christ, who had said to them, "Go ye and make disciples of all the nations **in my name.**"

Again, in *Oration in Praise of Emperor Constantine*, Chapter 16, Section 8:

> What king or prince in any age of the world, what philosopher, legislator or prophet, in civilized or barbarous lands, has attained so great a height of excellence, I say not after death, but while living still, and full of mighty power, as to fill the ears and tongues of all mankind with the praises of his name?

> Surely none save our only Savior has done this, when, after his victory over death, he spoke the word to his followers, and fulfilled it by the event, saying to them, "Go ye and make disciples of all nations **in my name**."

Eusebius never quotes Matthew 28:19 as *"in the name of the Father, and of the Son, and of the Holy Spirit"* as it appears in modern Bibles and Greek texts, but always with the words "in my name." Why? Did you ever wonder why they needed a new formula for baptism? All other scriptures command believers to be baptized "in the name of *Yeshua* (Jesus)."

> *Then Peter said unto them, Repent, and be baptized every one of you **in the name of Jesus Christ** for the remission of sins, and ye shall receive the gift of the Holy Ghost (Acts 2:38).*

Did Peter make a mistake? Did he forget what *Yeshua* (Jesus) told him and the others just prior to His ascension into heaven? Or could it be that the formula, "in the Name of *Yeshua* (Jesus)," was for the Jews, and the "Father, Son, Holy Spirit" formula was for gentiles? The next scripture shows others using this "incorrect" formula as well:

> *Who, when they were come down, prayed for them, that they might receive the Holy Ghost: 16 (For as yet he was fallen upon none of them: only they were **baptized in the name of the Lord Jesus**) (Acts 8:15, 16).*

Next we see Peter baptizing gentiles. Does he offer two formulas, one for the gentile and the other for the Jew?

> *For they heard them speak with tongues, and magnify God. Then answered Peter, 47 Can any man forbid water, that these should not be baptized, which have received the Holy Ghost as well as we? 48 **And he commanded them to be baptized in***

the name of the Lord. Then prayed they him to tarry certain days (Acts 10:46-48).

No, he doesn't. In fact, there's not a single recorded case of anyone being baptized in the *Byzantine formula*, "in the name of the Father and of the Son and of the Holy Spirit." Every baptism of record in scripture uses the formula, "in the name of *Yeshua* (Jesus)."

*When they heard this, **they were baptized in the name of the Lord Jesus** (Acts 19:5).*

The irony of the *Byzantine formula* is that no Jewish names are used. In fact, no names are used at all, just titles. The Hebrew Text known as Shem Tob mentioned earlier was also used by the Jews to discredit Christians and Christianity. While there are many questions about the text and its origin it, too, reads, "*in my name*." (Hebrew Gospel of Matthew. By George Howard. 2d ed. Macon: Mercer University, 1995).

> **CRUCIAL POINT:** The two major adjustments made in the Greek texts included the removal of Jewishness and the reinforcement of the Godhead doctrine (Trinitarianism) with the new baptismal formula.

We would do well to ask why the early Church tolerated such blasphemous corrupting of the Word of God. First, the Church had a new, charismatic leader who happened to be the Roman emperor, a man with a **"better revelation."** Does that sound like a Gnostic? Secondly, removing Jewishness from the scriptures rendered Constantine-style Christianity much less offensive to pagans, the bulk of whom despised Jews. Constantine was the ultimate politician, and he cultivated assimilation and mixture in his kingdom for the sake of peace among his other reasons. The more people found the gospel acceptable, the more likely they were to get saved. What could be better for the Church?

Constantine wanted the scriptures edited because the new religion was *his* religion; he sought ultimate control. Every similarity to Judaism, every Jewish custom, had to be purged. The question then remains, "Why are the original texts generally believed to have been written in Greek?" After Constantine, the Roman Catholic Church became the world's most powerful religious entity. At times it ruled the known world, and even today is the world's largest property owner. The future of the Roman Catholic Church's powerbase depended on anti-Semitic, Greek scriptures that removed all Jewish aspects from Christianity and reinforced its trinity doctrine.

For centuries, the Roman Catholic Church punished people with death for possessing any form of the scriptures. Even though they had been edited, they contained enough truth in the words to set a person free from the clutches of "Mother Church," therefore it was safer to insist that clergy maintain possession and interpret the holy truths for the people if anyone asked. Many "heretics" (Baptists, etc.) who did escape were able to hide from Roman Catholic authorities. But millions of others were slaughtered for the crime of simply disagreeing with the Church. In the 1960s, the Second Vatican Council admitted to killing ten million Jews between AD 1000 and 1900. It also admitted that the Church's anti-Semitism was "probably the root cause" of the Holocaust. The Catholic Church created a document known as *Nostra Aetate* in 1965 which acknowledges the Muslims and Jews and declared they had a right to their religious freedom. They also acknowledged the fact that all Jews were not Christ Killers and laid the groundwork for addressing the anti-Semitism that the Church was built on.

Another astonishing fact concerns the huge library in Vatican City where many of the much sought-after original manuscripts are hidden. Revealing these documents to the public would raise many questions in addition to defrocking the Church doctrinally. We now live in the age of information: *In the last days, knowledge will increase*. All of the facts discussed above are floating to the surface for everyone to discover for themselves. In Part 6, which deals with the Protestant Reformation, I will continue with texts and text translations.

In spite of all that has been said about tampering with the scriptures, this author nevertheless believes that nearly all of the

> **CRUCIAL POINT:** *The gentile Christians with their Roman Emperor reinvented both YHWH and Yeshua (Jesus) and then very carefully added just a few points into the originals to back up their plot.*

translations, no matter the text used, can help anyone who is led by the Spirit to understand sin, find the plan of salvation, and make heaven their home. Another point should be made here. There are more *deliberate* translation errors from Greek to English than from the original Hebrew and Aramaic into Greek.

Part of the Christian anti-Semitic propaganda is that *Yeshua* (Jesus) is *The Messiah King!* The gentiles even added to Yeshua's name in the Holy Scriptures. They added the word *Christ* to end of the name of Jesus *at least* 21 times and added *Lord* to the front of His name *at least* 72 times in the King James translation alone. Why? They claim it is to show that *Yeshua* (Jesus) is both the Lord *and* the Messiah. However, in reality it was done to drive the Jew away from the gospel and even further away from the church while robbing the gentiles of their authority and power. The word Messiah is only used twice in the KJV Old Testament, but Christ is inserted 522 times in the New Testament. It was blatant fabrication.

An even worse travesty is that not only did the Jews lose the correct pronunciation of YHWH, the Christians lost the name of His son, *Yeshua*. In fact, the false paradigm has so permeated the Christian world that they name their churches and even denominations after it—"*Christ Church*" and "*Church of Christ!*" Many, ignorant of His name, Yeshua, refer to Him as Christ. It's not His name, and it never was! It is so prevalent and it distracts from their points and well-intended messages. They don't realize that they have fallen prey to a semantics war and a plot laid by Satan himself. They also don't realize the consequences of losing the names. They wonder why they have no power. **If there is *no other name* by which men can be saved, shouldn't we make sure that name is correct? If we're told to approach the Almighty *in His name* don't you think it's important to do our best to have it correct?**

Constantine accomplished, by the power of the purse, what no other emperor could do with massive Roman legions; he gained imperial supremacy over the Church and changed its scriptures, its customs, and its God. In light of these "accomplishments," one wonders if Constantine was truly the born-again Christian that the Roman Catholic Church claims. Once again, let the facts speak for themselves.

Constantine Chronology *(continued)*

In AD 326, just a year after the so-called "divine council" of Nicea, Constantine ordered the execution of his eldest son Crispus, the one who had fought so gallantly beside him. The reason? Constantine was reportedly jealous of his son's popularity with his troops. Shortly thereafter, he ordered the execution of his wife Fausta. Reports that Constantine was known for fits of rage and murder were evidently true.

On May 11th, 330, Constantine officially dedicated the city of Constantinople. Although the emperor said that God had commanded him to build the city, in order to not offend the diverse cliques of his court; the dedication ceremonies combined pagan and Christian elements. (DiMaio, Zeuge, Zotov, Byzantion, 58[1988], 353ff, Mattingly and Warmington, OCD, 2 280; Jones, ibid., 281). Notable among the spectacular new buildings was a beautiful church with tombs specially built for the thirteen apostles. Sending out expeditions to find the bodies of the martyred apostles, he had their remains exhumed for burial in the tombs. You may well ask the identity of the thirteenth one. It was Constantine, of course. He declared that *he was the thirteenth apostle*, to be buried alongside the other twelve

Constantine's Death

Constantine was friendly and even helpful to Christians as early as AD 312, but the only record of his conversion to Christianity was his baptism by Eusebius, the Arian Bishop of Nicomedia, just weeks before his death on May 22, 337. Is it not significant that Constantine accepted baptism at the hands of an Arian bishop he had long ago banished and then reinstated? Was it because he didn't want to be baptized in the formula that he himself had created?

Constantine ruled the Western Roman Empire from AD 312-324, and the entire Roman Empire from 324-337. After he died, his empire was divided among his three remaining sons and a nephew. A bloodbath ensued, but Constantine's long-term legacy remained secure. He, more than any other emperor before or since, shaped the future course of western civilization. His views of the monarchy, recorded by Eusebius, were foundational to the concept known as the Divine Right of Kings, which gave an almost divine status to kings and queens. It prevailed in Europe throughout the Middle Ages, almost into the modern era.

> **CRUCIAL QUESTION:** *If the Church had already moved from Sabbath to Sunday, as we've all been taught, why did Constantine have to officially issue the Day of the Sun Edict 300 hundred years later in AD 322?*

> **CRUCIAL QUESTION:** *If the Church had already stopped observing the feasts, as we've all been taught, why did Constantine have to officially issue the Nicene Creed and the Easter Edict 300 years later in AD 325?*

> **CRUCIAL POINT:** *In fact, if the Church was doing all this 300 years before Constantine, he would never have issued any of his edicts and most of us wouldn't even know his name. So we see that Constantine, not Yeshua (Jesus) or his apostles, was responsible for the Sunday Sabbath, the Trinity, Easter, abandonment of the Feasts of the Lord, and the infected Roman Catholic Church.*

REVIEW: Constantine's 'Accomplishments' in Christianity

1. **Changed God's Sabbath:** He named Sunday for the sun god Apollo/Mithra, and declared it the official Sabbath of the Roman government. Shortly after the Council of Nicea, the bishops voted to make Sunday the official Sabbath for the Church also.

2. **Claimed Religious Authority:** He organized the Roman Catholic Church and appointed the first Pope.

3. **Established the Doctrine of Trinitarianism:** His sponsored creeds redefined God, Yeshua (Jesus) and the Holy Spirit as coequal and coexistent for the Christian world.

4. **Replaced Passover with Easter:** He replaced the biblical feast of Passover with the pagan holiday Easter, decreeing that the resurrection of Yeshua (Jesus) was to be celebrated on the day dedicated to the fertility goddess complete with symbols of rabbits and eggs.

5. **Rejected the Feasts of the Lord:** He single-handedly stopped the new Church from observing the Feasts of the Lord ordained by the Bible. Robbed of its Hebrew roots, the disconnected Church became paganistic in spirit and anti-biblical in its customs.

6. **Legislated Anti-Semitism:** Built the practice of hating Jews (the "cause of all evil") into the foundation of his new religion and it became popular on a worldwide scale.

7. **Legislated the Church:** Under his influence, the authority of the Church was reduced to an authority based on

edicts, not Scripture. *Thus by their fruit ye will know them. Mat 7:20*

8. Declared himself the 13th Apostle and became the "unofficial head" of the Church. Which raises another question: *Where did the "Christian Church" come from?*

Constantine and the Roman Catholics were craftier than the Jews in creating their own god and religious system. Roman Catholics modified/edited their scriptures, issued edicts, and as self-appointed "guardians" of much of the early writings and artifacts, made it extremely hard for ordinary people to obtain a copy of the scriptures for centuries. (Tragically, in one of the worst infectious outbreaks to date, they murdered tens of millions of Jews. (Read Vatican II – Murder of the Jews).)

The Jews created the Talmud, an entirely new scriptural authority. Roman Catholicism continued to evolve and make major changes, including the order of the priesthood, the infallibility of the Pope, Mariology, Transubstantiation (the Blessed Sacrament), as well as the confessional and purgatory doctrines. That's why I stated in the introduction, *"Christianity, in this specific case, Roman Catholicism, is not a Biblical religion in an apostate condition; it is a man-made religion."* Roman Catholicism is a copy of the religion of ancient Babylon, complete with a reinvented Levitical system of priests, bishops, and a Pope. Claiming to have a "better revelation," its celibate priesthood puts an air of superiority between priests and rank-and-file believers.

For changing times and laws, for being an example of how much evil one man can spread in a lifetime, we must salute the greatest Gnostic of all time—St. Constantine. What stage of infection do you think Constantine was at? To answer the question, let me summarize: the post Apostolic Christian Church was created by a pagan man who murdered his oldest son and wife. He cleverly slithered into the leadership role of the movement, altering its direction and fabricating its chief doctrines. His hatred of the Jewish people permeated the foundation of "his Christianity" and it lives on today as Replacement Theology, taught by many evangelistic denominations.

…Can anyone say "Outbreak"?

A Thought and Question for Christians

Is it an option to hate Roman Catholics? Should we take up arms against these people? The men who created this religion have been dead for nearly two thousand years, and the Catholics of today have little or no knowledge of their ancestors' acts. While several works have been published exposing the roots and pagan practices of Catholicism, most of it is hate driven and the majority of the Catholics never read it. I believe heaven will be filled with many wonderful Catholic brothers and sisters who knew nothing of this diabolical system, lived their lives and loved the Lord — in spite of their church. On the contrary we should pray for the salvation and enlightenment of every Catholic in the world. Mankind's real enemy is Satan, an adversary who is very effective. In the Garden of Eden, he asked Eve, *Did God say…?* To this day he still deceives us. I have believed lies. I have even taught them as truth. Maybe you have as well.

By now, you see how the five-step Edenic paradigm and the infection of religion have been at work in both Judaism and Christianity. There is nothing new under the sun. Christianity, however, has more *obvious* pagan practices than does Judaism. So, what do Christians need to do? May I suggest that you reread the prior *Review of Constantine's 'Accomplishments' in Christianity*, and take it to the Lord and ask Him to reveal His truth to you. Ask Him if what I have written are lies for my own agenda or if it is His truth that can and will set you free. Let the Spirit of the Almighty God speak to your heart, then do whatever He tells you to do.

As the Lord reveals His truths, you need a balanced method of returning to biblical practices. When the Children of Israel were delivered from bondage they always had to *walk* back to the Promised Land. They were not transported back. Why? The reason was to allow time for the paradigm change from bondage to freedom to take place. Sometimes they never did get there, refusing to change and left to wander in the desert for forty years as a result. It takes time for you and your family to adapt to change. May I suggest that you find a small spiral notebook and as the Lord reveals changes He wants you to make in your life, write them down. Ask Him to give you the steps out of bondage, or *Injections for the Infections,* and chart your path to freedom as He leads. The knee jerk method utilized by many is often a failure and usually misunderstood. The Lord is not the author of confusion. As you walk towards Him, He will walk towards you!

A Thought and Question for Jews

When you realize that Christianity has gone through the same evolutionary process that Judaism did, you can better understand the way modern, paganized Christians think. When you understand that there was a deliberate plan to make Christianity anti-Semitic by changing their doctrines, and even their Bible, you can see how effective the diabolical plan was. What you may not have seen before was the differences between the real "believer" who had a true relationship with G-d and the religious zealots who did not.

The most important thing for Jewish people to realize is that most who truly have a "born again" experience will become a friend and supporter of Israel, like the "righteous gentiles" throughout history. I'm not suggesting that these people will be perfect, nor that they will not ever offend or upset you. I am simply saying that they will usually have a love for the Jewish people that others will not have.

May I suggest that you ask the Almighty for the ability to discern between those who claim to be Christians and those who have had this experience of being born again so that you can discern between those you can trust and those who are wolves in sheep's clothing. Just as all Jews are not the same, neither are all Christians.

A PRAYER WE CAN ALL PRAY:

God, please forgive me for the lies that I have allowed to enter my life; lies that have taken root and grown into infections. I not only ask for forgiveness, I also ask You to remove the roots of these lies and the resulting infections. Purify my heart and mind. Forgive me for teaching others lies that I believed to be true at the time. I ask that You bring Your injection of revelation knowledge to each person that I misled, and free them from the curses of those lies. Teach me Your truths and shine Your light into my heart and my spirit. Breathe into me life—Your life. Mold me and shape me into a vessel usable in Your service. Lord, have mercy on me and the many others who have believed and taught lies. We pray for the deliverance, salvation and enlightenment of Roman Catholics, and for Protestant denominations around the world, the majority of which observe Roman Catholic doctrines. Please, send us all the Injections for the Infections. Lord, help me walk closer to You each day. Guide my steps and let them lead to Your side. Amen.

REFERENCES ON CONSTANTINE
==

M. Sordi, Constantine's conversion.
The Christians and the Roman Empire, [Norman, 1994], 13ff),
Barnes, Constantine, and Eusebius, 214ff.
Euseb., VC 4.1, 1.43. (Euseb., VC 2.22).
ibid,, 3.22. (ibid, 1.43), (ibid,, 4.28). (ibid, 4.4).

Add'l information—Roman Emperors—ORB Online Encyc.—C
Constantine I

Alfoldi, Andrew, *The Converison of Constantine and Pagan Rome,*
(Oxford University Press Oxford 1948).
Bacchiochi, Samuele, *From Sabbath to Sunday,* (The Pontifical
Gregorian University Press, Rome 1977).
Compton's Online Encylopedia, *Articles: Constantine. Easter* (AOL,
1994).
Cruse, Christian Frederick, *The Ecclesiastical History of Eusebius
Pamphilus.* (Baker Book House, Grand Rapids, Michigan 1990).
Dudley, Dean, *History of the First Council of Nice,* (Peter Eckler
Publishing Co. New York 1915).
Jones, A.H.M., *Constantine and the Conversion of Europe,_* (University
of Toronto Press, Toronto and Buffalo 1978).
Wheaton College online. Works of Eusebius
Early Church Fathers – www.ccel.org &
www.earlychristianwritings.com
Center for the Study of Early Christianity: Jerusalem office
www.csec.ac.uk/hq.staff.htm **www.earlychristianwritings.com**

APPENDIX A: DIDACHE
Of all the early Church documents that have been referenced, the
Didache is one of the most controversial. Its author(s) and date of origin
has never been established and what is so apparent to me seems to slip
many others' notes: *It is a Gnostic document!* Adding rules and having
"divine insights" to doctrines not covered in the scriptures is what
Gnosticism *was* and *is* all about. The Didache is carefully cloaked in
Scripture, then spits out rules and regulations on everything from alms
and prophets to re-describing sin. It's random and legalistic. It devises
rules for baptism including the mandate for, "running, warm" water. It's
a pitiful example of someone(s) wanting to have some sort of "spiritual
authority" or "spiritual revelation" to gain control over others. Read it in
its entirety. If you've ever read a Gnostic gospel, you will see the same
"blueprint" immediately. If you haven't read Gnostic works, ask yourself
these questions as you read through the material below. *Where did these
rules come from? How can they be verified? Who else in the Bible taught*

this? As you read these man made rules you will soon ask, "How would anyone put this document up there with the Torah, the Prophets, the Gospels and Epistles?" But, they did! Here lies the root of the Sunday Sabbath and the Trinity formula for baptism—Gnosticism.

DIDACHE: The Teaching of the Twelve Apostles

(from: <u>Apostolic Fathers</u>, Kirsopp Lake, 1912 (Loeb Classical Library))
Ascii file produced by Athenaeum of Christian Antiquity. Further editing by St. Columba Press.

CHAPTER 1

The Two Ways -- The Way of Life -- The explanation -- Almsgiving

1 There are two Ways, one of Life and one of Death, and there is a great difference between the two Ways. 2 The Way of Life is this: "First, thou shalt love the God who made thee, secondly, thy neighbour as thyself; and whatsoever thou wouldst not have done to thyself, do not thou to another." 3 Now, the teaching of these words is this: "Bless those that curse you, and pray for your enemies, and fast for those that persecute you. For what credit is it to you if you love those that love you? Do not even the heathen do the same?" But, for your part, "love those that hate you," and you will have no enemy. 4 "Abstain from carnal" and bodily "lusts." "If any man smite thee on the right cheek, turn to him the other cheek also," and thou wilt be perfect. "If any man impress thee to go with him one mile, go with him two. If any man take thy coat, give him thy shirt also. If any man will take from thee what is thine, refuse it not" -- not even if thou canst. 5 Give to everyone that asks thee, and do not refuse, for the Father's will is that we give to all from the gifts we have received. Blessed is he that gives according to the mandate; for he is innocent. Woe to him who receives; for if any man receive alms under pressure of need he is innocent; but he who receives it without need shall be tried as to why he took and for what, and being in prison he shall be examined as to his deeds, and "he shall not come out thence until he pay the last farthing." 6 But concerning this it was also said, "Let thine alms sweat into thine hands until thou knowest to whom thou art giving."

CHAPTER 2

The second part of the teaching

1 But the second commandment of the teaching is this: 2 "Thou shalt do no murder; thou shalt not commit adultery"; thou shalt not commit

sodomy; thou shalt not commit fornication; thou shalt not steal; thou shalt not use magic; thou shalt not use philtres; thou shalt not procure abortion, nor commit infanticide; "thou shalt not covet thy neighbour's goods"; 3 thou shalt not commit perjury, "thou shalt not bear false witness"; thou shalt not speak evil; thou shalt not bear malice. 4 Thou shalt not be double-minded nor double-tongued, for to be double-tongued is the snare of death. 5 Thy speech shall not be false nor vain, but completed in action. 6 Thou shalt not be covetous nor extortionate, nor a hypocrite, nor malignant, nor proud; thou shalt make no evil plan against thy neighbour. 7 Thou shalt hate no man; but some thou shalt reprove, and for some shalt thou pray, and some thou shalt love more than thine own life.

CHAPTER 3

Further advice to the catechumen

1 My child, flee from every evil man and from all like him. 2 Be not proud, for pride leads to murder, nor jealous, nor contentious, nor passionate, for from all these murders are engendered. 3 My child, be not lustful, for lust leads to fornication, nor a speaker of base words, nor a lifter up of the eyes, for from all these is adultery engendered. 4 My child, regard not omens, for this leads to idolatry; neither be an enchanter, nor an astrologer, nor a magician, neither wish to see these things, for from them all is idolatry engendered. 5 My child, be not a liar, for lying leads to theft, nor a lover of money, nor vain-glorious, for from all these things are thefts engendered. 6 My child, be not a grumbler, for this leads to blasphemy, nor stubborn, nor a thinker of evil, for from all these are blasphemies engendered, 7 but be thou "meek, for the meek shall inherit the earth;" 8 be thou long-suffering, and merciful and guileless, and quiet, and good, and ever fearing the words which thou hast heard. 9 Thou shalt not exalt thyself, nor let thy soul be presumptuous. Thy soul shall not consort with the lofty, but thou shalt walk with righteous and humble men. 10 Receive the accidents that befall to thee as good, knowing that nothing happens without God.

CHAPTER 4

The duty of the catechumen to the Church -- Against meanness -- Household duties -- Against hypocrisy

1 My child, thou shalt remember, day and night, him who speaks the word of God to thee, and thou shalt honour him as the Lord, for where the Lord's nature is spoken of, there is he present. 2 And thou shalt seek daily the presence of the saints, that thou mayest find rest in their words.

3 Thou shalt not desire a schism, but shalt reconcile those that strive. Thou shalt give righteous judgment; thou shalt favour no man's person in reproving transgression. 4 Thou shalt not be of two minds whether it shall be or not. 5 Be not one who stretches out his hands to receive, but shuts them when it comes to giving. 6 Of whatsoever thou hast gained by thy hands thou shalt give a ransom for thy sins. 7 Thou shalt not hesitate to give, nor shalt thou grumble when thou givest, for thou shalt know who is the good Paymaster of the reward. 8 Thou shalt not turn away the needy, but shalt share everything with thy brother, and shalt not say that it is thine own, for if you are sharers in the imperishable, how much more in the things which perish? 9 Thou shalt not withhold thine hand from thy son or from thy daughter, but thou shalt teach them the fear of God from their youth up. 10 Thou shalt not command in thy bitterness thy slave or thine handmaid, who hope in the same God, lest they cease to fear the God who is over you both; for he comes not to call men with respect of persons, but those whom the Spirit has prepared. 11 But do you who are slaves be subject to your master, as to God's representative, in reverence and fear. 12 Thou shalt hate all hypocrisy, and everything that is not pleasing to the Lord. 13 Thou shalt not forsake the commandments of the Lord, but thou shalt keep what thou didst receive, "adding nothing to it and taking nothing away." 14 In the congregation thou shalt confess thy transgressions, and thou shalt not betake thyself to prayer with an evil conscience. This is the Way of Life.

CHAPTER 5

The Way of Death

1 But the Way of Death is this: First of all, it is wicked and full of cursing, murders, adulteries, lusts, fornications, thefts, idolatries, witchcrafts, charms, robberies, false witness, hypocrisies, a double heart, fraud, pride, malice, stubbornness, covetousness, foul speech, jealousy, impudence, haughtiness, boastfulness. 2 Persecutors of the good, haters of truth, lovers of lies, knowing not the reward of righteousness, not cleaving to the good nor to righteous judgment, spending wakeful nights not for good but for wickedness, from whom meekness and patience is far, lovers of vanity, following after reward, unmerciful to the poor, not working for him who is oppressed with toil, without knowledge of him who made them, murderers of children, corrupters of God's creatures, turning away the needy, oppressing the distressed, advocates of the rich, unjust judges of the poor, altogether sinful; may ye be delivered, my children, from all these.

CHAPTER 6

Final exhortation -- Food, and `things offered to idols.'

1 See "that no one make thee to err" from this Way of the teaching, for he teaches thee without God. 2 For if thou canst bear the whole yoke of the Lord, thou wilt be perfect, but if thou canst not, do what thou canst. 3 And concerning food, bear what thou canst, but keep strictly from that which is offered to idols, for it is the worship of dead gods.

CHAPTER 7

Baptism

1 Concerning baptism, baptise thus: Having first rehearsed all these things, "baptise, in the Name of the Father and of the Son and of the Holy Spirit," in running water; 2 but if thou hast no running water, baptise in other water, and if thou canst not in cold, then in warm. 3 But if thou hast neither, pour water three times on the head "in the Name of the Father, Son and Holy Spirit." 4 And before the baptism let the baptizer and him who is to be baptized fast, and any others who are able. And thou shalt bid him who is to be baptized to fast one or two days before.

CHAPTER 8

Fasting -- Prayers

1 Let not your fasts be with the hypocrites, for they fast on Mondays and Thursdays, but do you fast on Wednesdays and Fridays. 2 And do not pray as the hypocrites, but as the Lord commanded in his Gospel, pray thus: "Our Father, who art in Heaven, hallowed be thy Name, thy Kingdom come, thy will be done, as in Heaven so also upon earth; give us to-day our daily bread, and forgive us our debt as we forgive our debtors, and lead us not into trial, but deliver us from the Evil One, for thine is the power and the glory for ever." 3 Pray thus three times a day.

CHAPTER 9

The Eucharist -- The Cup -- The Bread

1 And concerning the Eucharist, hold Eucharist thus: 2 First concerning the Cup, "We give thanks to thee, our Father, for the Holy Vine of David thy child, which, thou didst make known to us through Jesus thy child; to thee be glory for ever." 3 And concerning the broken Bread: "We give thee thanks, our Father, for the life and knowledge which thou didst

make known to us through Jesus thy Child. To thee be glory for ever. 4
As this broken bread was scattered upon the mountains, but was brought
together and became one, so let thy Church be gathered together from the
ends of the earth into thy Kingdom, for thine is the glory and the power
through Jesus Christ for ever." 5 But let none eat or drink of your
Eucharist except those who have been baptised in the Lord's Name. For
concerning this also did the Lord say, "Give not that which is holy to the
dogs."

CHAPTER 10

The final prayer in the Eucharist

1 But after you are satisfied with food, thus give thanks: 2 "We give
thanks to thee, O Holy Father, for thy Holy Name which thou didst make
to tabernacle in our hearts, and for the knowledge and faith and
immortality which thou didst make known to us through Jesus thy Child.
To thee be glory for ever. 3 Thou, Lord Almighty, didst create all things
for thy Name's sake, and didst give food and drink to men for their
enjoyment, that they might give thanks to thee, but us hast thou blessed
with spiritual food and drink and eternal light through thy Child. 4 Above
all we give thanks to thee for that thou art mighty. To thee be glory for
ever. 5 Remember, Lord, thy Church, to deliver it from all evil and to
make it perfect in thy love, and gather it together in its holiness from the
four winds to thy kingdom which thou hast prepared for it. For thine is
the power and the glory for ever. 6 Let grace come and let this world pass
away. Hosannah to the God of David. If any man be holy, let him come!
if any man be not, let him repent: Maranatha, Amen." 7 But suffer the
prophets to hold Eucharist as they will. 8 -- none –

CHAPTER 11

Traveling Teachers—Apostles—Prophets

1 Whosoever then comes and teaches you all these things aforesaid,
receive him. 2 But if the teacher himself be perverted and teach another
doctrine to destroy these things, do not listen to him, but if his teaching
be for the increase of righteousness and knowledge of the Lord, receive
him as the Lord. 3 And concerning the Apostles and Prophets, act thus
according to the ordinance of the Gospel. 4 Let every Apostle who comes
to you be received as the Lord, 5 but let him not stay more than one day,
or if need be a second as well; but if he stay three days, he is a false
prophet. 6 And when an Apostle goes forth let him accept nothing but
bread till he reach his night's lodging; but if he ask for money, he is a
false prophet. 7 Do not test or examine any prophet who is speaking in a

spirit, "for every sin shall be forgiven, but this sin shall not be forgiven." 8 But not everyone who speaks in a spirit is a prophet, except he have the behaviour of the Lord. From his behaviour, then, the false prophet and the true prophet shall be known. 9 And no prophet who orders a meal in a spirit shall eat of it: otherwise he is a false prophet. 10 And every prophet who teaches the truth, if he do not what he teaches, is a false prophet. 11 But no prophet who has been tried and is genuine, though he enact a worldly mystery of the Church, if he teach not others to do what he does himself, shall be judged by you: for he has his judgment with God, for so also did the prophets of old. 12 But whosoever shall say in a spirit `Give me money, or something else,' you shall not listen to him; but if he tell you to give on behalf of others in want, let none judge him.

CHAPTER 12

Traveling Christians

1 Let everyone who "comes in the Name of the Lord" be received; but when you have tested him you shall know him, for you shall have understanding of true and false. 2 If he who comes is a traveler, help him as much as you can, but he shall not remain with you more than two days, or, if need be, three. 3 And if he wishes to settle among you and has a craft, let him work for his bread. 4 But if he has no craft provide for him according to your understanding, so that no man shall live among you in idleness because he is a Christian. 5 But if he will not do so, he is making traffic of Christ; beware of such.

CHAPTER 13

Prophets who desire to remain -- Their payment by firstfruits

1 But every true prophet who wishes to settle among you is "worthy of his food." 2 Likewise a true teacher is himself worthy, like the workman, of his food. 3 Therefore thou shalt take the firstfruit of the produce of the winepress and of the threshing-floor and of oxen and sheep, and shalt give them as the firstfruits to the prophets, for they are your high priests.

4 But if you have not a prophet, give to the poor. 5 If thou makest bread, take the firstfruits, and give it according to the commandment. 6 Likewise when thou openest a jar of wine or oil, give the firstfruits to the prophets. 7 Of money also and clothes, and of all your possessions, take the firstfruits, as it seem best to you, and give according to the commandment.

CHAPTER 14

The Sunday worship

1 On the Lord's Day of the Lord come together, break bread and hold Eucharist, after confessing your transgressions that your offering may be pure; 2 but let none who has a quarrel with his fellow join in your meeting until they be reconciled, that your sacrifice be not defiled. 3 For this is that which was spoken by the Lord, "In every place and time offer me a pure sacrifice, for I am a great king," saith the Lord, "and my name is wonderful among the heathen."

CHAPTER 15

Bishops and Deacons -- Mutual reproofs

1 Appoint therefore for yourselves bishops and deacons worthy of the Lord, meek men, and not lovers of money, and truthful and approved, for they also minister to you the ministry of the prophets and teachers. 2 Therefore do not despise them, for they are your honourable men together with the prophets and teachers. 3 And reprove one another not in wrath but in peace as you find in the Gospel, and let none speak with any who has done a wrong to his neighbour, nor let him hear a word from you until he repents. 4 But your prayers and alms and all your acts perform as ye find in the Gospel of our Lord.

CHAPTER 16

Warning that the end is at hand

1 "Watch" over your life: "let your lamps" be not quenched "and your loins" be not ungirded, but be "ready," for ye know not "the hour in which our Lord cometh." 2 But be frequently gathered together seeking the things which are profitable for your souls, for the whole time of your faith shall not profit you except ye be found perfect at the last time; 3 for in the last days the false prophets and the corrupters shall be multiplied, and the sheep shall be turned into wolves, and love shall change to hate; 4 for as lawlessness increaseth they shall hate one another and persecute and betray, and then shall appear the deceiver of the world as a Son of God, and shall do signs and wonders and the earth shall be given over into his hands and he shall commit iniquities which have never been since the world began. 5 Then shall the creation of mankind come to the fiery trial and "many shall be offended" and be lost, but "they who endure" in their faith "shall be saved" by the curse itself. 6 And "then shall appear the signs" of the truth. First the sign spread out in Heaven, then the sign of the sound of the trumpet, and thirdly the resurrection of

the dead: 7 but not of all the dead, but as it was said, "The Lord shall come and all his saints with him." 8 Then shall the world "see the Lord coming on the clouds of Heaven."

NOTES: [1]This is the so-called "negative form of the Golden Rule." It is found in some manuscripts in the "Apostolic decrees" in Acts 15:28, and is, in various forms, met with in Jewish and early Christian literature.

[2]The Greek is literally "for thou art not even able"; but this makes no sense, and though an emendation is difficult the sense must be something like that given by the translation -- unless, indeed, the whole phrase be merely a flippant gloss, which has been erroneously taken into the

[3]On the ground of a comparison with Jude 22 f. etc., some think that "and some thou shalt pity" ought to be added.

[4]This is the traditional translation of epiousion, but it is by no means certain that it is correct. The word has from the beginning been a puzzle, and its meaning is not clearly known. See further any good commentary on the gospels.

[5]The translation fails to preserve the play on the words, which might be rendered "concerning the giving of thanks, give thanks thus, etc." But this would obscure the fact that eucharistia is here quite clearly "Eucharist" (cf. verse 5).

[6]A transliteration of Aramaic words meaning "Our Lord! Come!"

[7]It is unknown to what ordinance the writer refers.

[8]This passage has never been satisfactorily explained: it probably refers to a tendency among some prophets to introduce forms of worship, or of illustration of their teaching, of doubtful propriety, if so the reference below to the prophets of old is perhaps an allusion to Hosea (Hos. 1:2 ff.).

[9]Literally, "right and left understanding."

[10]The meaning is obscure; but there seem to be other traces in early literature of a doctrine that each curse also contained the elements of a counterbalancing power to salvation. There is a valuable and long note on the subject in Rendel Harris's edition of the Didache.

APPENDIX B: CREEDS THAT FOLLOWED THE NICENE CREED

It is odd that God never felt that He had to continually create scriptures to explain Himself. Yet for centuries after Constantine's death, different groups took turns re-interpreting and re-explaining the mysterious Trinity. Here are a few examples:

Apostles' Creed

I believe in God the Father, Almighty, Maker of heaven and earth: And in Jesus Christ, his only begotten Son, our Lord: Who was conceived by the Holy Ghost, born of the Virgin Mary: Suffered under Pontius Pilate; was crucified, dead and buried: He descended into hell: The third day he rose again from the dead: He ascended into heaven, and sits at the right hand of God the Father Almighty: From thence he shall come to judge the quick and the dead: I believe in the Holy Ghost: I believe in the holy Catholic Church: the communion of saints: The forgiveness of sins: The resurrection of the body: And the life everlasting. Amen.

The Athanasian Creed (Date: Unknown)

Essentially an amplification of the Nicene Creed, the Athanasian Creed received general adoption by the Western churches. The words of this creed are as follows:

We worship one God in trinity, and trinity in unity, neither confounding the persons nor dividing the substance. For the person of the Father is one; of the Son, another; of the Holy Spirit, another. But the divinity of the Father and of the Son and of the Holy Spirit is one, the glory equal, the majesty equal. Such as is the Father, such also is the Son, and such the Holy Spirit. The Father is uncreated, the Son is uncreated, the Holy Spirit is uncreated. The Father is infinite, the Son is infinite, the Holy Spirit is infinite. The Father is eternal, the Son is eternal, the Holy Spirit is eternal. And yet there are not three eternal Beings, but one eternal Being. So also there are not three uncreated Beings, nor three infinite Beings, but one uncreated and one infinite Being. In like manner, the Father is omnipotent, the Son is omnipotent, and the Holy Spirit is omnipotent. And yet there are not three omnipotent Beings, but one omnipotent Being. Thus the Father is God, the Son is God, and the Holy Spirit is God. And yet there are not three Gods, but one God only. The Father is Lord, the Son is Lord, and the Holy Spirit is Lord. And yet there are not three Lords, but one Lord only. For as we are compelled by Christian truth to confess each person distinctively to be both God and Lord, we are prohibited by the Roman Catholic religion to say that there are three Gods or Lords. The Father is made by none, nor created, nor begotten. The Son is from the Father alone, not made, not created, but begotten. The Holy Spirit is not created by the Father and the Son, nor begotten, but proceeds. Therefore, there is one Father, not three Fathers; one Son, not three Sons; one Holy Spirit, not three Holy Spirits. And in this Trinity there is nothing prior or posterior, nothing greater or less, but all three persons are coeternal and coequal to themselves. So that through all, as was said above, both unity in trinity and trinity in unity is to be adored. Whoever would be saved, let him thus think concerning the Trinity.

The Chalcedonian Creed (AD 451)

Eutichus, the founder of Eutichianism, argued that *Yeshua's* (*Jesus'*) human and divine natures merged to form a third composite nature.

The divine nature was so modified and accommodated to the human nature that Christ was not really divine...At the same time the human nature was so modified and changed by assimilation to the divine nature that He was no longer genuinely human.

Thus, according to this teaching, Yeshua (Jesus) was neither fully human nor fully divine. Eutichianism was condemned by the Council of Chalcedon in AD 451.

The Chalcedonian Creed reads as follows:

We, then, following the holy Fathers, all with one consent, teach men to confess one and the same Son, our Lord Jesus Christ, the same perfect in Godhead and also perfect in manhood; truly God and truly man, of a reasonable [rational] soul and body; consubstantial [co-essential] with the Father according to the Godhead, and consubstantial with us according to the Manhood; in all things like unto us, without sin; begotten before all ages of the Father according to the Godhead, and in these latter days, for us and for our salvation, born of the Virgin Mary, the Mother of God, according to the Manhood; one and the same Christ, Son, Lord, only begotten, to be acknowledged in two natures, inconfusedly, unchangeably, indivisibly, inseparably; the distinction of natures being by no means taken away by the union, but rather the property of each nature being preserved, and concurring in one Person and one Subsistence, not parted or divided into two persons, but one and the same Son, and only begotten, God the Word, the Lord Jesus Christ; as the prophets from the beginning [have declared] concerning Him, and the Lord Jesus Christ Himself has taught us, and the Creed of the holy Fathers has handed down to us.

The Westminster Confession of Faith (AD 1646)

The Westminster Confession arose from the stormy political scene in England during the reign of Charles I:

Charles met with resistance when he attempted to impose episcopacy on the Church of Scotland and to conform its services to the Church of England's Common Book of Prayer. A civil war erupted and Oliver Cromwell led the Puritan forces to victory. Charles I was beheaded in the process. In 1643 the English parliament commissioned the Westminster Assembly to develop the creed of the Church of England. The 121 English Puritan ministers met for 1,163 daily sessions from 1643 to 1649. The Westminster Confession of Faith, completed in 1646, affirmed a strong Calvinistic position and disavowed 'the errors of Arminianism, Roman Catholicism, and sectarianism.

Below is the Statement of God found in the Westminster Confession of Faith:

I. There is but one only living and true God, who is infinite in being and perfection, a most pure spirit, invisible, without body, parts, or passions, immutable, immense, eternal, incomprehensible, almighty, most wise, most holy, most free, most absolute, working all things according to the counsel of His own immutable and most righteous will, for His own glory; most loving, gracious, merciful, long-suffering, abundant in goodness and truth, forgiving iniquity, transgression, and sin; the rewarder of them that diligently seek Him; and withal most just and terrible in His judgments, hating all sin, and who will by no means clear the guilty.

II. God hath all life, glory, goodness, blessedness, in and of Himself; and is alone in and unto Himself all-sufficient, not standing in need of any creatures which He hath made, nor deriving any glory from them, but only manifesting His own glory in, by, unto, and upon them: He is the alone fountain of all being, of whom, through whom, and to whom, are all things; and hath most sovereign dominion over them, to do by them, for them, and upon them, whatsoever Himself pleaseth. In His sight all things are open and manifest; His knowledge is infinite, infallible, and independent upon the creature, so as nothing is to Him contingent or uncertain. He is most holy in all His counsels, in all His works, and in all His commands. To Him is due from angels and men, and every other creature, whatsoever worship, service, or obedience He is pleased to require of them. In the unity of the Godhead there are three Persons of one substance, power, and eternity; God the Father, God the Son, and God the Holy Ghost. The Father is of none, neither begotten nor proceeding; the Son is eternally begotten of the Father; the Holy Ghost eternally proceeding from the Father and the Son.

PART 6

REFORMATION ERA
AD 1400 - c.1700

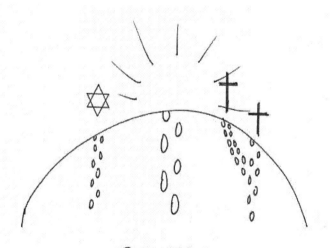

REFORMATION

DIDN'T THE REFORMATION FIX EVERYTHING?

At this point you may be thinking, "Okay, I get that the history of our faith was filled with a lot of problems. But didn't the Reformation solve them all?"

Vast numbers of books have been written about the Reformation, and although the short answer is no, in *no* way am I minimizing the importance of the corrections that did follow Martin Luther's historic act of nailing his 95 Theses to the castle church door in Germany. An adequate account of the enormous significance of that great era of history is beyond the scope of this book. The purpose of this section is

CRUCIAL POINT: *It was a "REFORMATION", that is, a "RE-FORM" of an existing system back toward the original, not a "FORMATION" of something new.*

to allow you to see what *did not* happen during that time. What infections survived? I want to use a "hypothetical" numeric example to illustrate the course of religious history. If the evolution of Rabbinic Judaism is perceived as seven steps to the left of God, then the evolution of Roman Catholicism would be seen as seven steps to the right of God. In this context, the Reformation would count as one step back towards God on the right side. (There is no idiom attached to "left" or "right," it's just allegoric—the point is the weight or impact of each. Although the Reformation was influential, it was far outweighed in impact by the corruption that had already taken place in both Rabbinic Judaism and Roman Catholicism.) To understand the purpose of the Reformation, we need to examine what they were actually seeking to reform and why it was in such desperate need of a course correction. What the Reformers did was to "re-form" or modify the existing religion — Roman Catholicism — to accommodate the new revelation or paradigm. Luther's new religion wasn't a new religion at all. It was merely "saved" Roman Catholics calling themselves Lutherans.

In contrast, what Constantine did (and the Rabbinical Jews for that matter), was to cannibalize an existing religious structure and create an entirely new religion utilizing some of the old terms. Constantine even used the same name: Christianity.

A Brief Look at the Evolution of the Infected Monster

I was recently at a conference and heard a man praising Constantine, "When he came to power there were only 4 million Christians, and when he died there were 60 million Christians." I had to laugh. Just like so many, he was quoting "revised" Catholic history as propagated by the infected monster, the Roman Catholic Church.

I have no idea about the accuracy of his numbers but I can attest to the fact that before Constantine came to power it was a capital offence, punishable by public execution, to be a Christian and by the time he died he had made it the strongest political party in the empire. Unfortunately, in the process he totally corrupted it, infecting it with a Stage V infection and single-handedly producing the worst killing machine that history would see for thousands of years. In two generations of Christianity, the Roman Catholic Church became the infamous bloody tyrant the world would come to fear. Personally, I don't see that as progress.

After Constantine's death, the Roman Catholic Church was recognized as the official religion of the empire. Because of its numbers, wealth, and political power, it was already the second most powerful organization on the planet. Only the Roman Empire had more power, and even mighty Rome would eventually bow to the Church.

The Roman Catholic Church rose to world power and for a period in time actually ruled the vast majority of what was known as the civilized world. With references like *Foxe's Book of Martyrs* and *Vatican II*, it's easy to say that the Roman Catholic Church murdered tens of millions of people and became one of the most brutal, cruel, deplorable, sadistic torturing machines in history. You have to put them up there with *Genghis Khan* and *Attila the Hun*, but what makes it worse, to me, is that it was all done under the counterfeit, sick, infected proclamation of Christianity. The only other religion that ever came close to this level of violence and bloodthirsty power is Islam, but historically it didn't have the same sophistication. (It is my belief that Islam is gaining that and the power to make another run at world domination.)

> **CRUCIAL POINT:** *When Constantine came to power, Christians were willing to die for their faith, but by the time Constantine died they were willing to murder for it. While that statement did not apply to everyone, it did apply to the religious system that Constantine created.*

Here is a partial list from one of the websites that claims to have the research of the doctrinal evolution of the Roman Catholic Church. Some of the dates are verifiable from the Catholic Encyclopedia. However, utilizing the infected records of infected organizations has been a frustration to this writer. There is ample evidence of historical revisionism, cover-ups, misrepresentations and various attempts to hide, or at least justify, previous actions and errors.

AD 379	Praying to Mary & Saints (prayers of Ephraim Syrus)
AD 389	Mariology begins with Gregory Nazianzen, who mentions in a eulogy how Justina had besought the Virgin Mary to protect her virginity
AD 416	Infant baptism by immersion commanded of all infants (Council of Mela, Austin was the principal director)
AD 430	Exaltation of Virgin Mary: "Mother of God" first applied by the Council of Ephesus
AD 502	Church clergy special dress code at all times
AD 519	Lent
AD 526	Extreme Unction (anointing of the sick)
AD 593	The Doctrine of Purgatory popularized from the Apocrypha by Gregory the Great
AD 607	First Pope: Boniface III is the first person to take the title of "Universal Bishop" by decree of Emperor Phocas
AD 709	Kissing of Pope Constantine's feet
AD 753	Baptism by sprinkling for those on sick beds officially accepted
AD 787	Worship of icons and statue approved (2nd council of Nicea)
AD 850	Burning of Holy Candles
AD 995	Canonization of dead saints, by Pope John XV

AD 998	Good Friday: fish only and the eating of red meat forbidden
AD 1009	Holy water
AD 1268	Priestly power of absolution
AD 1414	Laity no longer offered Lord's cup at communion (Council of Constance)
AD 1439	Doctrine of Seven Sacraments affirmed

From the year AD 325 (Council of Nicea), the power and doctrines of Constantine permeated the Roman Catholic Church as it continued to evolve. From its infected inception, the Roman Catholic Church's method of adapting easily to paganism allowed her to spread rapidly into other cultures.

Becoming more Babylonian each year, she gradually bore no resemblance at all to the movement begun by the Hebrew Messiah Lamb from Jerusalem. She did, however, retain two attributes of her founder, Emperor Constantine: She destroyed anyone who opposed her, and maintained her hatred for the Jews. It's one of the religions that seem to have been created and maintained in a Stage V infection.

Early Attempts at Reformation

Although the *Protestant Reformation* officially started in the 1500s, the fires of dissent started immediately after the Council of Nicea. Pastors and church leaders all over the empire disagreed with the edicts of AD 325, and began having "counter-councils" to refute such notions as Constantine's godhead doctrine. Because God always has a remnant unto Himself, these early Church leaders understood what Constantine's words meant; they refused to accept the teaching that *Yeshua* (Jesus) was identical to the Father.

The following is from Bernard Lonergan's book *The Way to Nicea* and is a partial list of councils called to refute the Nicene edicts with the references of each council:

7. Those who were dissatisfied with the Nicene Creed composed many rival creeds, in various places, at various times, and on various occasions, between the years 340 and 360.[22]

(1) The second council of Antioch, known as the Dedication Council, was held in 341. Four credal formulae are attributed to this council. Bardy (p. 122) thinks that the second of the four goes back to Ludan of Antioch, and he notes that the fourth did not emerge from the council itself, but was drawn up by four bishops a little later.[23]

(2) In 343, the Eastern bishops, refusing to enter into discussion with the "orthodox", who were gathered together in Sardica, withdrew to Philippopolis, where they held a council of their own and produced their own creed.[24]

(3) What is known as the Long-lined Creed, dating from the year 345, is an exposition of the faith prepared for the Emperor Constantius; four Eastern bishops brought it with them to Milan, where they sought to explain the Eastern theological standpoint to their Western colleagues and the Emperor Constans.[25]

(4) The first council of Sirmium, held in 351.[26]

(5) The second council of Sirmium, held in 357, produced a creed that Hilary called "the blasphemy of Sirmium".[27]

(6) The third council of Sirmium, held in 358, produced no new creed, but reaffirmed older ones, namely, those composed against Paul of Samosata and Photinus, and one of the creeds attributed to the second council of Antioch.[28]

(7) The bipartite general council, held at Rimini in the West and Seleuria in the East, is made up of many different episodes.

(a) The fourth creed of Sirmium, dated May 25, 359, was to be signed by all of the bishops, from the East and from the West alike. This was the emperor's way of preparing the ground for the council.[29]

(b) At Rimini, where more than 400 Western bishops had assembled, eighty Arians approved die fourth creed of Sirmium, on July 12, 359. The other bishops rejected it, and reaffirmed the faith of Nicea. Further, they excommunicated four bishops who were attached to the court of the emperor, namely, Valens, Ursacius, Germinius and Gaius; and they sent a deputation of ten bishops to the Emperor himself.[30]

(c) At Nike, in Thrace, on October 10, 359, the delegates from Rimini were forced both to revoke the above-mentioned excommunication and to subscribe to an ambiguously worded creed.[31]

(d) At Rimini, on the return of their delegates, the orthodox bishops, confused and deceived, submitted to the Emperor's demands [32] It is to this that Jerome refers when he says: "The whole world groaned, astonished to find that it was Arian".[33]

(e) The Eastern bishops came together at Seleucia, from September 27 to September 30, 359. There the Homoeousians revived the second creed of the Dedication Council, hoping to have it endorsed by the assembly; the Acacians, for their part, attempted to impose their own formula.[34]

(f) Delegates from both sides, (Homoeousians and Acacians) sent to the Emperor at Constantinople, were, given the choice of subscribing to an ambiguous credal formula, very similar to the one imposed on the Western bishops at Nike on October 10, 359, or of going into exile.[35]

Bernard Lonergan, *The Way To Nicea*, pgs. 78-80

[22] See Athan., *De synodis,* MG 26, 681-793; Hilar., *De synedis,* ML 10, 471-545; the ancient Church historians: Socrates and Sozomen, MG 67; Theodoret, MG 82; Hahn, *Bibliothek* der *Symbole.* Breslau, 1897; Hefele-Lecdercq, *Histore desconcilles,* I, 2, 633, 987, Paris, 1947. P. Smulders, *La doctrine trinitare* de S. *Hilaiire de Poitiers,* Rome, 1944, Anal. Greg. 32.

[23] The credal formula is to be found in Hahn, §§ 153-156, and Athanasius S§ 22-25. Sec Smuldcrs, pp. 33-24.

[24] The credal formula of this council is to be found in Hahn, § 158, and Hilary, § 34. See Smulders, pp. 25 ff. •

[25] Hahn, § 159; Athanasius, § 26; Smulders, p. 29 f.

[26] DS 139 f; Hahn, § 160; Athanasius, § 26; Smulders, pp. 29 ff.

[27] Hahn, § 161; Hilary, § 11; Smulders, p. 44.

[28] Sozomen, IV, 15; MG 67,1152; Smulders, p. 5.

[29] Hahn, § 163; Athanasius, § 8; Smulders, p. 57.

[30] Smulders, p. 58 f.

[31] This formula is to be found in Hahn, § 164; Theodoret, n, 16; MG 82, 1049; cf. Smulders, p. 59.

[32] Smulders, p. 60; cf. Hahn,§ 166; Jerome, *Dialogue against the Luciferans, IT, ML* 23, 710.

[33] Jerome, *ibid.,* 19, col. 181.

[34] The Acacian formula is to be found in Hahn, § 165; Athanasius, § 29; cf. Smulders, p. 61 f.

[35] This formula is to be found in Hahn, § 167; Athanasius, § 30; cf. Smulders,p. 65 ff.

Most people were taught that the edicts issued by the Council of Nicea were enthusiastically welcomed by all but the Arians. Lonergan's book is a record of the men who were not infected the same way and who did not agree with the Constantine doctrine known as Trinitarianism. The book also records the debates and individual doctrines presented at each of these councils.

From early in the twelfth century onward there were calls for reform. Between 1215 and 1545 nine church councils were held with church reforms as their primary intent. The councils all failed to reach significant accord (James Jackson, *The Reformation and Counter-Reformation*).

CHRISTIANITY EVOLVES FROM PAGAN ROMAN CATHOLICISM

The long period following the downfall of the Roman Empire in the west is known today as the Dark Ages. It was an era brought on, for the most part, by the Roman Catholic Church in Stage V infection; an era in which she tried to blot out all light and truth, and slaughtered anyone who dared disagree with her actions and teachings. The inquisitions were not only her wrath on those who opposed her, but also provided another way to continue her policy of purging the world of the Jews. Compared to the millions of innocent lives destroyed by the Roman Catholic Church in the name of Christianity, Hitler and Stalin combined barely scratched the surface.

Perhaps the most feared and infamous example of the Church's arrogance, suppression, and diabolical hatred was the centuries-long campaign known as the Crusades. Roman Catholic historians of the day portrayed the Crusades — the rescue of Jerusalem and the Holy Land from Islamic Arabs — as a lofty and sacred cause and an exercise in knightly chivalry. Absent from writings on the subject were the details including persecution of Jews, which were anything but noble.

On their way to drive the infidel Arabs out of Jerusalem, these holy fighters for the Cross decided to drive the Jews out of the lands through which they were marching. Jewish men were killed and Jewish women were raped all along the way to and from the Holy Land. In their wake were left not tens, hundreds, or thousands, but multiplied thousands of pregnant Jewish women and young girls. So many babies were born that the Jewish community had to determine what to do with this avalanche of half-breed children. What were they to do with the children? Were they to be raised as Jews or as gentiles?

The decision was an inclusive one. Jewish lineage was to be changed from the father to the mother so that any child born to a Jewish mother would be considered Jewish, and thereby afforded all the love, privileges, and heritage of a Jew.

To this day, the Jews still trace their lineage through the mother. When you ask them why, many either cannot or will not tell you. They may simply not know because they haven't been told, or they don't want to tell you. Imagine if your family lineage was traced back to an era of mass rape.

NOTE: Some historians claim that the lineage change took place after the destruction of the Temple in AD 70. Some Jewish scholars claim that that it has always been that way, but history suggests otherwise.

The Evolution of Protestantism: *The Modern Christian View*

In and of itself, the Reformation was a wonderful thing. After long centuries of containment and suppression in the Dark and later Middle Ages, the scriptures were read by hungry men and women and many sacred truths discovered. Church power was opposed; groups and denominations were formed, and more truth was taught than had been known since early Church times. Each revelation of truth was an *injection* for a specific *infection*.

However, with all of these wonderful events, it is important to remember that the reformers were coming out of the Roman Catholic Church; they were highly infected pagans. Secondly, they were *re-forming* Catholicism, not *returning to* a full Biblical worldview. In other words, they were adding a new room to the existing building. Along with their individual, vital revelations, they carried forward the rest of the infected pagan practices of Roman Catholicism. As we mentioned earlier, Martin Luther was one such reformer.

Martin Luther re-discovered the incredible revelation that an individual is saved by grace, not through or by the Roman Catholic Church. This is an unmistakable, monumental truth that comes straight from Scripture, a remarkable vision for someone locked inside the doctrines of the Roman Catholic Church. Martin Luther walked forward in the light that he had, but unfortunately brought with him the entire sack of Stage V, epidemic level, Roman Catholic paganism which included the anti-Semitism. How infected was Martin Luther? Did you ever wonder where Hitler got all his ideas regarding *The Final Solution*? How could Hitler be so demented? Let's examine one of his textbooks, written by none other than Martin Luther.

In 1543 the German leader Martin Luther advocated in his book, *DIE JUDEN UND IHREN LUEGEN (The Jews and Their Lies)*, the anti-Jewish measures that the Nazis followed almost to the letter. He wrote:

"First...set fire to their synagogues or schools and...bury and cover with dirt whatever will not burn, so that no man will ever again see a stone or cinder of them. This is to be done in honor of our Lord and of Christendom, so that God might see that we are Christians... [It would be good if someone could also throw in some] hellfire."

"Second, I advise that their houses also be razed and destroyed."

"Third, I advise that all their prayer books and Talmudic writings, in which such idolatry, lies, cursing, and blasphemy are to be taught, be taken from them...also the entire Bible...[The Jews] be forbidden on pain of death to praise God, to give thanks, to pray, and to teach publicly among us and in our country...[T]hey be forbidden to utter the name of God within our hearing...We must not consider the mouth of the Jews as worthy of uttering the name of God within our hearing. He who hears this name from a Jew must inform the authorities, or else throw sow dung at him when he sees him and chase him away. And may no one be merciful and kind in this regard.

". . . For they are a heavy burden, a plague, a pestilence, a sheer misfortune for our country."

"[Today's Jews] are nothing but thieves and robbers who daily eat no morsel and wear no thread of clothing which they have not stolen and pilfered from us by means of their accursed usury. Thus they live from day to day, together with wife and child, by theft and robbery, as arch-thieves and robbers, in the most impenitent security...If I had power over the Jews, as our princes and cities have, I would deal severely with their lying mouth...For a usurer is an arch-thief and a robber who should rightly be hanged on the gallows seven times higher than other thieves."

"<u>We are even at fault in not avenging all this innocent blood</u> of our Lord and of the Christians which they shed for three hundred years after the destruction of Jerusalem, and the blood of the children they have shed since then (which still shines forth from their eyes and their skin). <u>We are at fault in not slaying them.</u>"

Did you get that? *"We are at fault in not slaying them!"* What Stage of infection did Martin Luther have? Did he write this before or after his great revelation? It goes on and on with a systematic way of eradicating the Jews from the face of the earth. Why? It's the way he was taught *all his life.* It's what Constantine taught! It's what the Roman Catholic Church taught! It is the basis of Replacement Theology and it is still being taught by many good men who believe they love God. This is a perfect example of a man having a great revelation, obviously straight from God, while remaining anti-Semitic and trapped in the teachings from his past. It becomes obvious that one revelation of truth does not cure all of the infection.

At this point, please let there be no misunderstanding. The intention is not to condemn Martin Luther, to lessen his accomplishments or the price he paid for his convictions. And it does need to be said that before he went on a rant campaign that he was kind to them early on in his desire to evangelize them. It was when they did not respond the way he wanted that he reacted pretty much the way the Roman Catholic Church would—to try to destroy them. But this is not about one man. We are establishing the factual and natural progressions of the Reformation and the evolution of the epidemic. The Reformation was like a marathon relay race. Each runner took a baton and ran his particular part of the course, moving the team forward toward the finish line. And the astounding good news is that the Reformation race is still not finished; the Church that was saturated with paganism is still evolving from it.

An example of the pagan influence that infiltrated the Church and still remains is the deletion of the Shema from the first commandment of the Ten Commandments, or Decalogue. It seems unimaginable to us today, but the Shema , *Hear oh Israel, the Lord our God, the Lord is one*, was actually deleted by Roman Catholicism.

When asked what the greatest commandment was, *Yeshua* (Jesus) responded:

> *And Jesus answered him, The first of all the commandments is,* **Hear, O Israel The Lord our God is one Lord**: *30 And thou shalt love the Lord thy God with all thy heart, and with all thy soul, and with all thy mind, and with all thy strength: this is the first commandment (Mk 12: 29, 30).*

Few realize that when they quote the first commandment, they are quoting the Roman Catholic version, which was minus the first phrase. If you were not taught the first part of the first commandment, you should be asking, "Why not?" These are two answers: first of all, it was a reminder of Israel and secondly, it refuted the Trinity.

An interesting phenomenon of the Reformation was that the major struggles between Roman Catholics and Protestants involved the way we approach God and the way of salvation, but not over the way He *exists*. The infected doctrines were passed down with the good. Sad to say, but the same pattern is repeated today in most institutions of higher theological learning. Rather than learning to study, students are programmed with infected denominational doctrines, mostly TWIB doctrines. Now, a certain amount of basic doctrine should be taught, but students should learn to read the originals, bathe them in prayer and fasting, and hear the voice of God for themselves. This would give us men and women of God instead of "Infected Hot Dogs" from the Infected Hot Dog factories.

Another amazing and tragic shortcoming of institutions, and people in general, is the willingness to adjust Scripture to fit their own paradigms. But if you want to grow as a son or daughter of God instead of being religious, don't adjust the Scripture to fit your paradigm—adjust your paradigm to fit God's. Forget about the box you are building for God, and get into the one He has already built for you.

Here is an illustration of how ignorant we are of the boxes that we so easily build or have been built for us. If you have moved over to Sunday for your Sabbath, believe in the Trinity, and celebrate Easter and Christmas each year, are you a Roman Catholic? Your response may be "no," but the residue of Roman Catholicism is still so ingrained in

Protestantism that you could easily be labeled Methodist-Roman Catholic, Baptist-Roman Catholic, Pentecostal-Roman Catholic, or Presbyterian-Roman Catholic.

If you accept the foundations of a religion and practice them, are you not part of them? If a Baptist believed that Joseph Smith was a prophet from God, that the Book of Mormon was inspired by God, and that Salt Lake City was the New Jerusalem, would he not be a Baptist-Mormon, or perhaps a Mormon-Baptist? If a Methodist believed that Allah was the true God, that Mohammad was his prophet, and that the Koran was the inspired word of God, wouldn't it make him a Methodist–Muslim, or perhaps a Muslim-Methodist? If a Charismatic went to synagogue on the Sabbath, worshiped the Jewish God, and kept all the Jewish holidays, wouldn't he be a Charismatic-Jew, or perhaps a Jewish-Charismatic?

If you were a Protestant who worshipped the Roman Catholic God, had a Roman Catholic Sabbath, and celebrated Roman Catholic holidays, what would that make you? You probably haven't thought of this before from this perspective, but the Catholics have. They claim anyone who goes to Church on Sunday pays homage to the Catholic Church because *they alone* changed it to Sunday, without scriptural authority.

THE REFORMATION AND THE SCRIPTURES:
The Bible is Made Available to the Masses

In the sack of infected errors that the reformers brought with them was the belief that Greek was the language of the original New Testament manuscripts. Limited in knowledge as they were, they had no way of knowing that their Greek texts were translations from Hebrew and Aramaic.

The objective of reform scholars was to find the best and most accurate Greek text. Sincere men who loved God, they were committed to presenting to the entire world the texts and the truths they contained. It was and is a task of the noblest order. Greek became the subject of intense study at Church institutions that trained numerous critics and experts of the Greek language and customs. Seminaries and other religious educational institutions embraced the notion that the language of the Greek texts was the language of the originals. That's what we were all taught.

Begun during the Reformation, the debates over which texts are the purest have been ongoing for the last few centuries. Countless books and papers have been written on the subject, and scholars continue to pore over manuscripts with fine-toothed combs, longing for new breakthroughs in textual accuracy. They have even counted the "variants," (which none would call mistakes), between each of the manuscripts.

As of this writing, the gatekeeper and moderator of the quest for the purest Greek text is Kurt Aland. Mr. Aland and his wife Barbara, from Germany, have been the leading authorities on the Greek text and the evolution of New Testament historicity since the midway point of the last century. They have published several works on the Greek New Testament, including a favorite of mine, *The Text of the New Testament* (second edition). Keeping in mind that the

Alands believe that the originals were in Greek, students will find the references in this excellent textbook to be most helpful.

The Greek manuscripts are divided into two main groups. The largest group and the one with more copies available, is known as the Majority Text. The Majority Text includes all Byzantine texts that originated in Constantine's day; they are known as the Western Text since Rome was in the Western Roman Empire at that time. The second group of texts, the Minority or Eastern Text, was long considered by scholars to be corrupt because it varied greatly from the Western text.

The test for measuring whether a text was credible or corrupt was really quite simple. If the text agreed with the Majority text and did not contradict the pagan foundation of the Roman Catholic Church, it was credible. If it disagreed, it was considered corrupt. The same test holds true today, with the exception being the Nestle-Aland team which produced a Greek New Testament based on many of the earliest pre-Constantine, Alexandrian, or Minority texts. This text was used by the New International Version, NIV, and the New American Standard Bible, NASB. This caused a furor among the protective scions of textual criticism, the "infected gate keepers."

All the men and women who have officially collected, catalogued, and translated the Greek texts have been infected Roman Catholics or Trinitarians who keep the infected Roman Catholic foundations of faith. These include such storied scholars as Westcott-Hort, Tischendorf, Van Soden, and Nestle-Aland. Many such men have resisted Roman Catholicism, including the Papacy, and some have been persecuted by it; still they have held to its early infected foundations. Understandably then, it should come as no surprise to find in Greek texts and translations a bias that reflects the beliefs of the workers.

Keeping in mind that God's plan of redemption can be found in all of the translations, it is of more than passing interest to view the biases of certain translators. Take, for example, the rhetoric of those who hold to the "King James Version only" perspective. While no small amount of sincerity and earnestness characterizes these people, so also do lack of learning and a marked paucity of real biblical education. Several have started their own infected Bible schools to propagate their beliefs, thereby creating a false sense of academic respectability. They bash Roman Catholicism in general, but then claim that the Roman Catholic Church corrupted every translation of the Bible except the King James version.

A little knowledge is a dangerous thing. Those with little more than a smattering of skill in textual criticism claim, "The *Textus Receptus* was the only anointed Greek original." Further, they assert: "God protected that specific text from the Roman Catholic Church, thereby allowing the true word of God to be preserved and delivered into the hands of the faithful." In point of fact, however, the *Textus Receptus* was a New Testament Greek text compiled by Roman Catholic scholar-priest Desiderius Erasmus. Furthermore, it was dedicated to the Pope. To that end, we include this observation by Kurt Aland:

> Then at the beginning of the sixteenth century two editions appeared: printing was completed for the New Testament part of the Complutensian Polyglot on January 10, 1514, and the *Novum Instrumentum Omne* of Desiderius Erasmus, the great humanist of Rotterdam, was published and marketed by Johann Froben in Basel on March 1, 1516. Although Erasmus' edition was produced later, it is famous as the first edition (editio princeps) of the Greek NT, fulfilling the goal of its editor and of its publisher. Both men were

well aware that Francisco Ximenes de Cisneros (1437-1517), <u>Cardinal and Archbishop of Toledo</u>, had received a license to publish a multivolume polyglot Bible.' ...The final volume of the polyglot was completed on July 10, 1517, shortly before the death of Ximenes, but publication of the whole work was delayed until March 22, 1520, <u>when papal authorization for its issuance was finally granted (after the manuscripts loaned from the Vatican library had been returned to Rome)</u>.

The identity of these manuscripts..., but the sources used by Erasmus for his edition are known. He took manuscripts most readily available to him in Basel for each part of the New Testament (the Gospels, the Apostolos [Acts and the Roman Catholic letters], the Pauline letters, and Revelation), entered corrections in them where he felt it necessary, and sent them directly to the printer, who treated these manuscripts like any ordinary typesetter copy. In two manuscripts preserved at the university library the evidence of this incredible process can still be examined in all its detail (cf. plate 2). Erasmus was unable to find in Basel any manuscript of the Revelation of John, so he borrowed one from his friend Johann Reuchlin. Because its ending was mutilated, **Erasmus simply translated Rev. 22:16-21 from Latin back into Greek (introducing several errors). He modified the text elsewhere as well, correcting it to the common Latin version.** ..."thrown together rather than edited" was how Erasmus described it later). But it gained for Erasmus and Froben the fame (and financial profit) of publishing the first edition of the Greek New Testament.

The most serious defect of the first edition of the Greek New Testament was not so much its innumerable errors[2] as the type of text it represented. Erasmus relied on manuscripts of the twelfth/thirteenth century which represented the Byzantine Imperial text, the Koine text, or the Majority text — however it may be known[3]—**the most recent and the poorest of the various New Testament text types, and his successors have done the same. This was the dominant form of the text in the fourteenth/ fifteenth century manuscript tradition, and even where earlier uncial manuscripts were available they were not consulted.**

Although the eighth-century uncial E or Basiliensis (which would have given him only a slightly earlier form of the same Byzantine text) was available to Erasmus in Basel, and **Theodore Beza's** personal library contained both Codex Bezae Can-tabrigiensis (D^e ^{a}) and Codex Claromontanus (D^p),[4] both scholars ignored these resources. ...Textus Receptus is the name by which the text of Erasmus has been known ever since an enterprising publisher, Elzevir, characterized it in 1633 in the following words: "Textum ergo habes, nunc ab omnibus receptum: in quo nihil immutatum aut corruptum damus...Yet no real progress was possible as long as the Textus Receptus remained the basic text and its authority was regarded as canonical. The days of the fifteenth century were long past, when the text of the Latin Vulgate was accepted as sufficient.[9] Every theologian of the sixteenth and seventeenth centuries (and not just the exegetical scholars) worked from an edition of Greek text of the NT which was regarded as the "revealed text." This idea of verbal inspiration (i.e., of the literal and inerrant inspiration of the text), which the orthodoxy of both Protestant traditions maintained so vigorously, was applied to **the Textus Receptus with all of its errors**, including textual modifications of an obviously secondary character (as we recognize them today).[10]

[1]. This was the normative text in England until 1880. The Greek letter stigma (5) still used as a symbol for the Textus Receptus in critical editions originally meant the text of Stephanus.

[2]. *Many of* these were pointed out to Erasmus by his contemporaries; a nineteenth-century critic in England called it the least carefully printed book ever published.

[3]. For these terms, cf. p. 66, etc.

[4]. For the explanation of manuscript symbols, cf. pp. 72ff.

[6]. Cf. p. 4.

[7]. Cf pp. 3f.

[8]. E g., in the London Polyglot the Greek and Vulgate texts were accompanied by the Syriac, Ethiopic, and Arabic, while for the Gospels there was also a Persian version, each with its own Latin gloss.

[9]. Except for the Roman Catholic Church and its theology, which maintained this position considerably longer.

[10]. Cf.pp. 279ff.

Kurt Aland and Barbara Aland, *The Text of The New Testament*, pgs. 3-7

The Aland comments are indeed sobering. In summary, the *Textus Receptus,* the Greek text used to create the King James Version, was called *the least carefully printed book ever published*. It was a hastily gathered collection of Byzantine pieces, full of mistakes, and rushed into production for the purpose of monetary gain.

Many who still insist that the *Textus Receptus* is the only inspired text obviously have not studied the text's history. Not that it would make much difference if they did. Most of them, in their infected state of blindness, would doubtless disregard history, assert the mystery of God's ways, and persevere in their infected error. It was also done *by* the Roman Catholics *for* the Roman Catholics. Wouldn't it be good if people did their homework before wrestling over these kinds of issues?

CRUCIAL POINT: *God is in all the translations and most of the texts! We can pick up any translation, from the Roman Catholic Bible to the Living Bible (which is a paraphrase for children, not a translation), and—if the Spirit of God is drawing us—find God. When God draws his children, He will put in their path the tools needed to find Him.*

It amuses me to hear KJV-only zealots offering rewards to anyone who can show an error or contradiction in the King James Bible. Of course, this silliness should never make those of us who know where they are become a stumbling block to the weaker brethren. None of the *translations* are inerrant; only the originals are, along with the One who inspired them. I do believe God has a sense of humor.

Personally, I love my King James Version. I grew up with it, I study with it, and I teach from it. It's my personal favorite! I also know where most of the translation errors are. I understand the text, and it doesn't confuse me. That's the position I believe is the best — realize that little in this world is perfect, know where the landmines are, and just avoid them.

The Wrong Approach

There is a critical error in the very approach to Scripture translation. All the translations, except the Amplified Bible, are done on a word-for-word basis. That means the translators take the original word from the text and select the most accurate word in the language they are translating to. In many cases it can't be done. Hebrew is a very simple language, while Greek is very sophisticated. The simpler the language, the more complex the words have to be. Here are a few examples, including one that works in the word-for-word method and a few that don't:

Messiah is the theme of the New Testament; it comes from the Hebrew word *mashiach*, a verb which means *anointed*. The Greek word selected by the translators is *christos*, a verb which also means *anointed*. Here you have a "word for word" that works between Hebrew and Greek. Unfortunately, when it moved into English they didn't use the verb *anointed*, they changed it to a noun, a title, and did a transliteration to Christ.

The most quoted New Testament scripture is John 3:16: *For God so loved the world, that he gave his only begotten Son, that whosoever believeth in him should not perish, but have everlasting life.*

The Greek word used for "believeth" is *pisteuo*. 4100. *pisteuo, pist-yoo'-o*; from G4102; to have faith (in, upon, or with respect to, a person or thing), i.e. credit; by impl. to entrust (espec. one's spiritual well-being to Christ):--believe (-r), commit (to trust), put in trust with. This Greek word has a triune meaning: to rely on, to trust in, and to cling to, with an emphasis on trusting.

The Hebrew word that is translated "believe" is *aman*. 539. *aman, aw-man'*; a prim. root; prop. to build up or support; to foster as a parent or nurse; fig. to render (or be) firm or faithful, to trust or believe, to be permanent or quiet; mor. to be true or certain; once (Isa. 30 : 21; by interch. for H541) to go to the right hand:--hence assurance, believe, bring up, establish, + fail, be faithful (of long continuance, stedfast, sure, surely, trusty, verified), nurse, (-ing father), (put), trust, turn to the right.

Even the Hebrew word has a multiple meaning, so using the word-for-word approach in this case (going from the Hebrew culture/language to the Greek culture/language) worked. However, in the next step (moving to the English culture/language), you lose the meaning, thus the power, of the word — it becomes "acknowledge," not "trust."

Let me show you another one that doesn't work well. The Hebrew word for "peace" is *shalom*. 965. *shalowm, shaw-lome'*; or *shalom, shaw-lome'*; from H7999; safe, i.e. (fig.) well, happy, friendly; also (abstr.) welfare, i.e. health, prosperity, peace:-- X do, familiar, X fare, favour, + friend, X greet, (good) health, (X perfect, such as be at) peace (-able, -ably), prosper (-ity, -ous), rest, safe (-ly), salute, welfare, (X all is, be) well, X wholly.

The word *shalom* has so many facets to it. It refers to every aspect of your body, soul, and spirit. It reflects your relationship with God, nature, wealth, your family, and your neighbors. It is the most complete blessing you can pronounce on anyone. There is not a single Greek or English word that can communicate the power in the blessing of the Hebrew word *shalom*. It is just not possible.

There are several Greek words that represent the concept of peace. The Greek word most commonly translated for peace is *eirene*. 1515. *eirene, i-ray'-nay*; prob. from a prim. Verb *eiro* (to join); peace (lit. or fig.); by impl. Prosperity: — one, peace, quietness, rest, + set at one again. This is the word that many use to imply that Christians should be wealthy.

Another Greek word for peace is *hesuchazo*. 2270. *hesuchazo, hay-soo-khad'-zo*; from the same as G2272; to keep still (intrans.) i.e. refrain from labor, meddlesomeness or speech: — cease, hold peace, be quiet, rest. (Luke 14:4 KJV) *And they held their peace. And he took him, and healed him, and let him go.....*

Let us look at one more example of translations and translators. The words "power" and "authority" have similar but different meanings. In the King James Version (especially the New Testament) it is consistently mistranslated, leaving the reader without a clear picture of the meaning.

What's the point? These were not men who understood the spiritual authority of the believer, nor did they grasp the power of God and how it worked. We are just now beginning to understand d this realm, so it has become more important to us. *NOTE:* Except for the editing and removal of the New Testament's Jewishness, I believe the Hebrew/Aramaic-to-Greek translations are, in most cases, more accurate than the Greek-to-English translations.

At this point, an important issue must be clarified: Hebrew New Testaments exist, but they were translated into Hebrew from Greek, English, or a language that came from an original Greek manuscript, and then translated back into Hebrew.

George M. Lamsa's Peshitta version is one such example. Mr. Lamsa claims that the original Aramaic used for his translation was untarnished by man, that his Aramaic text was a copy that came straight from the apostles' pens. One wishes that were true; it would make the age-old quest much easier. But the Aramaic text used for the Peshitta New Testament translation was obviously Hellenized; it was either originally translated from the Greek, or translated and made comparable to the Greek. In any case, it is no better than the average Greek text. The Old Testament Peshitta is good for study purposes, but an English translation of the Masoretic text is just as good for reference.

I want to make a final point about the Reformation and the King James Version text. The Jerome Comma is the most blatant example of the Reformation refusing to abolish its anti-Semitic foundation and even perjuring itself to propagate the Trinity doctrine. I John 5:7 is not in any Aramaic texts and is proven by many sources to have been added in the 16th century. It is omitted by all Greek manuscripts prior, and by most of the Latin fathers. Sir Isaac Newton points this out in an essay he wrote: *An Historical Account of Two Notable Corruptions of Scripture* (London: John Green, 1841, pp. 1-2. See Snedeker, pp. 118-120.

How can you print Bibles and call them infallible when you know for a fact that I John 5:7 and the closing of the Lord's Prayer in Matthew 6:13 were both added? While many scholars did not know about the corruption of Matthew 28:19 "in my name," I've never met a scholar that didn't know about the other two. So, why continue to print Bibles that we *know without argument* are in error? Why don't we have the courage to make them as close to the original manuscripts as we possibly can so that the masses can have what was so painstakingly preserved (often by bloodshed) and handed down to us?

CRUCIAL POINT: *Every branch of Christianity begun by the reformers carried forward the early infected foundational doctrines of the Roman Catholic Church, thereby perpetuating them.*

Of course, not all agree with that assessment. In their pamphlet *The Trail of Blood*, Baptists claim that rather than coming from the Roman Catholic Church, they are a remnant that traces its lineage all the way back to the apostles. If such is true, how and when did they adopt most of the early infected foundations of Roman Catholicism, *the Trinity, Sunday Sabbath, Easter and Christmas*, just like everyone else?

A similarly purist claim is made by Mormons; they claim theirs is the true religion of God, and that it evolved from Judaism, but they also carry the infected Catholic doctrines.

Years ago, I met a zealous young Mormon who (when he found out I was Jewish) got all excited and asked if I had read the Book of Mormon. I had not, and he told me all about a Jewish man who left Jerusalem with his family, built a boat, sailed to America, and built colonies. With all the sincerity of a new convert, he told me that the Book of Mormon was a record of this Jewish expedition.

In due time, I read the Book of Mormon, and it is an absolute certainty that whoever wrote it had neither a Jewish heritage nor even a close Jewish friend. The writer was completely devoid of any knowledge of Jewish customs, textual criticism and was obviously just rewriting Roman Catholic doctrines.

In fact, that's what they have all done. Constantine, the rabbis, the Mormons, and Mohammad are all guilty of just about identical crimes.

1. They redefined God
2. They redefined *Yeshua* (Jesus)
3. They redefined the rules of salvation and damnation
4. They create new scriptures, books, and/or edicts with the claim of divine revelation
5. They point their finger at everyone else and condemn them for doing exactly what they did

While they all teach very different doctrines, I can honestly say it looks to me as if they all get their revelation from the same source. What did I say earlier? *All religion is an infection!*

I did like one of the Mormon doctrines where everyone "gets in," or goes to heaven. If you are going to make up doctrine, make it where everybody goes to heaven. Why not? That is much better than sending everyone to hell! You gotta love it!

KEY POINTS THE REFORMATION DID NOT ADDRESS

The achievements of the Reformation are numerous, and I rejoice that I live on this side of that great awakening. But I do need to list a few of the things left to do as we complete the final phase of the Reformation—although I would much rather see a Transformation!

1. The removal of anti-Semitism from the Church.

2. The restoration of the Hebrew idioms, customs, and paradigms of the Bible.

3. The removal of the Church's pagan foundation:

    A. The Trinity Doctrine
    B. Easter & Christmas
    C. Sunday Sabbath (return to the seventh day, or Saturday)

4. The return to the priesthood of every believer (Maybe the most important point of all).

5. Restoration of the Feasts of God.

The mistake that most people make is to believe that the light given to them is the *final* revelation. A wave of excitement rises, a new denomination begins, word spreads that the new group is better than the old one. It's a familiar scenario, one that explains why we have so many infected denominations.

Revelation is like a coconut. You taste the milk and find that it is sweet. Then you break open the shell and eat the sweet meat of revelation; it's a simple two-step process. Truth, however, is like an onion. Each layer is more truth. You can stop anywhere or keep going deeper. The revealed truth in each layer will take you deeper and deeper into the revelation knowledge of who God is.

All of this history, readily available for us to study, was hidden from the reformers. Imagine what they could have done with the benefit of the vast stores of information we can access with a couple clicks on a computer today. How many steps they would have taken back toward God had they been given even half of what we have? Thank you, Lord that we live in a day of information! Let us use it wisely!

This study is just a tiny part of an evolutionary process that continues to this day. May I ask you a personal question? Will you be the one who God uses to pick up the baton and carry us all into the next stage of our growth as we come into the maturity of Ephesians 4:13?

A PRAYER TO PRAY

Heavenly Father, King of the Universe, help me to know truth. Send me Your precious Holy Spirit, the Spirit of truth. Open my eyes and reveal to me Your truth, and remove from me the infection, the lies and misinformation I have believed and even taught others. Allow me to walk closer to You than I ever have. Draw me closer each day! Redeem my past and wash me in the blood of Your Son. Give me wisdom for this day, and for every day you give me on this earth. Forgive my condemnation of others. Help me be a vessel of love and grace. Amen!

PART 7

AGE OF ENLIGHTENMENT ERA
c. AD 1800

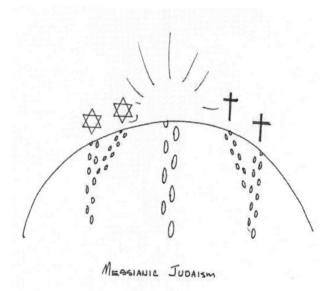

MESSIANIC JUDAISM

SEARCHING FOR THE CURE: *Is Messianic Judaism the Answer?*

Well, surely if the Reformation wasn't the *Injection for the Infection*, Messianic Judaism—which stresses a return to Jewish roots—must be...*right?*

First, let's define some terms. Saved Jews? There are two *basic* types of saved Jews: Christian Jews and Messianic Jews. Christian Jews are those who get saved, then join or affiliate with Christian Churches, practicing Christian traditions and customs. Messianic Jews get saved and then follow Jewish traditions and customs. There are varying degrees of Jewish identification with each one of these groups; but the operative word for both groups is *saved*.

Which group do I personally fit into best? I really enjoy any kind of service in which God is worshiped and the Word is taught, but my favorite services are those of the Messianic Jewish movement. There's just something special about the Messianic music and teaching, and the reading of the Torah. Although their doctrine is not pure, perfect, or free of paganism (they are infected, too!), it is what works best for me.

What am I saying here? Am I compromising by having fellowship with those who do not have *all* of the scriptures interpreted correctly? Those who are still infected? An old friend advised me years ago that if I ever found a perfect church, I should stay away from it, so *I* wouldn't mess *it* up. I have many theological friends and, honestly, none of us has it all correct; many don't even have *most* of it correct. We all have our own error-based views and misunderstandings. To one is given this, to another is given that. Neither Peter nor Paul had it all, and no one has since. *We all see through a glass darkly (I Cor. 13).*

I fellowshipped with and declared myself to be a Messianic Jew from about 1991 until about 2002. I went through the same process most Messianic Believers probably go through. In the beginning, I thought I was finally home. I loved it all. The traditions, the structure—even the all the garments that let me, and everyone else, know I was Jewish. Having come from a Pentecostal background, it was quite a change in many respects.

However, once I began to study the origins of our customs I began to realize that I was—again—having to repent for the actions I was so recently excited about. It seemed so right at the time. It was fulfilling for the moment. But then I started to become restless as my spirit began communing with my mind. I finally went on a quest to know what was from God and what was not. This desire to reconnect with God's original "ways and means" is really the greatest motivation for the work you now have in your hands.

The errors that I fell into caused me to see the importance of this book. I can say without a doubt, if any man is guilty, I am. If any has fallen short, it was me. If any has fallen into traps of emotion or zeal, it has been me. And it is I, Lord, who need mercy and grace to stand before You, for I made every mistake, adopting beliefs I had not examined in the light of Scripture first, and following after the clamor of self-anointed men. If you have the ability to learn from others' mistakes, please, learn from mine. There is no reason for us all to roll in the mud.

While I have basically removed myself from the title and official fellowship from the movement, in my heart I am most closely aligned to my Messianic Brothers. However, as my wife has so eloquently stated, "When they read your book, they will all hate you, so you won't have to worry about it any more." But I do worry about "it" because I don't want "it" (the truth), to offend anyone even though what has to be said may be painful. I do pray that once the issues have been broken open for dialogue and examination that eventually the truth will bring healing and — ultimately — restoration for us all.

Remembering our numeric example: if the Reformation was one step back toward God for Christians, then Messianic Judaism is one step back towards God for the Jewish community. Compared to *most* of Christianity, on the surface they are much closer to the purest form of biblical teaching and customs. But just as the Christians are still infected and practicing a lot of paganism, so are the Messianic Jews. Unfortunately, the paganism of the Jewish customs is so demonically woven into all the fabric of Rabbinic Judaism that it's hidden from most of the Messianics. They are unknowingly dragging the Babylonian infections right into their Messianic congregations and exposing their followers to them. In fact, it's become the touchstone of contention and many congregations have been split over it. It is the leading problem within the movement today. (More on this later.)

God must have a sense of humor during this age, this covenant of grace and personal priesthood, to allow us <u>all</u> to get so out of plumb. While the Christians have been evolving from the paganism of Roman Catholicism for hundreds of years, the more recently established Messianic Jews are just starting to evolve from the paganism of Rabbinic Judaism! In fact, many haven't even begun to "come out of her" while others are sadly turning right back into it. While there have been individual Messianic Jews since the days of *Yeshua* (Jesus), the Messianic Jewish Movement, as a denomination or unified religion, only came back on the scene in the 20th century and really began to pick up steam from 1967 on.

Once, while I was at a social gathering, a person who knew some of my background asked me to describe the Charismatic Movement. You will recall that from the age of nine I was raised by my mother, a wonderful Pentecostal believer who loved nothing more than to find a church where *the Spirit really moved*. I have seen the entire gamut, from the real deal to carnival barkers in preacher costumes.

"It's sort of like granola bars—a lot of fruits, nuts, and flakes," I told my questioner. "There are many wonderful people who have great zeal, but seem to make up many of their doctrines as they go." That same friend worked his way back over to me a little later and asked how I would describe the Messianic Jewish movement. I smiled. "Sort of like granola bars with chocolate chips." By that, I meant that I love my Messianic brothers, but we have our own fair share of eccentrics along with a fairly nice assortment of certifiable "wackos". We are *all* infected!

The Messianic movement does not exist in a vacuum; it undergoes continual pressure from three different groups: Jews, Protestant Christians, and Roman Catholics. The movement responds to these different groups in different ways, trying to be congenial to all three. It is an impossible task.

Just as in Christendom, Messianic Judaism has many splinter groups and sects, many different flavors. While they don't refer to themselves as such, inside the movement are a growing number of independent fellowships and two main denominations: the MJAA (Messianic Jewish Alliance of America), and the UMJC (Union of Messianic Jewish Congregations) and a third group evolving outside

Messianic Judaism that may or may not end up as a denomination, the MIA (Messianic Israel Alliance).

There are wonderful brothers and sisters in all the camps. As we look at the movement more closely, keep in mind that it is evolving under pressure on both sides—from pagan infected Christianity and pagan infected Judaism.

So…what do you think you will find there?

DOCTRINAL STATEMENTS OF THE MJAA & UMJC

Now, I want you to see that there is almost no difference between the doctrinal statements of these two denominations and the average Baptist or Pentecostal church. I've included them here so their positions are presented accurately. Much of it is basic Christianity with a Jewish emphasis, but please pay attention to the later remarks that introduce concepts found nowhere in the apostolic writings—and completely incompatible with them.

The following was taken from the website www.mjaa.org:

What is the MJAA?

The Messianic Jewish Alliance of America is the largest association of *Messianic Jewish* believers in *Yeshua* (Jesus) in the world. Established in 1915, the specific and special ministry of the MJAA is threefold:

1. To promote a clear and visible testimony to the fact that there is a large and growing movement of Jewish people who believe that Yeshua is the Jewish Messiah and Saviour of the world;

2. To bring together, in one organization, Jewish and non-Jewish people, of like faith and mind, with a shared vision for Jewish revival; and

3. Most importantly--To introduce our Jewish brothers and sisters to the Messiah Yeshua.

The MJAA is affiliated with Messianic Jewish Alliances in fifteen other countries, including Israel.

Why does the MJAA exist?

Over the last 1500 years, Jews have been frequently persecuted by those calling themselves *"believers";* in Jesus. This, coupled with the fact that the Jewish gospel has been presented in a manner that makes it appear non-Jewish, has led Jews to assume that to follow

Yeshua is to leave the faith of our Fathers and become non-Jews. These misperceptions have been used by the Adversary, Satan, to hinder the Jewish people from accepting their promised Messiah Yeshua. Therefore, it is critical that a **Jewish** organization exist as a witness to the Messiahship of Yeshua. The MJAA is that organization.

What does the MJAA believe?

We believe in *one G-d* as declared in the *Sh'ma* (Deuteronomy 6:4), who is *Echad* (a compound unity) and eternally existent in three persons: *G-d, the Father, G-d, the Son*, and *G-d, the Holy Spirit* (*Ruach HaKodesh*--Isaiah 48:16-17, Genesis 1:1, Exodus 3:6, Ephesians 4:4-6).

We believe in Messiah Yeshua's deity (Isaiah 9:6, John 1:1,4), His virgin birth (Isaiah 7:14), His sinless life, His atoning death (Isaiah 53, Psalm 22), His bodily resurrection, His ascension, and His future return in power and glory.

We believe that the Bible, consisting of the *Tanach* (Old Covenant Scriptures) and the *B'rit Chadasha* (New Covenant Scriptures), is the inspired, infallible, and authoritative Word of G-d (Psalm 119:89, Proverb 30:5-6, 2Timothy 3:16-17).

We believe in G-d's eternal covenant with Abraham, Isaac, and Jacob. We, therefore, stand with and support the Jewish people and the State of Israel and hold fast to the Biblical heritage of our forefathers.

The following taken from www.umjc.org/umjchome.htm:

Union of Messianic Jewish Congregations

The Union of Messianic Jewish Congregations was formed in 1979 to provide support and accountability for this expanding Messianic Jewish congregational movement, through the following five objectives:

- To further the initiation, establishment, and growth of Messianic Jewish Congregations worldwide.

- To be a voice for Messianic Jewish Congregations and Messianic Judaism worldwide.

- To provide a forum for the discussion of issues relevant to Messianic Judaism and Messianic Jewish Congregations.

- To aid in the causes of our Jewish people worldwide, especially in Israel.

- To support the training of Messianic Leaders.

DOCTRINAL STATEMENT

1. We believe the Bible is the inspired, the only infallible, authoritative Word of G-d

2. We believe that there is one G-d, eternally existent in three persons, Father, Son, and Holy Spirit.

3. We believe in the deity of the L-RD Yeshua, the Messiah, and His virgin birth, in His sinless life, in His miracles, in His vicarious and atoning death through His shed blood, in His bodily resurrection, in His ascension to the right hand of the Father, and in His personal return in power and glory.

4. We believe that for the salvation of lost and sinful man, regeneration by the Holy Spirit is absolutely essential.

5. We believe in the present ministry of the Holy Spirit by whose indwelling the believer is enabled to live a godly life.

6. We believe in the resurrection of both the saved and the lost; they that are saved unto the resurrection of life, and they that are lost unto the resurrection of damnation.

7. We believe in the spiritual unity of all believers in the L-RD Yeshua, the Messiah.

8. We believe in the process of discipline and conflict resolution taught in Matthew 18:15ff, as applicable to all congregants and leaders.

9. As Jewish followers of Yeshua, we are called to maintain our Jewish biblical heritage and remain a part of our people

Israel and the universal body of believers. This is part of our identity and a witness to the faithfulness of G-d.

(They are Trinitarians;
http://www.umjc.org/aboutumjc/theology/triunity.htm)

The biblical data we have teaches:
1. G-d is echad, ONE in a composite sense.
2. G-d has manifested Himself in three persons, Father, Son, and Holy Spirit.
3. G-d is eternally existent as one G-d in three persons.

DEFINING MESSIANIC JUDAISM

Let's get into the meat of what's really being taught in these camps. While the leadership both past and present does not speak for everyone, the documents of past presidents of the UMJC teaching are representative of the movement's beliefs and widely accepted among the Messianic Jewish congregations. You will find the following index at www.umjc.org/aboutmj/mjdefined.htm:

**DEFINING MESSIANIC JUDAISM (ADDENDUM 1 & 2)
COMMENTARY ON THE DEFINITION BY RUSS RESNIK**

(Click on DEFINING MESSIANIC JUDAISM to find the underlined and bolded statements that I would draw to your attention.

The following statement was affirmed by the Delegates to the 23rd Annual UMJC Conference on July 31, 2002

Defining Messianic Judaism
Mark Kinzer, Dan Juster

Basic Statement
Messianic Judaism is a movement of Jewish congregations and congregation-like groupings committed to Yeshua the Messiah that embrace the covenantal responsibility of Jewish life and identity rooted in Torah, expressed in tradition, renewed and applied in the context of the New Covenant.

Expanded Statement
Jewish life is life in a concrete, historical community. Thus, Messianic Jewish groupings **must be fully part of the Jewish people,** sharing its history and its covenantal responsibility as a people chosen by G-d. At the same time, faith in Yeshua also has a crucial communal dimension. This faith unites Messianic Judaism and the Gentile Christian Church, which is the assembly of the faithful from the nations who are joined to Israel through the Messiah. Together Messianic Judaism and the Gentile Church constitute the one Body of Messiah, a community of Jews and

Gentiles **who in their ongoing distinction and mutual blessing anticipate the shalom of the world to come. To attempt to anticipate this shalom within a local Jewish-Gentile congregation will diminish the "ongoing distinction" between Jew and Gentile that is necessary for "mutual blessing." Gentiles are certainly welcome within Messianic Jewish congregations, and often essential to the task of building these congregations, but the congregations remain *Jewish*, not expressions of "one new man" that is neither Jew nor Greek. Much of their life is based, not strictly on Scripture or on universal precepts for all believers, but on Jewish teaching and tradition. Gentiles moved by Ahavat Yisrael [Love of Israel] will participate in the Messianic Jewish congregation on these terms. **From Pg 3, Add 2, Pt 2 of the three common alternative models for Gentile involvement: Unity of Jews and Gentiles in Messiah.**

For a Messianic Jewish grouping (1) to fulfill the covenantal responsibility incumbent upon all Jews, (2) to bear witness to Yeshua within the people of Israel, and (3) to serve as an authentic and effective representative of the Jewish people within the body of Messiah, **it must place a priority on integration with the wider Jewish world. Such integration must then be followed by a vital corporate relationship with the Gentile Christian Church.**

The Messianic Jewish way of life involves an attempt to fulfill Israel's covenantal responsibility embodied in the Torah within a New Covenant context. Messianic Jewish halakhah is rooted in Scripture (Tanakh and the New Covenant writings), which is of unique sanctity and authority. However, it also draws upon **Jewish tradition, especially those practices and concepts that have won near-universal acceptance by devout Jews through the centuries. Furthermore, like most other branches of Judaism, Messianic Judaism recognizes that halakhah must be dynamic as well as faithful, for it involves the application of the Torah to a wide variety of changing situations and circumstances.**

(END OF WEB QUOTES)

Wanting to remain a Jewish organization dedicated to the evangelism of the Jews, the MJAA limits its membership to Jews. Some find such a membership policy offensive, but it is clearly stated in the MJAA's documents of purpose. When UMJC split from the MJAA, it opened its membership to gentiles. There are several differing ideals and doctrines between the MJAA and the UMJC; this work is not trying to show preference or guide the reader to either.

What the document *Defining Messianic Judaism* states first and foremost is that Messianic Jews want to think, act, and look "Jewish," believing it to be the way to attract and evangelize the Jewish people. We are not debating that approach, merely stating the fact. Unfortunately, most cannot tell the difference between rabbinical paganism and biblical traditions; until this publication, there was little on the subject. Another interesting fact is that between 80-90 percent of the Jews in the world today are secular and don't wear any of the rabbinic religious garb, therefore the Messianic Jews are dressing and looking *rabbinic*, not *Jewish*.

Second, Messianic Jews have had to be "Christians" (even though many reject the term), as most have come into the faith through evangelization. To be otherwise, the movement would have been branded a cult, and cooperation would have been non-existent. This explains why most Messianic Jews are Trinitarians.

Third, Messianic Jews try to please, be acceptable to, and fellowship with Roman Catholics. This is a new effort that has evolved since the reign of Pope John Paul II. Pope John Paul II was the first Pope to admit to and apologize for the Church's hatred and crimes against the Jews. Next to the rebirth of the nation of Israel, to me, this acknowledgement is the most astonishing thing that has happened in my generation.

Finally, one of the most troubling aspects of the addendum is the statement that Jewish and gentile congregations are to wait separately in their distinct roles until the "ha olam" (world to come) to experience "shalom" and the "one new man" expression. They are encouraged *not* to seek for it in a local Jewish-gentile congregation, although it is acknowledged that gentiles are "often essential to the task of building these congregations" for the Jewish believers. This approach, while understandable as Messianic Judaism attempts to present a Jewish rather than Christian façade to unsaved Jews, is in direct conflict with the entire New Covenant principles. It is a particular affront to the work of Yeshua, whom they claim to preach:

> *For he is our peace, who hath made both one, and hath broken down the middle wall of partition between us; 15 Having abolished in his flesh the enmity, even the law of commandments contained in ordinances; for to make in himself of twain **one new man**, so making peace; 16 And that he might reconcile both unto God in one body by the cross, having slain the enmity thereby (Eph 2:14-16):*

I think this is about as clear as it can be made. This is just one of many blatant examples of Scripture being ignored or dismissed with a religious sounding excuse. Unfortunately, what no one seems to realize is that the Messianic Jewish community has been spiritually hijacked by a group of rabbinic demons. These demons have infected the minds of these teachers. Many also don't realize as believers and followers of Yeshua they are actually denying Him by every rabbinic teaching they practice. They defile themselves and the congregations as they teach them to eat regurgitated dog vomit—Rabbinic Judaism!

But it is happened unto them according to the true proverb, the dog is turned to his own vomit again; and the sow that was washed to her wallowing in the mire (2 Peter 2:22).

Please understand that I am not accusing or maligning the majority of sincere individuals seeking to lead these congregations—many Messianic Jewish leaders do not realize what they are doing and where they are leading the sheep.

Recently, I read a document prepared by a Messianic Jewish leader who claimed that all forms of Judaism evolved from the rabbinical system except the Messianic movement. Unfortunately, he is not correct. The Messianic Jewish movement is a direct descendant with the majority of its infection still intact. How sad it is that they don't know that they have infected doctrines as everyone continues to dance towards the edge of the cliff!

The former UMJC Executive Director, in his *Defining Messianic Judaism Addendum 2*, made two explosive statements regarding Jewish identity: first, he declared that *"One who discovers a Jewish ancestry and feels drawn to identify with the Jewish people should be encouraged to learn and grow in awareness and practice. The time may come when we have within Messianic Judaism a ritual of return to Jewishness. But without some form of ritual and communal recognition, such an individual should simply describe himself as having Jewish ancestry and a love for the Jewish people, not as being Jewish himself"* (italics & emphasis mine). Second, he went as far as to suggest that **the Messianic movement could adopt a form of conversion to their religion similar to that of the Orthodox community which includes circumcision.**

He takes the infection to new levels as he encourages conformity to Rabbinic Judaism and even goes to the point of saying that they, the Messianic Jewish movement, *"need to provide communal rabbinic leadership to guide the members of the Messianic Jewish family."*

So how on earth is this leader going to put Messianic Judaism under their authority and still be under the New Covenant?

CRUCIAL POINT: *Rabbinic Judaism doesn't even have a Covenant to operate under. It has rejected both the Old and New Covenants!*

Do you see how deeply the Messianic movement is infected and in need of immediate examination and realignment with the Word? It's almost as if they are racing back to dive under the veil of darkness and blindness that YHWH delivered them out from through His Son. Please pray for the Spirit of Truth to sweep through the Messianic community and bring a revival of repentance. Pray that they begin to communicate with the Holy Spirit so that the blindness will be removed.

We repeat here: The UMJC and MJAA leadership does not speak for all of the Messianic Jewish community, nor do all agree with them.

CONTRASTS WITHIN MESSIANIC JUDAISM

POSITIVE ASPECTS:
Of the many positive aspects, I will list the ones that
Christians might not be aware of:
1. They proclaim *Yeshua* (Jesus) as the Son of God and
   the Messiah (several views of what that means exist
   within the movement.)
2. They keep the biblical Sabbath.
3. They "keep" the Torah in a Messianic way.
   (This varies greatly from group to group.)
4. They keep the Feasts of the Lord.
   (Some are more rabbinic than others.)
5. Wonderful praise and worship music and dance are
   common in many congregations.
6. An emphasis is placed on intensive Bible study.
7. An open-ended atmosphere of questioning and
   discussion is encouraged (such would be considered
   rebellious or even heretical in many churches).

NEGATIVE ASPECTS:
The movement's attachment to Rabbinic Judaism is strong,
as evidenced by the following practices:
1. Many still wear the kippah (yarmulke), or skullcap,
   trying to keep their Jewish traditions. Most do not
   know its origin or its rabbinical anti-Christian
   symbolism.
2. Most still keep the feasts in rabbinical order and with
   rabbinical traditions, particularly Rosh Hashanah and
   Passover. Most have never thought about the pagan
   roots of Rabbinic Judaism and do not examine its
   practices in light of the scriptures.
3. Some believe the teachings of the Talmud are
   inspired, and try to live by them. While this is not the

dominant teaching, it does exist in larger numbers than some would think. Here are just a few examples:

    A. Use of the Siddur and rabbinical prayer books.

    B. Study and application of the Mishnah and Gemara (and rabbinic commentaries).

    C. Chanting the Amidah (the "standing prayer").

4. Many still follow the rabbinical kosher laws instead of the biblical ones. The meat and dairy laws are the most blatant non-scriptural examples.

5. In accord with rabbinical heresies, many claim or imply that saved Jews are superior to saved gentiles; they use the passage in Ephesians about saved gentiles becoming the "commonwealth of Israel" as though saved Jews are somehow not in the same group, and thus superior to saved gentiles.

6. Most are Trinitarians.

7. Some are Arians (Believe Yeshua, or Jesus, is a created being, *not* deity.)

8. Some are Modalists. (Believe the Father came as the Son and returned as the Holy Spirit. One Being manifesting in three different modes.)

9. Many are rabbinical-ists, or legalists. This group poses the greatest threat to Messianic congregations and the spiritual battle in many congregations is intense. The infection has gone wild. Tragically, some have gone through splits on this issue.

10. Most congressional leaders call themselves or allow others to call them "Rabbi" in direct contrast with the biblical instruction given by Yeshua (Jesus) himself in Matthew 23.

If you are going to blatantly refuse to obey the words of Yeshua (Jesus), why call yourself *Messianic?* Again, this movement goes directly against the scriptures and excuses itself with religious sounding justifications such as, "the title 'Rabbi' meant something else back then." No, it didn't! It is and was the term used for the teachers of Pharisaical congregations, Rabbinic Judaism! Why do we refuse to hear the Lord on the simplest matters? (More on this later.)

While many Messianic Jewish congregations are comprised—surprisingly—of a majority of gentiles, the congregations I have been to make a clear distinction between saved Jews and saved gentiles. There is a two tier system which makes non-Jews second class citizens and perpetuates the rabbinic arrogance of their fathers towards the gentiles. This is absolute heresy and infection of the highest level, and should be rebuked until driven from the ranks. Sadly, instead, I see the opposite—division in the Body being encouraged with Jewish evangelism being used as the "end that justifies the means." Interestingly, both of these denominations seem to be dying on the vine. While ten years ago their numbers were rising quickly, today they are barely maintaining status quo and even declining in some quarters. While numbers are not the only measuring sticks, overall they are important markers.

I believe with all my heart that the Messianic Movement had a divine call to "come out from" religious paganism and restore the biblical Hebraic Roots of our faith—and then to share those lost traditions with the world wide church. Ponder this: if they had continued on their original biblical course and not gotten caught in the infected trap of rabbinical-ism, would YHWH have used the movement to help restore the revelation knowledge of The Kingdom of God to us all? Would they have become the empowered, "Kingdom witness" the rabbinic community needs so desperately? Could it still happen? I believe it could!

A LOOK AT THE MIA

The other group mentioned, the MIA, (Messianic Israel Alliance) is a very loose knit group, and not a denomination at this writing. The majority is non-Jewish, who believe that, in Messiah Yeshua (Jesus Christ) they are members of the commonwealth of Israel and belong to His Eternal Kingdom (Eph2:11-22; John 18:36) — hence the name Messianic Israel.

They also believe many of them could be part of the myriads of biological descendants once promised to Abraham— but that, regardless of genetic background, all true Believers in Messiah are full members of Yeshua's assembly of the firstborn (Gen 15:4-5; Rom 4:19-22; Gal 3:26-29; Heb 12:23). Joseph was Jacob's firstborn heir, Ephraim was Joseph's heir, and the Father calls "Ephraim" His "firstborn" (Gen 48:19,22; Deu 21:17; 1 Chr 5:1-2; Jer 31:18-19). Messianic Israel believes that many of them could be of once hidden but now restored Ephraim (the former Northern Kingdom of Israel), because the Ephraimites were scattered among every Gentile nation, yet were destined to one day return to the Father (Hos 1-2; 5:3; 8:8; Amos 9:9; Zec 10:6-9; Rom 9:23). Messianic Israel sees themselves as part of the "stick" of Joseph/Ephraim and "his companions," and desire to be rejoined with brother Judah, being made one in the Father's hand (Eze 37:15-28). As members of Firstborn Israel, they want to be a true brother to Judah, but without compromising their faith in Messiah.

While they have evolved from the Messianic Jewish community and are still struggling with some of the issues in that movement, they are substantially less infected as a group than either the UMJC or the MJAA. Even though this statement may not be taken as flattery (by either group), the leadership of the MIA does try to adhere to the Word. They are clearly making an attempt to walk with God as they seek to identify what they should and should not be doing. It's refreshing to see any group emerge that attempts to be self-examining as they proceed.

Different customs are allowed among their members: some are more rabbinic, most are less. To this writer, one of the most refreshing aspects of this group is they have overcome the heresy that Jews are better in some way than Believers who are former Gentiles. They hold the Jewish people and the Nation of Israel in very high esteem, but do not think they are "inherently better." They think Ephraim and Judah should regard each other as "family," but with different opinions about Scripture and Messiah.

The original founders of this group, Angus and Batya Wootten, began teaching about "Ephraim" and "both the houses of Israel" (Gen 48:19; Isa 8:14; Rom 11:25) in 1983. Some Messianic Jews immediately twisted their teachings, then made their false accusations a point of contention. Batya wrote her first book on the subject in 1988, and they began hosting conferences soon afterward. Years later, others began calling the teaching the "Two House" doctrine, but Angus and Batya contend that Messianic Israel is called to be "One House," and thus feel the title does not fit.

Enemies of the teaching falsely call it a heresy rather than a legitimate interpretation of Scripture. Personally, I have found it humorous for the most infected to accuse others of having an infected doctrine. What I found even more humorous was that the blasphemous doctrine everyone was clamoring about, that only the Lost Tribes of Israel could be saved, wasn't even in the book that caused the uprising. It was alleged! Everyone was drawing lines in the sand and excommunicating the Ephraimites over hearsay and rumor. What a bunch of spoiled children we are.

I remember the look in Rabbi Joseph's eyes as he told me of all the family he had lost in the Holocaust. He, being an Orthodox rabbi, was explaining to me why he even tolerated me. His daughter had become a Messianic Jew.

"It is our custom to 'cut-off" anyone in our families who becomes a Christian or a Messianic." He pointed his finger at me and his eyes narrowed and filled with tears. "But after all I lost...nothing will ever take another family member from me! *Nothing!* Do you understand me?!"

Why can't we love each other like Rabbi Joseph loved his daughter? Why can't we have so much passion for each other that what we believe is secondary to the love we communicate to one another? Do you think Rabbi Joseph's daughter ever questioned if her daddy loved her?

This writer is not endorsing any of these movements, or trying to lead the readers to or away from any of these movements or denominations. These are my observations at this point in time. If you are involved in any of these movements, then I pray that you research the points brought up in this work and become part of *"the Injection for the Infection."* I pray for the leadership of all of these groups and that they find cures for all of these issues so they may bring their congregations to *Walk with God*.

Sensitive Issues Of The Messianic Jewish Movement

Once, while visiting a Messianic Jewish home, the conversation turned to the subject of a Messianic Jew being called a Christian. It is an emotional subject, one that provokes many kinds of responses, some of them offensive.

Hannah is the sweetest lady in the world next to my wife. If you looked for a hundred years, you could not find a better example of the perfect wife, mother, and sister. Raised in a good Jewish home, one day she received *Yeshua* (Jesus) as her Lord and Savior. To this day Hannah is jubilant to be both a Jew and a Christian. She bubbles because she is saved **and** because she is called a Christian. At a public gathering one time, Hannah saw a Messianic Jewish "celebrity" being asked by a fan if they were a Christian. This person responded in an ungracious way, almost biting the head off of the questioner with a sharp "No!" and Hannah was offended. Whatever else in life I do, I do not want to offend Hannah.

There are many Messianic Jews who struggle with the paradox of what to be called. Fueling the fire is the age-old mantra of "Christians hate Jews, Christians kill Jews, and Christians call Jews 'Christ Killers.'" With that being the case, then why would Jews want to call themselves Christians? Many Christians condemn Messianic Jews for celebrating the feasts and the Sabbath, which is one more reason for Jews to eschew the name Christian. But, many Christians don't understand all of that.

FACT: More Jews have been killed by Christians than by any other group, religion, or culture.

FACT: The Holocaust was perpetrated by self-styled Christian Lutherans.

FACT: America has become the greatest friend of the State of Israel and the Jew.
A. Today, many Americans are pro-Israel; before World War II, anti-Semitism was common across the country.

> B. The Christian Knights of the Klu Klux Klan
> are still alive and well in America; so too are
> skinheads and many anti-Semitic groups and
> churches.

In a Jewish mindset, for a Jew to call himself a Christian is to be a traitor to all he has ever known. Furthermore, most Messianic Jews don't worship on Sunday, and most do not celebrate Easter and Christmas which is what Christians do. Why give yourself a label that does not match what you believe and practice?

In fact, 99.9% of all Christians who ask questions are not aware of all of these complexities. Usually, they are just excited to find Jewish believers and want to celebrate with them. Shouldn't we Messianics be more sensitive to them, responding with maturity and love: "Yes, I am a Born again Believer! Praise the Lord, Jesus is my Savior or Messiah." Shouldn't we work *not* to offend each other? Hopefully as we mature in the love of the Lord, we become quicker to extend that same love to others whether we agree on the finer points of the faith or not. So the next time questions come up, raise the bar, and show a little grace and compassion to the person asking or answering.

Are Messianic Jews Actually Jews?

While the Messianic Community is aware of the following details, many outside our camp are not; therefore I will lay a little groundwork. Many Messianic Jews want to be called and referred to as "Jews." Rabbinical Jews claim Messianic Jews can't be Jews because they have accepted *Yeshua* (Jesus) as their Messiah. There are "Jews" (referring to the descendants of Abraham) who are religious, and those who are not. Some would call them Israelites, referring to the nationality of that race. Of course, the former UMJC Director states that "Jewish Identity is not racial." However, if it were not then his entire commentary would be about nothing. Then, of course, there are Rabbinical Jews, representing the religion. Many Ultra-Orthodox Jews claim that none but themselves are Jews.

What most Messianic Jews whom I have contact with are wanting is acceptance from Rabbinic Judaism, the religion, as a fourth branch of Judaism, just as Reformed Judaism and Conservative Judaism are accepted. It seems to be a fight to be accepted by the religious Jews. If you've gleaned enough truth about Rabbinic Judaism, you are probably asking yourself, "Why?" The answer is: "It's part of the infection.

CRUCIAL POINT: *The people of God are starving for HIM and HIS ways, not rabbinical customs. Teaching Gentiles (and Jews) to observe rabbinical traditions in many cases is just trading one form of infected paganism for another.*

In my earlier years I actually agreed with it. I thought, "I'm as Jewish as the next guy." In fact, I wanted everyone's approval, the Jews and the Christians. But I realized — as I began compiling this information — that Rabbinic Judaism is as far to the left of God as Ecumenical Christianity is to the right. In fact, they are both ditches that run along either side of the "narrow way" that we are called to walk. Neither Rabbinic Judaism nor Ecumenical Christianity has enough biblical doctrine to be called biblical and neither teach men how to walk with God. Why would I want the recognition of dead, infected religions? I didn't realize it then, and most of my brethren who want it now don't realize it either. Most

Christians and Jews alike have little or no knowledge of their religious roots, and how infected we all are.

The Difference Between Being Jewish and Being Hebrew

This may be a shock to some of you, but Abraham, Isaac, and Jacob were not Jewish. They were Hebrews. The word *Jew* evolved after the northern part of Israel was carried off into captivity. All that was left were the people living in Judah. After a while the people became known as Jews because of the name of their tribe and country, Judah. Now, semantically speaking, the only Jewish roots of Christianity we have are pagan and Pharisaical.

At first this may seem like an irrelevant point, but as we delve a little deeper I don't think it will turn out to be so. As I hear the proclamation, "We must return to our Jewish roots!" I realize most preachers making this statement don't know the difference and only know the Rabbinical Jewish way of celebrating anything, including the feasts. Their zeal and passion is outrunning their knowledge. Teaching gentiles (and Jews) to trade a pagan Easter for pagan Passover Seders, or to trade a pagan Christmas for a pagan Day of Atonement doesn't bring anyone closer to God.

Most of my Messianic brothers are even celebrating the pagan Rosh Hashanah (New Year) in the fall with the pagan rabbinical community instead of the spring when our God told us to celebrate it. I know this sounds hard but Rabbinic Judaism changed the Feasts of the Lord into rabbinical heresy. To whom and to what does the following passage apply?

> *And what agreement hath the temple of God with idols? for ye are the temple of the living God; as God hath said, I will dwell in them, and walk in them; and I will be their God, and they*

shall be my people. [17]*Wherefore **come out from among them,
and be ye separate,** saith the Lord, and **touch not the
unclean thing;** and I will receive you,* [18]*And will be a Father
unto you, and ye shall be my sons and daughters, saith the
Lord Almighty (2 Cor 6:16)*

Is this just to the gentile? Is it talking about gentile
paganism only, or could it refer to rabbinical paganism, as
well? Are *your* rabbinic traditions a stench in the nostrils of
the living God *(Amos 8:10-11 & Jude 1:12)*?

> **CRUCIAL POINT:** In my opinion, the ROOT
> infection of Rabbinic Judaism is far more
> dangerous than the infection of pagan Christianity.

Why do I say that? Like a snake, Rabbinic Judaism
slithered into the Jewish culture and cloaks itself as if it were
the truths of God Almighty. It is not just errors. It is
blasphemy and heresy! Why are we teaching it to others as
if it were God's commands? The Messianic community is
transmitting rabbinic heresy as if it were truth. We are
spreading the infection. You can't have *the Lord's* Passover
without a lamb—it isn't possible! Yet the traditional Seder
has replaced it with a lamb bone and an *egg*. Where did the
egg come from? Why do we ignore YHWH's choice of the
head of the year? Rosh Hashanah is not in the fall! And
exactly why are we fasting and mourning on Yom Kippur?
   *Lord, help us! We, your children, are still polluting Your
customs and teaching others to do so. Help us come out from
Babylon! Remove from us the infection, and teach us Your ways!
Thank You for mercy and a covenant where we can learn to honor
You by obeying Your instructions.*
   Don't let the following verse apply to you:

> *Woe unto you, scribes and Pharisees, hypocrites! For ye*
> *compass sea and land to make one proselyte, and when he is*
> *made, ye make him twofold more the child of hell than*
> *yourselves.* [16]*Woe unto you, ye blind guides…(Mat 23:15).*

I was a blind, infected guide and had to repent from teaching errors. Most of us are guilty. If you are, do not try to protect a faulty position out of pride or fear. Simply repent and ask forgiveness. He is merciful and quick to forgive!

The people need to be returned to the *Hebraic Roots,* which is where *Yeshua* (Jesus) and Paul were trying get the Jews to return. And (in contrast to the pg 3 item in the Defining Messianic Judaism Addendum, which states that "It is not the mission of Messianic Judaism to call gentiles to Torah and Jewish Roots") I believe the Lord is calling us *all* back to Him! *"Come out from among them, and be ye separate!"* is not a request from the Lord for a select few — it's a command to us all!

Should Messianic Jews (*Believers*) Wear a Kippah?

Whether or not Messianic Jews should wear a Kippah, or head covering, is a very sensitive subject. Many say yes, some say no. Some wear it wanting to continue in the Jewish traditions and hoping to make Jewish visitors comfortable. Opinions range from wearing it with the belief it is required, to wearing it just because everyone else does.

As I stated earlier, the Messianic Jewish community is evolving and many people feel differently about each of these customs.

What We Know About the Kippah

The kippah, as it exists today, was developed in central Europe in the 1600s to 1700's in the same general locale that the Hassidic movement came from. Although there is much debate about the exact origins and motivation for the kippah, 17th century Russian scholar David Haley suggested that Jews should always keep their heads covered in order to distinguish themselves from the Christian majority (from www.Jewishmag.com). There was also a controversy over the "covering of the head" back in Apostle Paul's day. The Pharisees were already teaching that men should cover their head while they read the scriptures or prayed.

Rabbi Hayim Donin in his book *To Be a Jew* quotes Orach Chayim 2:6, "It is a custom not to walk under the heavens bareheaded." and Shabbat 156b "Cover your head, so that the reverence of Heaven be upon you." Rabbi Donin goes on to say about the kippah, "No religious significance is attached to this particular type of head covering." It is just a Rabbinical Jewish tradition! So why do *any* believers wear them? Every reference I've found to the purpose of the kippah, as well as everyone I've asked, referred to the primary purpose as a "sign of their covering," while a secondary purpose was to show respect to God. The key word here is *covering*. To the gentile believer it usually means very little.

To the believer, it boils down to this: "the sign of their covering" is referring to the individual's trust in the rabbinic system as their covering for salvation. I hear the cries, "That's not what it means to *me*!" But that *is* what it means to the Orthodox community who created them. The Messianic community condemns the Christian community for worshiping on the pagan holidays, Christmas and

Easter, while the Christians of today are saying, "That's not what it means to *me!*"

I appreciate that the Messianic Jews want to do all they can to look and act rabbinic in an honest effort to make the non-believing Jews feel comfortable. I'm simply asking the question, "Why are you wearing an anti-Christian symbol that states Rabbinic Judaism is your covering?" I understand that Paul taught that while in Rome he did all he could to be Roman so he could win some to the Lord. Do you think he participated in pagan practices to accomplish that? Do you think he wore pagan god jewelry, wardrobe or symbols to look like he fit in?

The Lord Himself made the first covering for Adam and Eve in the garden. God killed something (a lamb?) and took the skins to make their *covering*. In the everlasting covenant God provided Himself a Lamb whose blood is *the covering* for us all.

I fear most don't realize how anti-Christ the kippah actually is and how offensive it must be to the Lord. But even this has to come through revelation.

Let's Deal With the Excuses

The only scriptural precedent used for wearing the kippah is the head covering worn by the high priest whenever he went into the Holy of Holies under the Mosaic Covenant.

1. The High Priest had not been *born again*. Have you?
2. He was the High Priest. Are you the High Priest?
3. He was performing Levitical Ceremonies. Are you?
4. He was under the Mosaic Covenant. Are you?

Be careful how you answer these questions. The old covenant? The Levitical system? Your High Priest? While we are individually kingly priests, we have only one High Priest and that is *Yeshua* (Jesus).

The other excuse is that the scripture verses below were dealing with the custom of male prostitutes in Corinth when Paul wrote this letter. Let's examine the Scripture and see if there is any reference in any way to that issue.

Let the Scriptures Speak to the Kippah

> *But I would have you know, that the head of every man is Christ; and the head of the woman is the man; and the head of Christ is God. :4 Every man praying or prophesying, having his head covered, dishonoreth²⁶¹⁷ his head. :5 But every woman that prayeth or prophesieth with her head uncovered dishonoreth²⁶¹⁷ her head (I Cor. 11:3)*

Did you see any reference to the traditions, customs or problems in Corinth? Do you see any reference to anything that could be referred to as a "local issue"? None! It's all religious mumbo-jumbo to make excuses to break the Lord's commandments. This passage is about our Head and how men dishonor our Lord by this practice.

Let's examine the Scripture.

The word used for dishonor is G2617 kat-ahee-skhoo'-no From G2596 and G153; to shame down, that is, disgrace or (by implication) put to the blush: - confound, dishonour, (be a-, make a-) shame (-d).

To begin with, Paul sets forth the relationship between *Yeshua* (Jesus) and every man. Just as *Yeshua* (Jesus) is subject to God, and God is His Head, man should be subject to *Yeshua* (Jesus) as **He** is our head.

What if your wife prays or prophesies with her head uncovered? As in hair or otherwise? She is dishonoring and is making ashamed *you!* If she is single, she is dishonoring and making ashamed *Yeshua* (Jesus).

Now, I don't know how much clearer it needs to be put. What else needs to be added to this directive? Paul went on and explained why this was important as he repeated his directive to his brethren in Corinth.

> *For a man indeed ought not to cover his head, forasmuch as he is the image and glory of God (Co 11:7):*

Don't you see? It's about honoring God as the Creator. It's about honoring *Yeshua* (Jesus) as the sacrificed Lamb and it's a statement of faith we trust YHWH for our covering.

You may reply, "I'm just wearing it for my identity or to show respect to the Jews!" Then, at the very least, do you remove your kippah when you pray or cite the Aaronic Blessing? If not, then you have a problem and are in direct conflict with Scripture.

The real question should have been, "Should Messianic Jews follow *any* rabbinical traditions?" The kippah was developed by Rabbinical Jews, so that *is* the real question. Do you remember how Yeshua spoke to the Pharisees (soon to be Rabbinical Jews)?

> But <u>**woe unto you, scribes and Pharisees, hypocrites!**</u> *For ye* **shut up the kingdom of heaven against** *men: for ye neither go in yourselves, neither suffer ye them that are entering to go in. 14* **Woe unto you, scribes and Pharisees, hypocrites!** *For ye* **devour widows' houses,** *and for a pretence make long prayer: therefore ye shall receive the greater damnation. 15* **Woe unto you, scribes and Pharisees, hypocrites!** *for ye* **compass sea and land** *to make one proselyte, and when he is made, ye make him* **twofold more**

the child of hell than yourselves... 24 <u>**Ye blind guides,**</u> *which strain at a gnat, and swallow a camel...33* **Ye serpents,** *ye generation of vipers, how can ye escape the damnation of hell?*

> **CRUCIAL POINT:** If Yeshua (Jesus) is your Head, you are dishonoring and making Him ashamed if you, as a man, pray or prophesy with your head covered. Is that clear enough?

What About Being Called Rabbi?

And love the uppermost rooms at feasts, and the chief seats in the synagogues, 7 And greetings in the markets, and **to be called of men, Rabbi, Rabbi. 8 But be not ye called Rabbi:** *for one is your Master, even Christ; and all ye are brethren. 9 And* **call no man your father** *upon the earth: for one is your Father, which is in heaven. 10* **Neither be ye called masters:** *for one is your Master, even Christ.... (Matt 23: 6)*

The earliest manuscripts have *Rabbi* for the first *masters, repeating the statement, "Neither be ye called Rabbi, for one is your Master.*

Now I have to say this in all humility and with the knowledge that it applies to me, as well: the shepherds will be judged harsher than the sheep. But that is exactly why we need to have this dialogue in the first place. We are all responsible for the instructions that were given to us — and preserved through bloodshed and great sacrifice — no matter how irresponsibly we have handled them down through the centuries. We need to hold one another accountable.

Yeshua (Jesus) Himself taught this doctrine and it is an affront to Him and His Commandments for a believer to be called Rabbi. He included the title Father that the Catholics use. This should be obvious—he did not want any religious teacher to be called Rabbi or Father. *Yeshua* (Jesus) made it a commandment, *"Be ye not called!!!" Thou Shalt Not!!!*

CRUCIAL POINT: *The title Rabbi has (both past and present) a connotation of a "Master Teacher", specifically teaching the heretical, blasphemous doctrines of Rabbinic Judaism.*

Let's ask this question, "Did Yeshua (Jesus) know there would be a Messianic movement 2000 years later? Did He know that the pastors and teachers would run around with the title of Rabbi? Did He say, "until the Messianic Movement comes back, don't be called Rabbi?" Did He say, "If your word Rabbi has a different connotation then it's okay to be called Rabbi?" Or did He say, "Be not called!"?

A final point to consider is the fact that Rabbi is *not* a New or Old Covenant a. definition, b. calling or c. ministry. (Rabbinic Judaism isn't, either.) While the title of Rabbi, as a congregational spiritual leader, has its roots in the Hebrew language, it is a cultural, rabbinic, non-biblical, idiom.

SO, why would any New Covenant Believer want to be, or allow himself to be, called Rabbi, in direct disobedience to Yeshua's (Jesus') clear commandment? How are we still doing this and calling ourselves His disciples?

HOP-SCOTCH COVENANTS:
Which Covenant are we under? Should we be Torah Observant?

One of the most effective "stealth" methods utilized in the infection is to either add new words with distorted definitions, or to scramble or change the definition of an existing word.

For example, Christians came up with the term *dispensation* as a way to reorganize time as well as explain, validate and manipulate their doctrines. God's Feast system, which represented His divine appointments and timing for mankind, was cast aside. With the new infrastructure, they could explain away or add whatever they wanted, while completely ignoring the covenants of YHWH.

On the other side of the aisle, the rabbinic community had added the Oral Torah to God's written word, and now the Messianic Community is scrambling the covenants and manipulating the word "Torah."

This is one of Satan's greatest tools: *confusion*. Confusion destabilizes and distorts the foundations of truth so that people become frustrated and exhausted in their attempts to interpret God's instructions. Trying to live uprightly, but not knowing whom or what to believe, many give up and just take the path of least resistance, blindly following the crowd.

Let's take a quick look at the two most controversial arguments in the covenant debate: the book of Hebrews and the writings of Paul (Shaul). Both the Rabbinic and the Messianic community have done everything they can to discount, omit, disclaim or ignore Paul's (Shaul's) epistles, along with the book of Hebrews (generally accepted as written by either Paul (Shaul) or Luke).

Why? Could it be because this body of work—if correct—completely destroys Rabbinic Judaism and the compromises that many of the Messianic community have taught their constituents to obey?

An Important Note: Many of the leaders of MJAA and the UMJC have made public record of their desire for Messianic Judaism to become accepted, by Rabbinic Judaism, as the "Fourth Branch of Judaism." For this to happen, the Messianic Community must justify the Rabbinical Dog Vomit that they are teaching their followers in order to comply with and submit to the authority of the rabbis. What exactly does that do to Yeshua (Jesus) and His role as our High Priest?

Paul (Shaul) was the most educated and zealous Pharisee (Rabbinic Jew) of his time. Paul (Shaul) knew every trick, every deception, every mis-teaching and every lie that the rabbinic community was spreading throughout the entire Roman world. He was the "point man" of this specific battle—the Ph.D., the expert on all the infected teachings the rabbinic community was pumping into the synagogues and into the growing body of the New Kingdom priests. Paul (Shaul) was the only disciple of the remaining eleven with the education and training to know how to combat Rabbinic Judaism. While Luke had an education, it appears he was most likely a Sadducee, which the other disciples also appear to be, not Pharisees or Rabbinic Jews (although many of today's Jewish documents and writings have rewritten the history on many aspects of the Pharisees vs. Sadducees issues). In regard to understanding the law, nobody knew it better than Paul (Shaul). He was Gamaliel's star pupil *(Acts 22:3)*, in his own words, a "Hebrew of Hebrews," "touching the righteousness which is in the law, blameless" *(Phil 3:6)*. However, YHWH led Paul down to the desert of Arabia *(Gal 1:17)* where he was deprogrammed and taught a more correct understanding of the plan and purpose of the law. A crucial point here is that YHWH did not make a mistake by appointing Paul to write much of the New Testament, a.k.a. The New Kingdom Covenant Torah!

In short, Paul (Shaul) was the only one alive who was qualified to deal with the complexities of the issue. He was also the disciple who "established the law through faith *(Rom 3:31)*. So, what will you do with Paul (Shaul)? Pick through his doctrines like a can of mixed nuts, keeping what you want and rejecting what you don't want? It will not work. Unfortunately, you must either treat his work as canon, or rip it out of your Bible completely.

Don't think Paul was a lone voice. Yeshua (Jesus) covered in detail the rabbinical heresies in Matthew 23. We bring this out for your further study, and while you are reading the Hebrew and Pauline references, continually keep in mind what Yeshua said in the horrific indictment of Matthew 23:8-33. In fact, you may want to read that once or twice before you read the other scriptures.

Read this section with the understanding that we'll cover it in much greater detail in *What Do We Do Now?* while understanding that YHWH has never changed, nor has His statutes.

WHICH COVENANT?

Earlier, we described covenants as vehicles designed by YHWH in which the terms and conditions of His relationship with man are defined. There are those who teach that the Mosaic Covenant is still intact and in effect, and that the New Covenant was merely added on. Then there are those who teach a two-covenant system, one for the Jew and another for the Gentile. Others are teaching that the New Covenant is just a "renewed" covenant while still others teach it is a "revised" covenant.

Yet in almost every Scripture passage where the term "new covenant" is used, the word translated "new" is the Greek word *kainos* (Strongs #2537). *Kainos* means "new in kind and quality." Let me put this in terms we can understand: We're not talking about an old pickup truck getting a new paint job; we're talking about the pickup truck becoming a fighter jet! It is now a completely different vehicle. It is superior in every way. So we must be wary of religious infection negating the glory and power of the New Covenant. By confusing or misinterpreting this single issue, everything else can be distorted.

First of all, the Mosaic Covenant, "the Law," never represented YHWH's ultimate goal for the children of Israel. The law was given to instruct them in the principles of life and redemption, and to reveal to them their sinfulness. The goal has always been for YHWH's people to walk with Him in intimacy—remember the way it was in the Garden of Eden? This is why the Apostle Paul would later write how YHWH had "made us adequate as servants of a new [*kainos*] covenant, not of the letter but of the Spirit; for the letter kills, but the Spirit gives life" *(2 Cor. 3:6)*. Much confusion exists regarding which covenant to follow, but it's not that difficult to understand. YHWH wants sons and daughters who hear His voice, and desire to walk with Him in the "cool of the day" *(Gen. 3:8)*. The law did not bring that restoration of intimacy; in fact, it was given to reveal the absence of that very thing.

The book of Hebrews deals pretty thoroughly with this misunderstanding.

But now hath he obtained a more excellent ministry, by how much also he is the mediator of a better covenant, which was established upon better promises. 7 For if that first covenant had been faultless, then should no place have been sought for the second. 8 For finding fault with them, he saith, Behold, the days come, saith the Lord, when I will make a new covenant with the house of Israel and with the house of Judah: 9 Not according to the covenant that I made with their fathers...13 **In that he saith, A new covenant, he hath made the first old.** *Now that which decayeth and waxeth old is ready to vanish away (Heb 8:6).*

The temple was about to be destroyed, and the impossibility of continuing to live in the Mosaic Covenant was staring everyone in the face. A study of the book of Hebrews and Galatians should convince you of at least two

---

CRUCIAL POINT: *It is time to allow all that can be shaken to be shaken—including all those pet ideas and concepts that have never been fully examined in the light of Scripture. It is time to PICK YOUR COVENANT AND LIVE IN IT.*

---

things. The first is that the priestly order has changed — *Yeshua* (Jesus) is our only High Priest—and the law has been changed (transformed). Hebrews 7:12 makes this clear: "For the priesthood being changed, there is made of necessity a change also of the law." We need to spend more time rejoicing in and exploring the glorious aspects of the New Covenant, rather than trying so desperately to keep placing ourselves back under that which is inferior.

It's time to stop playing "Hop-Scotch" Covenants.

Remember, the words *Law* and *Torah* are often used interchangeably by the Rabbinic Jewish world. Though they deny it, the Talmud or Oral Law (Oral Torah, as they refer to it) is what they consider "Judaism," and that is what they are really selling. What they are teaching is not even the Law (Torah) or the Covenant that YHWH made with the Children of Israel at Mt. Sinai — rather, it is a Satanically inspired Babylonian forgery which interprets the written Law (Torah) of Moses and rips it into heresy and blasphemy against YHWH, *His* covenants and *His* Son.

The following scriptures make the argument so clear that those without blinders on wonder what the argument is about. Messianic Judaism, while embracing *Yeshua* (Jesus) as the Son of God and the Lamb of God, has been totally infected with Rabbinical Jewish dog vomit for so long it has actually become "unclean"! The Holy Spirit is calling *Yeshua's* (Jesus') Bride, "to come out of her" — referring to the Babylonish system of entanglement and corruption — and be cleansed. Let the Word of YHWH wash all of us!

(I have attached Torah to the word Law and changed the word Christ to Yeshua for clarity.)

> *If therefore perfection were by the Levitical priesthood, (for under it **the people received the law (Torah)**, what further need was there that another priest should rise after the order of Melchisedek, and not be called after the order of Aaron? 12 For the priesthood being changed, there is made of necessity **a change also of the law (Torah)** (Heb 7:11).*

> *But now hath he obtained a more excellent ministry, by how much also he is the mediator **of a better covenant**, which was established upon **better promises**. 7 For **if that first covenant had been faultless**, then should no place have been sought for the second. 8 For **finding fault with them**, he saith, Behold, the days come, saith the Lord, when I will make*

a new covenant with the house of Israel and with the house of Judah (Heb 8:6):

For **the law (Torah) having a shadow of good things to come,** *and not the very image of the things,* **can never** *with those sacrifices which they offered year by year continually* **make the comers thereunto perfect** *(Heb 10:1).*

Then said he, Lo, I come to do thy will, O God. **He taketh away the first, that he may establish the second.** *10 By the which will* **we are sanctified** *through the offering of the body of Jesus Yeshua once for all (Heb 10:9).*

"He taketh away the first, that he may establish the second." If English is a language that you are well versed in, I don't think this statement requires interpretation. How do men of reasonable intelligence read all these simple, straightforward scriptures and still come up with such convoluted messages? The only answer that could possibly make sense is that the religious infection has been used to blind them to the truth. Just as YHWH put a veil on Judah concerning the scriptures, once an individual has been infected with the religious spirit, Satan wastes no time using it to blind them to the truth. Many good people who are otherwise highly intelligent live in this infected blindness all over the world.

ARE YOU WALKING UNDER THE CURSE OF THE LAW (TORAH)?

For **as many as are of the works of the law (Torah) are** **under the curse***: for it is written, Cursed is every one that continueth not in all things which are written in the book of the law (Torah) to do them. 11 But that* **no man is justified**

> *by the law (Torah) in the sight of God, it is evident: for,*
> *The just shall live by faith. 12 And the law (Torah) is*
> *not of faith: but, The man that doeth them shall live in them.*
> *13 Yeshua hath redeemed us from **the curse of the law***
> ***(Torah)**, being made a curse for us: for it is written, Cursed is*
> *every one that hangeth on a tree:14 That the blessing of*
> *Abraham might come on the Gentiles through Jesus Yeshua;*
> *that we might receive the promise of the Spirit through faith*
> *(Gal 3:10).*

We need to get this straight: *No one* is, or can be, "under the Law" or the Mosaic Covenant. YHWH saw to it that there is no temple, no Levitical system, and no altar to sacrifice on, which is the only way it can be done. *So stop saying it!*

WHAT HAPPENED TO YOU? DID YOU RETURN TO JUDAISM?

> *O foolish Galatians, **who hath bewitched you**, that ye*
> *should not obey the truth, before whose eyes Jesus Yeshua hath*
> *been evidently set forth, crucified among you? 2 This only*
> *would I learn of you, **Received ye the Spirit by the works***
> ***of the law (Torah), or by the hearing of faith? 3 Are ye so***
> ***foolish? having begun in the Spirit, are ye now made***
> ***perfect by the flesh** (Gal 3: 1).*

This isn't hard to understand, either. We enter the Kingdom by faith in Yeshua, and we become more like Yeshua as we continue to trust Him and yield to the inner leading of the Holy Spirit. The Holy Spirit is more than able to customize your personal program of sanctification.

Don't Return to the Rabbinical Dog Vomit

> *But now, after that ye have known God, or rather are known of God,* **how turn ye again to the weak and beggarly elements, whereunto ye desire again to be in bondage?** *10 Ye observe days, and months, and times, and years. (Gal 4:9, R.D.V.)*

The "weak and beggarly elements" can refer to a variety of things, the keeping of pagan observances being one of them, but in this context it is referring to a legalistic perversion of YHWH's appointed times that the Pharisees (Rabbinic Judaism) had already distorted. The "observation" of these appointed times has nothing to do with your salvation or standing with God. Salvation is only by grace through faith (see Rom. 11:6). "Observation" is what is done under legalism and carries with it righteousness through your own works. It's another trap! That being said, many in the Christian world misinterpret this scripture claiming that it eliminates all teaching in the Torah. No, the teachings in the Torah contain eternal principles of life and wisdom that help us to understand YHWH's nature, and His great plan of redemption. Just don't pervert it into something it is not. We will cover this more fully in *What Do We Do Now?*

> *Am I therefore become your enemy, because I tell you the truth (Gal 4:16)?*

> *Tell me,* **ye that desire to be under the law (Torah), do ye not hear the law (Torah)**?*22 For it is written, that Abraham had two sons, the one by a bondmaid, the other by a freewoman. 23 But he who was of the bondwoman was born after the flesh; but he of the freewoman was by promise. 24*

*Which things are an allegory: **for these are the two covenants**; the one from the mount Sinai, which gendereth to bondage, which is Agar. 25 For this Agar is mount Sinai in Arabia, and answereth to Jerusalem which now is, and is in bondage with her children (Gal 4:21).*

Now we, brethren, as Isaac was, are the children of promise. 31 So then, brethren, we are not children of the bondwoman, but of the free (Gal 4:28).

WHAT DO WE DO WITH THOSE TEACHING RABBINIC JUDAISM, AKA "JUDA-IZERS"?

What Did Paul Say?

*And that because of **false brethren** unawares brought in, who came in privily **to spy out our liberty** which we have in Yeshua Jesus, **that they might bring us into bondage**: 5 To whom we gave place by subjection, no, not for an hour; that the truth of the gospel might continue with you (Gal 2:4).*

*Stand fast therefore in the liberty wherewith Yeshua hath made us free, and **be not entangled again with the yoke of bondage**.(RDV) 2 Behold, I Paul say unto you, that **if ye be circumcised, Yeshua shall profit you nothing**. 3 For I testify again to every man that is circumcised, that he is a debtor to do the whole law (Torah). 4 **Yeshua is become of no effect unto you**, whosoever of you are justified by the law (Torah); **ye are fallen from grace** (Gal 5: 1).*

A little leaven leaveneth the whole lump (Gal 5:9).

*I would **they were even cut off** which trouble you. 13 For, brethren, ye have been called unto liberty; only use not liberty for an occasion to the flesh, but by love serve one another. 14*

For all the law (Torah) is fulfilled in one word, even in this; Thou shalt love thy neighbour as thyself (Gal 5:12).

What Did Yeshua (Jesus) Say?

*Then spake Jesus to the multitude, and to his disciples, 2 Saying, The scribes and the Pharisees sit in Moses' seat:… 7…, and **to be called of men, Rabbi, Rabbi. 8 But be not ye called Rabbi**: for one is your Master, even Yeshua; and all ye are brethren. 9 And **call no man your father** upon the earth: for one is your Father, which is in heaven. 10 **Neither be ye called masters**: for one is your Master, even Yeshua….13 But <u>**woe unto you, scribes and Pharisees, hypocrites!**</u> For ye **shut up the kingdom of heaven against** men: for ye neither go in yourselves, neither suffer ye them that are entering to go in. 14 <u>**Woe unto you, scribes and Pharisees, hypocrites!**</u> For ye **devour widows' houses**, and for a pretence make long prayer: therefore ye shall receive the greater damnation. 15 <u>**Woe unto you, scribes and Pharisees, hypocrites**</u>! for ye **compass sea and land** to make one proselyte, and when he is made, ye make him **twofold more the child of hell than yourselves**…24 **<u>Ye blind guides</u>, which strain at a gnat, and swallow a camel**…33 **<u>Ye serpents, ye generation of vipers</u>, how can ye escape the damnation of hell?** (Mat 23:1-33)*

Let me see if I can interpret Yeshua's real thought here. Let's review the quotes:

*13 But <u>**woe unto you, scribes and Pharisees, hypocrites!**</u> For ye **shut up the kingdom of heaven against** men: for ye neither go in yourselves, neither suffer ye them that are entering to go in.*

*14 **Woe unto you, scribes and Pharisees, hypocrites!** For ye devour widows' houses, and for a pretence make long prayer: therefore ye shall receive the greater damnation.*

*15 **Woe unto you, scribes and Pharisees, hypocrites**! for ye compass sea and land to make one proselyte, and when he is made, ye make him **twofold more the child of hell than yourselves**...*

*24 **Ye blind guides, which strain at a gnat, and swallow a camel**...*

*33 **Ye serpents, ye generation of vipers, how can ye escape the damnation of hell?** (Mat 23:1-39)*

Do you think anyone needs this to be interpreted for you? Do you think studying it in the Hebrew or Greek would change any context or reveal some deep hidden meaning?

CRUCIAL QUESTION: Will teaching Rabbinic Judaism get you or your disciples into heaven? In my opinion, the type and shadow set here are the Pharisees as the Rabbinic Jews and the Scribes as the legalistic Christians. Religion is the infection! Doctrines of men will lead you to HELL!

HOW MUCH CLEARER CAN WE MAKE THIS???

__I do not frustrate the grace of God__: for if righteousness come by the law (Torah), then Yeshua is dead in vain (Gal 2: 21).

We had better read — and reread — Galatians 2:21, examining our lives to see if we are frustrating God. If you grasp the meaning and power of this scripture, it should sober your perspective and make you carefully examine your doctrines. Whatever you do, make sure you are not declaring with your teaching that Yeshua died in vain!

> *Is the law (Torah) then against the promises of God? God* **forbid: for if there had been a law (Torah) given which could have given life, verily righteousness should have been by the law (Torah).** 22 *But the scripture hath concluded all under sin, that the promise by faith of Jesus Yeshua might be given to them that believe.* **23 But before faith came, we were kept under the law (Torah), shut up unto the faith which should afterwards be revealed. 24 Wherefore the law (Torah) was our schoolmaster to bring us unto Yeshua, that we might be justified by faith. 25** <u>**But after that faith is come, we are no longer under a schoolmaster**</u> **(Gal 3:21).**

The overriding purpose of the law (or "schoolmaster") was to show us how much we need Yeshua the Lamb. Instead of a group of laws and ordinances outside of us that we try to follow, (Have to!) in the New Covenant, we now walk by faith and through HIM; and from the love that is imputed into our hearts from an inward power, we live to please HIM, (Get To!) and with our actions fulfill *all* the principles of the Torah and Law. Yeshua is "the Word," *Logos* in Greek (John 1:1). He is the expression and message of the unseen God. He is the "Living Torah," to put it in more Hebraic terms. What an awesome thing to have the Holy Spirit, the Living Torah Himself, living inside us to lead and

CRUCIAL POINT: *Infected doctrines put man back under the Mosaic Covenant system or doctrines, frustrate YHWH, blaspheme His Son Yeshua, and endanger the one doing the teaching. Remember that teachers are held to higher accountability standards!*

guide. True spirituality is the expression of the Holy Spirit, Yeshua's life, in us. If we fall into the mode of legalistic observance (I HAVE to do this, and I HAVE to do it this way or I'm condemned!), we are attempting to express — and even legislate — our own <u>human righteousness</u>. The last time I checked, we don't have any *(Rom 3:23).* All we can do is let HIS life come forth through us.

> *But we have this treasure* [His Holy Spirit] *in earthen vessels, that the excellency of the power <u>may be of God, and not of us</u>* (2 Cor 4:7).

What About the Natural-Born and the New Covenant?

> *Who also hath made us able ministers of the new testament; not of the letter, but of the spirit: for the letter killeth, but the spirit giveth life. 7 But if the ministration of death, written and engraven in stones, was glorious, so that the children of Israel could not stedfastly behold the face of Moses for the glory of his countenance; **which glory was to be done away**: 8 How shall not the ministration of the spirit be rather glorious? 9 For if the ministration of condemnation be glory, much more doth the ministration of righteousness exceed in glory. 10 For even that which was made glorious had no glory in this respect, by reason of the glory that excelleth. 11 **For if that which is done away was glorious, much more that which remaineth is glorious**. 12 Seeing then that we have such hope, we use great plainness of speech: 13 And not as Moses, which put a vail over his face, that the children of Israel could not stedfastly look to the end of that which is abolished: 14 But **their minds were blinded**: for until this day remaineth the same vail untaken away in the reading of the old testament; **which vail is done away in Yeshua**. 15*

But even unto this day, when Moses is read, the vail is upon their heart (2 Cor 3: 6).

*** CAUTION! CAUTION! CAUTION! ***
How do we handle brethren who are caught up in these errors? ...You'd better do it with love!

---

*Brethren, if a man be overtaken in a fault, ye which are spiritual, **restore** such an one in the spirit of meekness; considering thyself, lest thou also be tempted. 2 **Bear ye one another's burdens, and so fulfil the law (Torah) of Yeshua*** (Gal 6 1).

Don't make the mistake of haughtiness or arrogance. YHWH will not tolerate pride, no matter which covenant you choose to live under. It's possible to be very unrighteous in our righteousness. Correction must always be brought forth in love and humility.

You will notice a common theme communicated in Paul's epistles: *the law has been fulfilled and transformed in Yeshua.*

Yeshua is the End (Termination/Goal) of the Mosaic Law (Torah)

*Brethren, my heart's desire and prayer to God for Israel is, that they might be saved. 2 For I bear them record that they have a zeal of God, but not according to knowledge. 3 For they being ignorant of God's righteousness, and **going about to establish their own righteousness**, have not submitted themselves unto the righteousness of God. 4 **For Yeshua is the end [telos, Strongs# 5056] of the law (Torah) for*** *righteousness to everyone that believeth (Rom 10:1).*

The Greek word *telos* can be translated as "end" in the sense of termination or completion. It can also be translated as "goal" or "purpose." All of the above definitions might apply in this case. As it relates to righteousness, Yeshua is the end or completion of the law. We need look no further than what He did for us on the cross. But we also know that "the eternal wisdom of the law" has not come to an end. It has been transformed into something dynamic and alive through the Holy Spirit; so in that sense Yeshua, and His life in us, was always the goal of the law.

CRUCIAL POINT: *We may not realize it, but the doctrines we teach either honor Yeshua's blood or they negate its importance and blaspheme the covering that YHWH provided. That sacrifice made by both Father and Son should be in the forefront of our minds as we search for doctrinal truths.*

The Mosaic Covenant was a *Have To* Covenant!

Today there is no identifiable Aaronic Priesthood or Levitical System, no temple or possible way to keep any Levitical rites or ordinances. There is no way to keep the Civil or Judicial system. It is completely impossible to obey or fulfill the "The Law", the *Mosaic Covenant* in a literal way! Impossible!

I believe there are dimensions of restoration regarding Israel that few of us consider. I'm sure there are Levites, Gadites, Issacharites, and people from all the tribes of Israel alive today. Some of them are found within the New Covenant and are actively involved in ministry. The book of Ezekiel speaks of a restored temple and sacrificial system, all of which will serve as a memorial to the redemptive ministry of Yeshua.

CAN WE BE "TORAH OBSERVANT" UNDER THE NEW COVENANT?

Another religious term embraced in the Messianic movement is that of being *Torah observant*. While this phrase may sound upright and impressive, it has some very dangerous teeth.

Organizations, congregations and individuals are using this expression about themselves to convey the idea that they are "following and obeying the Torah." By using this term it gives zealous men and women a sense of righteousness. (Hmmm, does this ring a bell?) Torah observance is claimed by many wonderful people wanting to please God and show the importance of teachings in the Torah. Unfortunately, its use implies two things: first, that the Torah supersedes the rest of Scripture, and second, you can't please God without following the Torah.

There are several problems with this concept. First of all, each group creates and interprets what *Torah observant* means for them, personally. There is no standard. Although individual interpretation is encouraged by this writer, this term is used in so many ways, it's hard to give it a real definition or identify the specific doctrines that are inclusive of the term.

Second, the majority of congregations that teach Torah compliance are typically not Torah observant at all. They are rabbinic system observant! Many wear kippot, tallitot and follow many of the rabbinic traditions. Most of them keep the rabbinic calendar, rabbinic feasts and *none of them* have a lamb at Passover! In light of this, why do they call themselves Torah observant? They, of course, believe they are. The majority are good, sincere people trying to figure out how to serve and obey YHWH. It didn't help that infected Christian churches all but threw out the teachings in the Torah, or "Old Testament" as it is called, causing many to over-correct without understanding as they left to join Messianic congregations.

For others, the term *Torah observant* is just another way for the enemy to add more infection and create a feeling of superiority of one individual, or group, over another. Either way, it just becomes another form of legalism to end up creating arrogance and self-righteousness. We already have way too many things creating that problem for us as it is.

We have the same problem being "Torah observant" that we do with being "under the Law." It can't be done! There is no Levitical system, no Levitical or Aaronic Priesthood, no temple or any way to keep any of the Levitical rites or ordinances, and no way to keep the civil or judicial system—it's another infected rabbit trail!

> *But when I saw that they walked not uprightly according to the truth of the gospel, I said unto Peter before them all, If thou, being a Jew, livest after the manner of Gentiles, and not as do the Jews, why compellest thou the Gentiles to live as do the Jews? 15 We who are Jews by nature, and not sinners of the Gentiles, 16 Knowing that* **a man is not justified by the works of the law (Torah)**, *but by the faith of Jesus Yeshua, even we have believed in Jesus Yeshua, that we might be justified by the faith of Yeshua, and* **not by the works of the law (Torah)**: *for by* **the works of the law (Torah) shall no flesh be justified** *(Gal 2: 14).*

> *For I* **through the law (Torah) am dead to the law (Torah)**, *that I might live unto God (Gal 2:19).*

WHAT WAS THE LAW (TORAH) FOR?

For if the inheritance be of the law (Torah), it is no more of promise: but God gave it to Abraham by promise. 19 **Wherefore then serveth the law (Torah)? It was added because of transgressions, till the seed should come to whom the promise was made; and it was ordained by angels in the hand of a mediator** *(Gal 3:18).*

The law was "added because of transgressions." That's an important point. After the Ten Commandments were spoken forth on Mt. Sinai — a covenant which the Israelites affirmed by responding "all that the Lord hath spoken we will do" *(Exo 19:8)* — it was only a short time later that the Israelites would break the covenant. Remember that part about the golden calf? As a result, additional instructions, rules, and regulations were added in order to further explain covenant life, proper conduct, and the principles of redemption. Nothing wrong with that. However, YHWH knew all along about the stubborn hearts of His people. He knew they wouldn't be able to "keep" the law, therefore, the law provided a legal framework through which the Israelites would be convicted of their sin and declared guilty.

"The Law," (Torah) or Mosaic Covenant was moral, dietary, familial, Levitical, ceremonial, civil, and agricultural — it touched every aspect of life.

Which part do you think you could keep today?

Why do you think YHWH wiped the Temple out and drove the Israelites from the land for nearly two thousand years? So no one could "keep Torah" — *The Law!* They would be forced to look to their Lamb for true salvation.

Let's take it to the daily, practical level. When was the last time you went to a stoning? Or were required to participate in the purification process of washing in ashes or dipping so many times? When was the last time you tried to get a thief to pay you back three times for what he stole from you? Or had your slaves observe the Sabbath? When was the last time you celebrated a Jubilee and forgave everyone's debts who owed you a dime and gave back all the land you had bought from other families? This entire concept of being Torah observant is insanity and it's just another way the infection perverts the mind and reintroduces self-righteousness by works of the flesh. Adherents of Rabbinic Judaism aren't Torah observant, and neither are Messianic/Hebrew-roots believers. It is all just more rabbinical...(Don't make me say it!)

"Torah," the Law, cannot be kept in the literal sense or a biblical sense. It's completely impossible. It can only "be kept" from the heretical, fabricated doctrines of Rabbinic Judaism with the distortion of current interpretation and teaching. It's just another label that God didn't endorse. We need to realize it's another deception in man's endless quest to justify himself.

But The Wolves Say...

Those proclaiming they can show you "how to keep Torah" are either zealous without understanding, or wolves sent in to devour and place back into (Rabbinic Judaism) bondage those foolish Galatians who will fall prey to Satan's snares. Don't be trapped! They love to quote scriptures like this.

> *Blessed are they that do his commandments that they may have right to the tree of life, and may enter in through the gates into the city (Rev 22:14).*

The wolves say you have to keep, or "observe" Torah to qualify for your rewards. They use the word *lawless* to describe those who do not follow their interpretation of the Torah. Obviously there are commandments in the New Kingdom Covenant and important teachings in the Torah.

The wolves will tell you all about the great wisdom, stories and history they glean out of the Talmud, (Oral Law). Let me state for the record that I have two Babylonian Talmuds. And I will tell you that there are great stories, debates, historical records, doctrinal discussions and the opinions of more rabbis than you can count. The Talmud is full of nuggets from man's knowledge and information smattered with great heresy and blasphemy. Why would you study this instead of God's word? Studying the Talmud instead of Scripture is like eating out of a trash dumpster behind the restaurant when there is a super buffet inside. Looking outside God's instructions won't help you walk in the New Covenant or improve your spiritual maturity.

WHAT DO WE DO WITH THE TORAH?

Many believers are still asking the question, "What do we do and how do we do it?" The bottom line is, *YHWH has never changed, nor will He.* If He didn't like something back then, He doesn't like now, nor will He like it in the future. We respect and learn from the Torah. It was, and is, our school master. It teaches us the basics of what YHWH likes and hates. Without the Torah we don't truly know how to love God! We will cover this in detail in the next section.

> ***Blotting out the handwriting of ordinances*** *that was against us, which was contrary to us, and **took it out of the way, nailing it to his cross;** 15 And having spoiled*

*principalities and powers, he made a shew of them openly, triumphing over them in it. 16 **Let no man therefore judge you** in meat, or in drink, or in respect of an holyday, or of the new moon, or of the sabbath days: 17 **Which are a shadow of things to come**; but the body is of Yeshua (Col 2:14).*

What we do have is a living, breathing God. His Spirit is supposed to be breathing through us and teaching us His ways. And yes, we need to value and honor the Torah, which is full of wonderful teachings and lessons for us all to learn. It will always be a viable part of Scripture and should be a part of our lives. But, if you want to be *observant*, be *YHWH* observant. That's what *Yeshua* (Jesus) came to "disciple" you in, and the Torah was to point us, like a

CRUCIAL POINT: *Did you know that the Sabbath, the Ten Commandments, tithing, the dietary laws, and the Feasts of the Lord were actually "pre-law" practices and commandments? They were all established before the Mosaic Covenant.*

schoolmaster, to YHWH until the "Living Torah" arrived. He would then teach us how to live out or fulfill *the laws of God*, which are written on our hearts. The new covenant is a "**get to**" covenant! Yes, Christians (for the most part) have either totally ignored the teachings in Torah or considered the teaching for the Jews only and Rabbinic Judaism has completely perverted them. That results in confusion for a lot of people struggling to sort it all out.

SO, WHAT DOES APPLY TO US TODAY?

Are there parts of the Torah we're obligated to keep? How does this work? To some it is confusing and to others it's clear as a bell. There seems to be a different opinion from every group out there.

What we will try to do is to clearly lay out the basics. I will make a summary statement that covers these concepts and then give you the background information to support the summary.

God, YHWH, has laid out, in His marvelous collection of Holy Scriptures, a complete description of what He likes and doesn't like, and of what He approves and disapproves. YHWH said that He never changes. He is the same "yesterday, today and forever." What *has* changed are the covenants we live under. Each covenant contains conditions, rules, and statutes that allow the followers of God, YHWH, to enjoy fellowship with Him. Understanding which covenant you live under and which of those details are applicable to you is part of what this study is about.

SUMMARY STATEMENT: *New Covenant Believers are directed to keep Four Foundational Commandments. Indeed, all the other commandments and teachings in the Bible fall under the "Big Four." They Are:*
1. *Love God*
2. *Love your Neighbor*
3. *Love the Brethren*
4. *Share your Faith with others*

The last three commandments seem fairly simple and straightforward while the first one is a little more complicated and causes the most confusion. The question becomes, "How do we love God?" We know that the scriptures clearly teach us that our obedience is the evidence of our love. Yeshua told His disciples in John 14:15, *If ye love me, keep My commandments.* So which of His commandments apply to us today under this New Kingdom Covenant?"

There are two specific groups that have muddied the waters considerably: the Christian Church with its doctrines, and Rabbinic Judaism with its doctrines. The majority of the Church either implies or directly states that the Old Testament and "the Law" are completely disconnected from our lives as believers in *Yeshua* (Jesus). Rabbinic Judaism claims that all of the Old Testament is applicable, BUT only through their Babylonian interpretation with the "Oral Law."

I want to remind you here of the three covenant eras. The first we called Pre-Mosaic Era, the second is the Mosaic Era, and the third is the New Covenant/Kingdom Era. They are critical to this part of the study.

THE PRE-MOSAIC ERA

It's important to notice what was established BEFORE the Mosaic Covenant was established on Mt. Sinai with the seed of Abraham, the Hebrew people who became the nation of Israel. I'll also have you recall that there was a priestly order in existence before the Aaronic Priesthood, and that original priesthood was the Melchizedek Priesthood *(Gen 14)*. Abraham (and also Levi who was in the loins of Abraham at the time) tithed to this great king-priest *(Heb 7:9-10)*. This original Kingdom Priesthood (Royal Priesthood) is the priestly order of Yeshua of Nazareth today. This is what is being restored in the New Covenant; therefore, it is extremely important to acknowledge these ancient commandments and teachings. They include:

Sabbath *Gen 2:1-3, Exo 16:23, 25, 26, 29, 20:8*

Sacrificial Offerings *Gen 4:1-7, 22:2-8, 35:14, Exo 18:12*

Dietary Parameters *Gen 7:1-3*

Tithes *Gen 14:18-20, 28:22*

Blood Covenant *Gen 15:8-9, 18*

Feasts *Exo 12:1-8, 14, 17, 24 15-20*

Dedication of the Firstborn *Exo 13:12*

Divine Health *Exo 15:26b*

Kingdom/Royal Priesthood *Exo 19:4-6, 8*

Ten Commandments *Exo 20: 1-17*

God's commandments and statues are revealed in Exodus 15:26a – 16:4b – 16:28 – 18:16, 18:20, five times! How did Moses know of God's commandments and statutes and why was Moses teaching them to the children of Israel *before* the Covenant on Mt. Sinai? Why didn't the children of Israel know them, if Moses did? His father-in-law!

CRUCIAL POINT: *IMPORTANT ENOUGH TO REPEAT:*
Established "Pre Mosaic Covenant" was the Sabbath, Offerings, Sacrifices, Dietary Parameters, Tithes, Covenants, Feasts, God's commandments and statues, Kingdom Priesthood and the Ten Commandments.

All of these commandments and teachings were established back before the Children of Israel were offered the covenant so none of them were new. They are simply God's laws and statutes. They haven't changed nor were they "added" into the Mosaic Covenant.

MOSAIC COVENANT ERA

What happened when the Hebrews refused the Kingdom Covenant in Exodus 20:18-21? They did NOT realize the plan God had for them in becoming a "kingdom of priests and a holy nation" *(Exo 19:6)*. YHWH then established a priestly order and temporary system, all of which was a step backwards, a crude system teaching and pointing to the future Everlasting Covenant and the fullness of God's plan for His people.

The Levitical system (which included the Aaronic Priesthood) taught us many powerful truths. The most important three are 1) Humanity's sin was a problem, and this problem had to be dealt with. 2) The penalty of sin could only be satisfied through outpoured life—blood. 3) YHWH would forgive sin and restore relationship.

Myriad ritualistic details were established in regard to teaching and explaining each of these concepts, but these rituals were temporary in the sense that they looked forward to a greater fulfillment, a fulfillment we enjoy today in the New Covenant. Yeshua the Lamb has fully dealt with the problems of humanity in regard to being restored in right relationship to God.

Certainly, many pre-Mosaic laws and statutes were reestablished in the Mosaic Covenant, and these endure today; but in 12-1400 years from the time these details were given, the people were scattered, the temple destroyed and many of the specifics became impossible to carry out.

Since the Hebrews rejected the Kingdom Covenant on Mt. Sinai they were not made into Kingdom Priests. Instead, the entire Levitical System with the Aaronic Priesthood was established as a temporary replacement to instruct them, and to prepare them for the ultimate solution that YHWH would provide.

So the question becomes, when YHWH told the Hebrews living under the Aaronic Priesthood, with its Tabernacle/Temple-based system of sacrifices and offerings, "to do these things *forever*," did He know that it would one day be impossible, once the nation and system were wiped out? Of course He did. Do you see the difference between the permanent and the temporary? I hope so.

Added to the Mosaic Covenant were:

- Details of How to Keep the Sabbath and descriptions of different kind of Sabbaths.*
- Details about the Feasts of the Lord.*
- Details on the Dietary Laws.*
- Details on Tithes and offerings.*
- Details on the Moral Laws.*

* Every one of these were and are the statutes of our God. Just as He has never changed, His Laws don't either.

The entire Levitical system; civil laws; judicial system; agricultural Laws—the rest of these were part of that temporary system that went with the temporary covenant that was established on Mt. Sinai. While there are many wonderful principles within the temporary system, their application has been removed until the millennial reign when ceremonial aspects will be reintroduced for that period.

NEW COVENANT/KINGDOM ERA

In our New Kingdom Covenant we move into a dynamic rarely seen before. If you could take the positive attributes of Enoch, Noah, Abraham, Moses, David and Daniel, then roll them into one statement I believe it would come out something like this: They were great men *of* God who had a special relationship *with* God. This is what YHWH is offering you in the Kingdom—the New Covenant-intimate relationship! Everyone would be "born into" the Kingdom of YHWH as a Holy Priest and would have a personal relationship with Him. It's not a Jewish thing or a Christian thing, it's a God thing. This is why I said earlier to stop trying to convert people. We are *reborn* into the Kingdom, not converted to it. It's so exciting to know we all become an intricate part of the same love-centered family. (I wish we *could* convert people to that, but we can't.)

NEW COVENANT & THE FOUR KINGDOM BASICS

For those new to the faith, I want give you a very simple primary guide to fulfill all the other commandments. You'll see it is really nothing more than expounding on what *Yeshua* (Jesus) Himself said. As James gave the early gentile believers four basic rules to follow before they had a New Testament to study, the following is what I call the Four Kingdom Basics. With these four as a guide, you'll find all the other teachings fall under them. Whenever you get confused, or find yourself getting dry from too much knowledge-seeking and not enough relationship building, simply go back to your basics.

FIRST TWO COMMANDMENTS

*Then one of them, which was a lawyer, asked him a question, tempting him, and saying, 36 Master, which is the great commandment in the law? 37 Jesus said unto him, Thou shalt **love the Lord thy God** with all thy heart, and with all thy soul, and with all thy mind. 38 This is the first and great commandment. 39 And the second is like unto it, Thou shalt **love thy neighbor** as thyself. **40 On these two commandments hang all the law and the prophets** (Mat 22:35-40).*

The more we love YHWH, the more we want to learn what His statutes and commandments were and are. As His Spirit teaches us and guides us, we learn how to walk in each one of them. All of the scriptures are resources for us. While they include the Sabbath, Offerings, Sacrifices, Dietary Parameters, Tithes, Feasts, the Kingdom Priesthood and the Ten Commandments, don't try and master them all at once. I have some suggestion in the last chapter that may help. Study YHWH's scriptures and trust in YHWH's Holy Spirit to guide you. Please Him and everything else will work out. Be true to Him and yourself and you will do just fine.

In loving our neighbor we learn how to be good citizens, friends and stable pillars for our community. We become the well of hope and love that the world is truly seeking after. We become the godly examples, the righteous of our generation, the mighty men and women of valor.

Since our neighbors also include those who may hate or despise us, it is a wonderful opportunity to learn true forgiveness and grace as we cleanse our own hearts and hands and operate in our role of ministers of reconciliation (2 Cor 5:18).

THE THIRD COMMANDMENT

*A new commandment I give unto you, That ye **love one
another; as I have loved you, that ye also love one
another**. 35: By this shall all men know that ye are my
disciples, **if ye have love one to another** (John 13:34).*

*Herein is my Father glorified, that **ye bear much fruit**; so
shall ye be my disciples. 9 As the **Father hath loved me**, so
have **I loved you**: continue **ye in my love**. 10 If ye keep my
commandments, ye shall **abide in my love**; even as I have
kept my Father's commandments, and **abide in his love**. 11
These things have I spoken unto you, that **my joy might
remain in you**, and that **your joy might be full**. :12 **This is
my commandment, That ye love one another, as I have
loved you.** 13 Greater love hath no man than this, that a
man lay down his life for his friends. 14 Ye are my friends, if
ye do whatsoever I command you. 15 Henceforth I call you
not, servants; for the servant knoweth not what his lord
doeth: but I have called you friends; for all things that I have
heard of my Father I have made known unto you. 16 Ye have
not chosen me, but I have chosen you, and ordained you, that
ye should go and bring forth fruit, and that your fruit should
remain: that whatsoever, ye shall ask of the Father in my
name, he may give it you (John 15:8).*

Isn't it interesting that Yeshua had to make this a new
commandment? This is not our neighbor, it's our
brotherhood. The rest of the Kingdom Priests. All of New
Covenant Israel! Why did He have to do this? Are we that
bad or is Satan and the infection so capable of causing us to
mistreat each other?

Of the Christians it is said, "They are the only army in
the world known for executing their wounded." The

majority of the denominations condemn all the other denominations to Hell.

Of the Jews, rarely do you find even toleration of other sects, much less love. "They're not Jews!" is the cry heard over and over.

What have we created? It certainly isn't love. If it's not love, it's *not* the New Covenant!

THE FOURTH COMMANDMENT

And he said unto them, **Go ye into all the world, and preach the gospel to every creature.** *16 He that believeth and is baptized shall be saved; but he that believeth not shall be damned (Mark 16:15, 16).*

Did you see the word convert anywhere? Let's do a scriptural review of the description of *Yeshua's* (Jesus') ministry, found in Isaiah 61:1: The *Spirit of the Lord GOD is upon me*; because the LORD hath anointed me *to preach good tidings unto the meek*; he hath sent *me to bind up the brokenhearted, to proclaim liberty to the captives,* and *the opening of the prison to them that are bound*; 2 **To proclaim the acceptable year of the LORD,** Now *Yeshua* (Jesus) makes this proclamation for Himself in his own hometown. He was proclaiming YHWH's Kingdom and love while meeting the needs of the people wherever He went.

These should be our own:

> *When we preach good tidings unto the meek;*
> *When we bind up the brokenhearted,*
> *When we proclaim liberty to the captives,*
> *When we open the prison to them that are bound,*
> *When we proclaim the acceptable year of the LORD*

When was the last time you were digging around to find better ways to do these? Now, *these* things are worth discussing and debating over.

> *And these signs shall follow them that believe; In my name shall they cast out devils; they shall speak with new tongues; 18 They shall take up serpents; and if they drink any deadly thing, it shall not hurt them; they shall lay hands on the sick, and they shall recover (Mark 16:17, 18).*

Mark 16:17 is supposed to be a description of someone who believes and is walking in the New Covenant, the Kingdom Covenant! Is that you? Would you like it to be? When was the last time you realized that your primary calling as a New Covenant priest was to share YHWH's love and to meet the needs of others?

KINGDOM COMMANDMENTS REVIEW

The New Covenant (Kingdom Covenant) rests on four Foundational Pillars (Kingdom Commandments):

1) Love God
2) Love your Neighbor
3) Love the Brethren
4) Share YHWH's Love with Others and Meet their Needs

Remember, YHWH has never changed, nor have his statutes. The Sabbath, tithing, dietary laws, the Feasts of the Lord and the Ten Commandment were all established before the Mosaic Covenant, "the Law," was enacted. They are all "Pre-Law" or "Pre-Mosaic Covenant" commandments of YHWH. They will be His statutes forever.

THE CONCLUSION OF "THE LAW" AND BEING "TORAH OBSERVANT"

Where is boasting then? It is excluded. By what law? of works? Nay: but by the law of faith. 28 Therefore we conclude that a man is justified by faith without the deeds of the law. 29 Is he the God of the Jews only? is he not also of the Gentiles? Yes, of the Gentiles also: 30 Seeing it is one God, which shall justify the circumcision by faith, and uncircumcision through faith. 31 Do we then make void the law through faith? God forbid: yea, we establish the law (Rom 3:27).

Both the circumcision (Jews) and uncircumcision (non-Jews) are justified by faith. There is only ONE way to be reconciled to God, and only ONE way to walk with God — through the "law of faith" (vs. 27). It was always supposed to be that way. Paul tells us that we don't "make void the law through faith," but rather, "we establish the law." This is what *Yeshua* (Jesus) was telling us in Matthew 5:17: "Think not that I am come to destroy the law, or the prophets: I am not come to destroy, but to fulfill." The law of faith predates and undergirds the Mosaic law.

Paul goes on to solidify this understanding of the "law of faith" in Romans chapter 7. As you read the following scripture, keep in mind that this is describing a very legal aspect of our redemption.

Know ye not, brethren, (for I speak to them that know the law,) how that the law hath dominion over a man as long as he liveth? 2 For the woman which hath an husband is bound by the law to her husband so long as he liveth; but if the husband be dead, she is loosed from the law of her husband. 3 So then if, while her husband liveth, she be married to another man, she shall be called an adulteress: but if her husband be dead, she is free from that law; so that she is no adulteress, though she be married to another man. 4 Wherefore, my brethren, ye also are become dead to the law by the body of Yeshua; that ye should be married to another, even to him who is raised from the dead, that we should bring forth fruit unto God (Rom 7:1).

The law, which was given by YHWH, established His righteous standard, which all of us have failed to attain to because of our sin. Therefore, all were bound by the law in the sense of being judged guilty by it. But in the plan of genius implemented by our Heavenly Father, YHWH sent forth His Son Yeshua, the "last Adam," who kept the law perfectly and fulfilled ALL the law's righteous requirements. Only Yeshua qualified to serve as the unblemished Lamb of God. Because Yeshua's sacrifice on our behalf was accepted by the Father, the law has no legal jurisdiction or power over those who embrace the New Covenant. The law was kept perfectly, and the keeper of the law died — end of legal obligation — "It is FINISHED" *(John 19:30).*

We must understand that Yeshua went to the cross because of OUR sin. All our sins, past, present, and future, were laid on Him while He hung on that cross. We must acknowledge Yeshua's death on the cross, but we must discern ours as well. This is part of the message of the mikveh ritual (water baptism). But the primary focus of the mikveh is that not only did we die with Yeshua, we are raised up with Yeshua as new creations! We now live in the resurrection life of His Holy Spirit.

I am crucified with Yeshua: nevertheless I live; yet not I, but Yeshua liveth in me: and the life which I now live in the flesh I live by the faith of the Son of God, who loved me, and gave himself for me" (Gal 2:20).

Therefore if any man be in Yeshua, he is a new creature: old things are passed away; behold, all things are become new (1 Cor 5:17).

Through Yeshua, we died and were resurrected!

In the law, we read that an adulterous woman was to be put to death. Also, if a woman was divorced by her husband, it was illegal for the man who had divorced her to later take her back as his wife if she had been with another man (see *Lev 20:10; Deu 24; Jer 3*). As it relates to the New Covenant, since both Yeshua and the believer have died, they are legally free from the earlier covenant. Their earlier obligation to the law is broken, and there is nothing to prevent the two from once again becoming one in holy matrimony. Halleleujah!

In the rest of Romans 7, Paul clarifies our new relationship to the law. There was never anything wrong with the law — "the law is holy, and the commandment holy, and just, and good." It was sin that was the problem. But now, in *Yeshua* (Jesus), we are free from sin's power, and we stay free as we walk according to the leading of the Holy Spirit. Paul writes, "For I delight in the law of God after the inward man" *(Rom 7:22)*. Indeed, as new creations in *Yeshua* (Jesus), we do delight in the law of God. We understand that the eternal principles and wisdom of the law are within us, waiting to be expressed as we walk in love. The key, of course, is that this can only be done in the power of the Spirit. Anytime we revert back to flesh, we will fail.

CRUCIAL POINT: *Don't get caught up in the infected battle of semantics or secret meanings. You have the Spirit of the Almighty as your teacher. Learn to hear His voice, and spend time with Him daily.*

What Did Yeshua Mean When He Said "Till All Be Fulfilled?"

Think not that I am come to destroy[2647] the law,[3551] or the prophets:[4396] I am not come to destroy,[2647] but[235] to fulfill.[4137] Mat 5:18 For verily I say unto you, Till heaven and earth pass, one jot or one tittle shall in no wise pass from the law,[3551] till all be fulfilled[1096] (Mat 5:17).

G4137 πληρόω plēroō *play-ro'-o*

From G4134; to *make replete*, that is, (literally) to *cram* (a net), *level up* (a hollow), or (figuratively) to *furnish* (or *imbue, diffuse, influence*), *satisfy, execute* (an office), *finish* (a period or task), *verify* (or *coincide* with a prediction), etc.: - accomplish, X after, (be) complete, end, expire, fill (up), fulfil, (be, make) full (come), fully preach, perfect, supply.

G1096 γ ginomai *ghin'-om-ahee*

A prolonged and middle form of a primary verb; to *cause to be* ("gen"-erate), that is, (reflexively) to *become* (*come into being*), used with great latitude (literally, figuratively, intensively, etc.): - arise be assembled, be (come, -fall, -have self), be brought (to pass), (be) come (to pass), continue, be divided, be done, draw, be ended, fall, be finished, follow, be found, be fulfilled, + God forbid, grow, happen, have, be kept, be made, be married, be ordained to be, partake, pass, be performed, be published, require, seem, be showed, X soon as it was, sound, be taken, be turned, use, wax, will, would, be wrought.

What Did Yeshua Mean When He Said "It Is Finished!"?

Joh 19:30 When Jesus[2] therefore had received the vinegar, he said, It is finished:[5055] and he bowed his head, and gave up the ghost.

G5055 τ teleō *tel-eh'-o* From G5056; to *end*, that is, *complete, execute, conclude, discharge* (a debt): - accomplish, make an end, expire, fill up, finish, go over, pay, perform.

So what is it that you think *Yeshua* (Jesus) didn't complete or fulfill? What is it that you need to add to the puzzle that He didn't already provide?

> *Now the God of peace, that brought again from the dead our Lord Jesus, that great shepherd of the sheep, through the blood of the everlasting covenant (Heb 13:20),*

YHWH decided to have His Everlasting Covenant with us, one where He wrote His laws on our heart. If you want to reject that and return to a prior covenant where you can find a list of do's and don'ts because you believe that will make you righteous unto Him, you really need to rethink that. The Torah is valuable as it teaches us what He likes and doesn't like. It's a great reference source — but it won't make you holy.

Through our faith in YHWH, through our regenerated hearts with His law written there by His Spirit (Jer. 31:33), we obey His voice and keep all the principles of the law. Indeed, the letter of the law has been transformed into dynamic principles of life that find their fullest expression when we love YHWH and love our neighbor. Love is the essence of who our Creator is, and love is the essence of His New Covenant life in us.

We have been trapped by our enemy into debating the milk of the word. Paul (Shaul) wrote,

> *But I fear, lest by any means, as the serpent beguiled Eve through his subtlety, so your minds should be corrupted from the <u>simplicity</u> that is in Christ"* (2 Cor 11:3).

Satan has successfully manipulated and confused the most elementary truths. He has worked very hard to create infected wedges between us to divide us into religions and denominations. *It truly is an epidemic!* How I wish we were discussing more exciting things — like how to raise the dead, heal the sick and cast out demons, rather than which covenant should we be living in.

SUMMARY

THERE IS A NEW COVENANT — Hebrews 8-9

a)   Not an extended or amended covenant
b)   The old has been FULFILLED AND done away with.

In both Jeremiah 31:31 and Hebrews 8: 6-10, YHWH states He is going to make a NEW COVENANT with Israel and Judah. He didn't say He was going to extend, revise, add to it or make two of them. The Hebrew children had rejected and insulted YHWH in every way humanly possible. YHWH even went to the point of divorcing them and sending them away from the land — but He never abandoned them. Then YHWH sent His Son to establish a brand new covenant so He could have mercy on them and extend His love to the gentiles. Do you really want to challenge that?

The Holy Spirit is calling Yeshua's Bride, "to come out of her" and be cleansed. Let the Word of YHWH wash you!

MY THOUGHTS: MESSIANIC JUDAISM

Personally, I am deeply concerned for the Messianic movement. In the early years I was so excited about where it was headed, but it has stalled as many began returning to the Rabbinic Judaism they were coming out of. Can you hear the demons laughing, watching the Messianic community practicing traditions that the demons taught their ancestors in Jerusalem 2000 years ago? It breaks my heart.

If Messianic Judaism, (comprised of UMJC, MJAA, and independents following their lead) is going to grow (or even survive), its leadership must either get into an injection program or be completely replaced by YHWH. If you are an intercessor, please put these leaders on your prayer list. There are some great men and women of YHWH in these organizations and they desperately need our prayers. (Because the MIA is not actually a Messianic Jewish denomination, some of these comments are not applicable. However, it still struggles with some of the same issues and they could also use your prayers.)

Part of the problem is that most of these leaders don't know where to lead the people. All they have ever known is Judaism or Christianity. They know that pagan Christianity is wrong but their replacement religion isn't much better. The Messianic movement is "wandering in the desert." Truly, it is *feeding the sheep rabbinic dog vomit and calling it manna from heaven!*

What they need to do is seek YHWH and ask Him to help them lead their people out of infected rabbinical bondage while avoiding the infections of Christianity. The problem is, everyone wants to have a distinctive NAME and LOOK. YHWH provides for neither.

All "religious" names are pagan! All "religious" looks are pagan. Remember YHWH's covenant with Abraham? Remember the sign of His covenant? YHWH added the middle part of His own name to their names and gave Abraham a mark — circumcision — that cannot be shown to anyone. That is our God! That is His way! He does not change! You can add the H to your own name if you like but in the everlasting covenant, circumcision is of the heart and *that* is even harder to see than the mark of Abraham's covenant. YHWH wants it between you and Him — no one else!

We as believers are supposed to let our light shine. We are to be a city on a hill. It's supposed to come from the inside, not the outside. Not a phony religious crutch. We need to look and dress like the people we're around. Without crutches, we would then rely on our hearts being so changed that people can see it shining through our eyes. They need to see the love of YHWH in our eyes, to hear the joy of the LORD coming through our conversations, and even through our trials. The world is groaning for us to grow up into the fullness of the stature of our big brother. You won't do that with Tzit Tzit, tallitot and kippot!

I have made many mistakes and errors on my own journey seeking truth. I have fallen into deception and my zeal has outrun my knowledge more often than I want to admit. I've had to have sooo many injections for sooo many infections that there was a time I felt like a spiritual pin cushion. Therefore, I have both the scars and the understanding not to judge nor condemn, but to exhort and encourage others to "get up and out" of the mud we *all* fall into. I continue to seek the Lord and stay open to areas I still don't have quite right, and I welcome opportunities to re-examine set beliefs with any new light that may be cast on a particular subject. Our loyalty is not to a doctrine, theology or movement—it is to the truth of our living, breathing God, whenever and wherever we find it.

I sense in my spirit that God is calling us all back to Himself. I believe the last revival will be a revival of Spirit and Truth and we are entering into it now. It doesn't matter which camp you are in, it only matters that you begin walking towards God. The bride *He* is preparing won't have a spot or wrinkle, so I can see we all have a long way to go. Most of us are so infected and need many injections. But praise be to the Lord God Almighty! He is calling, washing, and covering us so that we might become that complete, mature, loving gift to His Son. I'm excited about what He is doing in this last hour as the age of the gentiles comes to an end *(Rom 11:25)!*

I pray that I will live to see the day when a body of believers, completely purged of infected paganism, worships our God in spirit and in truth. I don't know if it will ever happen this side of perfection, or if God has even ordained it. But what an anointing it would be!

While I have tried not to offend anyone—Jew, Christian, or pagan—it is nearly impossible considering the subject matter and information I've unearthed. Yet even if we disagree on doctrine, it is still my goal to explain our differences so we can *all* understand each other and try to respect each other. With that respect we should all be crying out, "Infection! Infection! Stop the infection!"

I'm not guilty yet, but I pray that before I die I can be accused of the following scripture: *By this shall all men know* *that ye are my disciples, **if ye have love one to another** (John 13:25).*

I pray you feel the love, even when it's confrontational.

A PRAYER FOR THE MESSIANIC MOVEMENT

Father, I thank You for the Messianic movement and all of the brethren involved. I pray a very special blessing on them. First, I pray the Spirit of Truth to indwell the leaders and congregations. I ask You to send Your Holy Spirit to each one individually and teach them all you would about Yourself, Your ways, Your statutes and how they can please You. Give them strength and courage to live in and walk in all that You teach them. I pray for grace and mercy on each one as they endeavor to walk with You. Draw them closer and closer each day. Lord, I pray You would open the windows of heaven and pour out from Your abundance all of the physical blessings and favor on them, allowing them the resources necessary to carry out Your plan for that movement. I pray a Spirit of Joy upon them that they may carry forth the message in Joy. I pray a Spirit of Love upon them that their hearts be so full of love that it overflows into their lives, their actions and reactions. Abba, purge the infections from us all! Lord, I pray that You rebuke the spirit of anger, pity, pride, arrogance and jealousy where You may find it. I pray You rebuke the spirit of confusion, deception and witchcraft. I pray You rebuke the spirits of religion no matter the source, Christian or rabbinical. Father, I ask You to send great leaders for this movement who hear Your voice, who will lead Your children into the paths of righteousness. Father, I thank You that we live in this information age and I pray You continue the revelation of Yourself to us all. Inject us all with the truth of Your Spirit and Your Presence. Amen.

PART 8

LAST ERA BEFORE THE MILLENNIUM

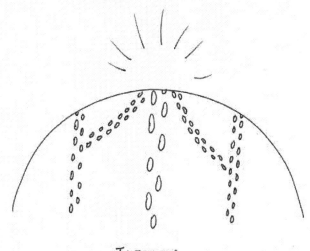

INJECTION

IS THERE A CURE?

Rabbinic Judaism took nearly 400 years to evolve from the Pharisees of Babylon to the religion it is today. Christianity did about the same. Both religions have continued to evolve, sometimes becoming more infected, sometimes less.

How long will it take us to get rid of the infection, the corrupt doctrines, that keep us from *Walking with God*? Some of us never will get there. Others will persevere and push their way into the presence of the Almighty.

I have a friend who likes to say, "It's just a mystery. We'll never understand God until we get to heaven!" While this is partially true, there remains much written in the scriptures about God. If He didn't want us to know about Him or His nature, why are there so many descriptions of Him in the context of His dealings with mankind?

Of course, we will never totally understand it *all* until we are face to face with Him.

However, we *are* commanded to *study to show ourselves approved, rightly dividing the word of God, workmen that should not be ashamed (2 Tim 2:15)*. Furthermore, we are told *to ask, to seek, to knock*. If understanding God to the best of our abilities and being able to explain Him to others is not the most important doctrine of our faith, I don't know what is. Remember, infected minds have been defining God for us all during the past 2,000 years, and our ignorance only fans the flames of godless leadership.

It would do us all well to remember the following passage in John 4: 23-24:

> *But the hour cometh, and now is, when the true worshippers shall worship the Father in spirit and **in truth**: for the Father*

*seeketh such to worship him. 24 God is a Spirit: and they that worship him must worship him in spirit and **in truth**.*

Why was "in Spirit and in truth" repeated in this verse? Because of its importance.

When I was studying with Rabbi Joseph one day, I asked if we could study the passage in Genesis 1:26 stating, *And God said, Let us make man in our image, after our likeness.*

"Oh!" he said. "You think Jesus is the One He was talking to in the Garden! That's where you're going with this!"

"Well, that's not what I wanted to study," I replied, "but if you do, we can. I wanted to study about God's likeness and image."

When Rabbi Joseph discussed the things of God, it was usually with a mixture of vehemence and solemn conviction.

"God doesn't have a body!" he said. "He's not like that. He doesn't have a form or shape. He's a spirit!"

"So God's a blob?" My question was calculated to upset my gentle, kind, and patient teacher. I succeeded.

"No!" he exclaimed, his voice rising. "God is not a blob! How can you say such a thing?"

"I didn't say it," I replied. "You did!"

"I didn't say God was a blob!"

I stood my ground. "You said he didn't have a body or form. That's a blob!

Now his vehemence rose in crescendo to its full force. *"I DIDN'T SAY BLOB! THAT'S NOT WHAT I SAID!"*

In all of our years studying together, I only upset the gracious Rabbi Joseph twice. This was one such occasion. He was sparked by the pain and frustration I feel when I realize that the Jewish people, just like Roman Catholics and

Protestants, have been robbed of so many real truths about *their* God. Each of these religions has a rehearsed, infected, theological-sounding formula while elucidating their view of God. Small wonder one cannot understand it! God has been made out to be some impersonal, mystical cloud that exists in a dimension that cannot be grasped by "the common man." He must be comprehended and reached only with the help of a rabbi, a priest or a pastor — none of whom comprehends Him, either.

Adherents of both rabbinic Judaism and Christianity were trapped, deceived, infected and robbed of the very same thing. Both groups lost the Kingdom of God, and finally lost the Kingdom principles to focus on their own kingdoms.

...for ye shut up the kingdom of heaven against men: for ye neither go in yourselves, neither suffer ye them that are entering to go in (Mat 23:13).

It's like the correct pronunciation of the name of YHWH. They have lost it!

Yet throughout the generations of rebellion and apostasy, there always survives the remnant. It's no different today. There are a few out there laboring in the fallow fields, digging up the precious principles of the Kingdom. They have been made aware of the missing pieces. Others are being stirred in their spirit, recognizing that YHWH is bringing us back into alignment with His Word and back into the fullness of His New Covenant.

I like to call it *the New Covenant Awakening*.

INJECTIONS FOR THE INFECTION

INJECTION 1:
THE TRUTH ABOUT HOW GOD EXISTS

Our purpose here is to show how God exists. The Greek text will be used for the New Testament, proving that the editing of the text did not hide the real God of Abraham.

Throughout this part of the study, I will use the numbers and definitions from *Strong's Exhaustive Concordance*. Definitions are placed below each section to clarify and reveal individual word meanings in selected scriptures. From time to time there is a variant between *Strong's* and the Hebrew text. Only those pertaining to this study will be noted. The following are complete definitions from *Strong's*. After the complete definition has been given, I will use an abbreviation.

> *In the beginning **God**** created the heaven and the earth. 2 And the earth was without form, and void; and darkness was upon the face of the deep. And the **Spirit of God**** moved upon the face of the waters. 3 And **God**** said (Gen 1:1-3),*

****GOD** - 430. 'elohiym, el-o-heem'; plur. 410 of ; gods in the ordinary sense; but spec. used (in the plur. thus, esp. with the art.) of the supreme God; occasionally applied by way of deference to magistrates; and sometimes as a superlative:--angels, X exceeding, God (gods) (-dess, -ly), X (very) great, judges, X mighty.

SPIRIT - 7307. ruwach, roo'-akh; from H7306; wind; by resemblance breath, i.e. a sensible (or even violent) exhalation; fig. life, anger, unsubstantiality; by extens. a region of the sky; by resemblance spirit, but only of a rational being (includ. its expression and functions):--air, anger, blast, breath, X cool, courage, mind, X quarter, X side, spirit ([-ual]), tempest, X vain, ([whirl-]) wind (-y).

Understanding YHWH & ELOHIM

The word pronounced "Jehovah" in English is a translation of *YHWH* in Hebrew. The Jews have lost the exact pronunciation for *YHWH,* therefore no one knows for sure how it is actually spoken. What a tragedy to lose the original pronunciation! In the ongoing debate the two most common pronunciations are: *Yah-weh,* and *Yah-veh.* Jews often substitute the words *Adonai,* or *Lord,* and *HaShem,* (Hebrew for *The Name)* in place of *YHWH.* A third pronunciation being debated is *Ye-Ho-vah,* similar to Jehovah.

YHWH, also known as the Tetragrammaton (Greek for "the four letters"), is the Father's proper first "name." With the Hebrew letters in His name, *YHWH,* you can spell "I was! - I am! - I will be!" He is complete, lacking nothing! YHWH has life within Himself!

If you were to properly address a letter to the Father, the one we all address as Father God, it would be to *YHWH ELOHIM.* This word *ELOHIM,* which is properly translated God, is plural! That the word is plural is more than just interesting. You see, all the grammatical forms in the sentences using the word *Elohim* are singular. Therefore, Moses either made some mistakes as he wrote, or in fact, his God was plural. *YHWH ELOHIM* states that *YHWH* (Father) is a pluralistic being.

As a means of introduction to the next section, I must first pose the following questions to you:

- Could it be that there are in Him, *YHWH*, a complete male and a complete female?

- Could it be that "He" is referenced only because of the preeminence normally accorded the male gender? Now, before you say I am crazy for even considering such questions, ponder this next part of the study.

What Did *They* Create

Many years ago, as I was studying the Bible with my wife, she asked me a funny question: "Honey, was Adam both male and female? It sounds like it here in Genesis." "What are you talking about?" I replied, somewhat taken aback.

In answer to my question about what *they* created, let us look at the creation of Adam. Was Adam made in the likeness and image of God *before* or *after* Eve was taken from his side? The answer is *before*! Was he a plural being just like his Creator? Where did Eve come from? Did God take more dirt and create a new creature, or did He remove the female from Adam?

Some years after my wife asked that initial question, she was pleased when Rabbi Joseph provided an answer that was in accord with what she had thought in the first place. Citing Orthodox Jewish teaching, Rabbi Joseph related that Adam was fully male *and* female prior to the removal of Eve. In other words, Adam was a plural being before Eve was taken from inside him. That is why Adam was referred to as "them" in Genesis 1:27; *So God created man in his own image, in the image of God created he him; male and female created he them.* This verse, as well as the following passage in

Genesis 5:1, prompts the question, "Is Adam a *Him* or a *Them*?"

In Chapter One we are given a complete overview of creation. In Chapter Two the story continues: they have the first Sabbath, God makes the garden and puts man in it. He opens up Adam and takes Eve out of and for Adam. In Chapter Three the serpent comes in and spoils everything. In Chapter Four we find the story of Cain and Abel. In Chapter Five we are given the lineage and generations of Adam.

Now this is a very complex word study and I pray I don't lose you here:

> *This is the book of the generations of Adam. In the day that God created man, in the likeness of God made he <u>him</u>; 2 Male and female created he them; and blessed them, and called their name Adam, in the day when they were created (Gen 5:1).*

Consider this part of the above verse: . . . *and called* their (plural) *name Adam* (singular). Most people have never considered the implications of a pluralistic being, much less that God or Adam could be one. Therefore let us look at the Hebrew word for name. *SHEM* is the common term in Hebrew for *name*. *Ha Shem* is Hebrew for *The Name*.

> **NAME** 8034. shem, shame; a prim. word [perh. rather from H7760 through the idea of definite and conspicuous position; comp. H8064]; an appellation, as a mark or memorial of individuality; by impl. honor, authority, character:-- + base, [in-] fame [-ous], name (-d), renown, report.

The Hebrew word "Adam" can be used to represent the human race or it can be used as a proper name for one person. It is quite clear in Genesis 5:2, "...*and called their name Adam,*" that it is a name.

Misunderstanding Genesis chapters one, two, and five occurs when people do not realize that Adam was a pluralistic being, both male and female, just like his Creator. Grasping this concept, we can better comprehend the Creator, *Elohim,* our pluralistic—but not dual—God.

> *And the* **LORD*** **God** *formed* **man*** *of the dust of the ground, and breathed into his nostrils the breath of life; and* **man** *became a living soul. 8 And the* **LORD*** **God** *planted a garden eastward in Eden; and there he put the* **man** *whom he had formed...15, And the* **LORD*** **God** *took the* **man***, and put him into the garden of Eden to dress it and to keep it (Gen 2:7, 8, 15)*

> ***Lord** 3068. YHWH - Yehovah, yeh-ho-vaw'; Eternal; Jeho-vah, name of God:

> **Man** 120. 'adam, aw-dawm'; from H119; ruddy, i.e. a human being (an individual or the species, mankind, etc.):--X another, + hypocrite, + common sort, X low, man (mean, of low degree), person.

> *And Adam gave names to all cattle, and to the fowl of the air, and to every beast of the field; but for Adam there was not found an help meet for him. 21 And the LORD God caused a deep sleep to fall upon Adam, and he slept: and he took* **one*** *of his* **ribs****, and closed up the flesh instead thereof; 22 And the* **rib***, which the LORD God had taken from man, made he a woman, and brought her unto the man. 23 And Adam said, This is now* **bone of my bones***, and* **flesh*** *of my flesh: she shall be called Woman,* **because she was taken out of Man.**

*24 Therefore shall a man leave his father and his mother, and shall cleave unto his wife: and they shall be **one flesh** (Gen 2:20-24).*

Rib 6763. tsela', tsay-law'; or (fem.) tsal'ah, tsal-aw'; from H6760; a rib (as curved), lit. (of the body) or fig. (of a door, i.e. leaf); hence a side, lit. (of a person) or fig.

Flesh 1320. basar, baw-sawr'; from H1319; flesh (from its freshness); by extens. body, person; also (by euphem.) the pudenda of a man:--body, [fat, lean] flesh [-ed], kin, [man-] kind, + nakedness, self, skin.

When did God create Adam? The sixth day! When did God create the Garden of Eden? When did God let Adam name the animals? When did God put Adam to sleep and take Eve out of him? Unless all of these events were all on the sixth day, *before* the first Sabbath, then God created a plural being and named him (or them) Adam. God referred to "him" as "them," just as He Himself is *Elohim*, pluralistic.

The following affirmation in Genesis 2:23 by Adam states that woman was taken out of man: *"This is now **bone of my bones**, and **flesh of my flesh**: she shall be called Woman, because she was taken out of Man."* Obviously, flesh and bone were removed from Adam; the female was removed from the male. Adam then looked like us, not *exactly* like God anymore. As a result, was it Adam's *likeness* or *image* that was changed—or were they both changed?

This profound statement, made by the man who had the woman taken out from him, is a key to understanding the relationship between the old plural man and new singular man with his creator.

What then did "They" (Elohim) create on that sixth day? They created a copy of themselves: a complete male/female unit, a pluralistic being, spoken to in singular male gender as Adam, but referred to as a "them", just like Elohim. Furthermore, like Elohim, Adam was created with life within himself, able to reproduce by himself.

Only when they are sexually together do a man and a woman become one flesh; at that moment they are complete and reflecting what they were originally. This is the reason God hates fornication and adultery. We wonder why our sex drives are so strong. One reason is that it's the only time we are "echad!"

"... *and they shall be **one*** flesh.*" *Gen 2:24. . . AND THEY SHALL BE ECHAD!*

One 259. 'echad, ekh-awd'; a numeral from H258; prop. united, i.e. one; or (as an ordinal) first:--a, alike, alone, altogether, and, any (-thing), apiece, a certain [dai-] ly, each (one), + eleven, every, few, first, + highway, a man, once, one, only, other, some, together.

> **QUESTION TO PONDER:** *When we get to heaven, will we be like we are now, or will we be male/female as Adam was in the beginning? Have you ever noticed that many of the men who have feminine characteristics are some of the most creative people? Have you ever wondered why?*

REVIEW: *Letting Scripture Bring it all Together:*

*So God created man in his own image, in the image of God created he him; **male** and **female** created he **them** (Gen 1:27).*

*And the **LORD* God** formed **man*** of the dust of the ground, and breathed into his nostrils the breath of life; and **man** became a living soul. 8 And the **LORD* God** planted a garden eastward in Eden; and there he put <u>the</u> **man** whom he had formed ... 15, And the **LORD* God** took <u>the</u> **man**, and put <u>**him**</u> into the garden of Eden to dress it and to keep it (Gen 2:7, 8, 15).* (**note references are singular)

*And Adam gave names to all cattle, and to the fowl of the air, and to every beast of the field; but for Adam there was not found an help meet for him. 21, And the LORD God caused a deep sleep to fall upon Adam, and he slept: and he took **one*** of his **ribs***, and closed up the flesh instead thereof; 22, And the **rib**, which the LORD God had taken from man, made he a woman, and brought her unto the man. 23, And Adam said, This is now **bone of my bones**, and **flesh* of my flesh**: she shall be called Woman, **because she was taken out of Man.** 24, Therefore shall a man leave his father and his mother, and shall cleave unto his wife: and they shall be **one flesh** (Gen 2:20-24, 20).*

CRUCIAL POINT: *Adam, the first "man" was a pluralistic being, male/female just like his Creator was. Eve was inside Adam, before the "rib operation," which is why Adam was referred to as "them" and "they." God is a pluralistic, male/female being and created us in His image.*

*This is the book of the generations of Adam. In the day that God created man, in the likeness of God made he <u>**him**</u>; 2 Male and female created he them; and blessed <u>**them**</u>, and called <u>**their name Adam**</u>, in the day when <u>**they**</u> were created (Gen 5:1).*

God Reveals Himself

Our first view of God in Genesis 1 is as Creator, and in Genesis 2 as Companion in the Garden of Eden. Soon after, we see Him as Judge: in the garden with Adam and Eve, in the incident of Cain and Abel, and then again in the worldwide flood of Noah's day. Eventually we find God tracking down Abram in the Middle East and sending him to the land of Canaan to establish covenant with him and his descendents. Four hundred years later, God finally begins to reveal Himself to Moses, who records it all for us.

The Revelation of God's Name: "Who Are You?"

In these next scripture verses, *Strong's* falls short of its usual reliability in translating the Masoretic Hebrew text.

> *And Moses said unto ***God, Behold, when I come unto the children of Israel, and shall say unto them, The **God of your fathers hath sent me unto you; and they shall say to me, What is his name? what shall I say unto them? :14 And **God said unto Moses, I AM THAT I AM: and he said, Thus shalt thou say unto the children of Israel, I AM hath sent me unto you. :15 And **God said moreover unto Moses, Thus shalt thou say unto the children of Israel, The *LORD **God of your fathers, the **God of Abraham, the **God of Isaac, and the **God of Jacob, hath sent me unto you: this is my name for ever, and this is my memorial unto all Generations (Exo 3:13-15).*

Strong's reads as follows:

> **I AM** 1961. hayah, haw-yaw'; a prim. root [comp. H1933]; to exist, i.e. be or become, come to pass.
> ***Lord** 3068. YHWH Yehovah, yeh-ho-vaw'; from H1961; (the) self-Existent or Eternal; Jehovah, Jewish national name of God:--Jehovah, the Lord.

God 430. 'Elohiym, el-o-heem'; **plural** of H433;

The original Hebrew has the following:

***God** 419 El, ale, short form for God(s)

****God** 433 elowah, el-o'-ah

NOTE: The translators only reflect *Elohim*, not *El* or *Elowah*. Why? While the significance doesn't show up here, it does allow you to see a pattern where three different words were used by Moses in the original, but translators decided to use only the word *God* for all three. With Hebrew being a crude language with very few words compared to Greek or English, wouldn't it be of great consequence that Moses used three different words referring to the one we call God? What have we lost not being taught these attributes of God? Can there be only one El or Elowah, or is it only Elohiym that there is one of? This is part of the problem we all share in our understanding about the word *God*.

Another mystery about this passage is that it is translated *I AM THAT I AM.* The proper translation is actually *I WILL BE THAT I WILL BE.* Just as the real pronunciation of His name was lost, the tense was lost, as well. Both Jews and gentiles adopted the same error. Most translations read *I AM* instead of *I WILL BE.* The Karaites are the only group I am aware of that translates this correctly. Why?

God Reveals His Image!

After revealing His name, God reveals to Moses that He has a body, *an image,* in Exodus 24: 9-11.

Then went up Moses, and Aaron, Nadab, and Abihu, and seventy of the elders of Israel: 10 And they saw the **God of Israel: and there was under his feet as it were a paved work of a sapphire stone, and as it were the body of heaven in his clearness. 11 And upon the nobles of the children of Israel he laid not his hand: also they saw **God, and did eat and drink.

This scripture tells us that 74 men *saw God,* meaning that <u>HE</u> had a body and that <u>HE</u> had feet! There are those who say God could take on any form at any time. This is, of course true, but could He, or would He do that when Moses asked to see Him in His glory?

*And he said, Thou canst not see **my face**: for there shall **no man see me, and live.** 21 And the *LORD said, Behold, there is a place by me, and thou shalt stand upon a rock: 22 And it shall come to pass, while my glory passeth by, that **I will put thee** in a cleft of the rock, and will cover thee with **my hand** while **I pass by**: 23 And I will take away **mine hand**, and thou shalt see **my back parts**: but **my face** shall not be seen (Exo 33:20-23).*

This scripture states that ***God has a face, a hand and back parts. THIS IS THE REVELATION OF GOD'S IMAGE.* We are "created in His *image.*" HIS FORM, HIS LIKENESS! God has a body that can be seen by humans!** Yet we hear people clamoring, "God is a Spirit! He has no body!" Why do we accept this infected idea so easily when the scriptures clearly refute it?

Of all of history's recorded meetings of God and man, this is surely the most intimate. Prior to this event, Moses had seen God's power and heard His voice many times; he had learned to love and respect YHWH, God of the universe. Moses had become God's personal messenger. The other 73 men saw God without His Glory. Moses wanted more; he wanted to see God in His glory. We are all commanded to *ask, seek and knock* after the things of God. Here is a man doing just that. Would God respond to this intimate request of Moses with a "composed image" of Himself, a form that was not really Him? I quote God: *"I will cover you with my hand while I pass by: And I will take away my hand, and you shall see my back parts: but my face shall not be seen."*

Notice the various parts of God's body, including His face. Yes, God has a face! If He didn't, He would not have told Moses that he could not see it. Later, God warned that looking at His face would bring death. *God is not a man, that he should lie (Num 23:19).*

FACT: Angels are spirits and they have bodies.

*And the ass saw the angel of the LORD **standing** in the way, and his sword drawn **in his hand**: and the ass turned aside out of the way, and went into the field: and Balaam smote the ass, to turn her into the way (Num 22:23).*

FACT: Cherubim are spirits and they have bodies.

And every one had four faces, and every one had four wings. 7 And their feet were straight feet; and the sole of their feet was like the sole of a calf's foot: and they sparkled like the colour of burnished brass. 8 And they had the hands of a man under their wings on their four sides; and they four had their faces and their wings. 9Their wings were joined one to another; they turned not when they went; they went every one straight forward. 10 As for the likeness of their faces, they four had the face of a man, and the face of a lion, on the right side: and they four had the face of an ox on the left side; they four also had the face of an eagle (Eze 1:6-10)

FACT: Seraphim are spirits and they have bodies. Some have four wings and some have six wings.

And every one had four faces, and every one had four wings (Eze 1:6).

Above it stood the seraphims: each one had six wings; with twain he covered his face, and with twain he covered his feet, and with twain he did fly (Isa 6:2).

ALL SPIRITS HAVE BODIES! Nowhere in the scriptures is a spirit described as a kind of formless cloud floating around. Each creature is described in detail to show the variety of God's created spirits. It would seem that the more wings the creature has, the more power it has. Just because they are invisible to humans does not mean they have no bodies. The only formless thing I can find in the scriptures is the Holy Spirit, and He is omnipresent.

> **CRUCIAL POINT:** It is a FACT that one day you will stand before this God. His face will either smile or frown. His hands will either open to beckon you to come or be closed in a fist to send you away. We will all give an account of our lives and time spent on this planet—how each of us utilized this body, this created image of the Father.

In review, let us list the facts about God's body:

- ☛ **FACT:** God has a face!
- ☛ **FACT:** God has hands!
- ☛ **FACT:** God has "back parts"!
- ☛ **FACT:** God has a body, an image in whose likeness we were created!

It is taught by some that *Yeshua* (Jesus) was the one who appeared to Moses on Mount Sinai, not *YHWH*. Further, it is taught that it was *Yeshua* (Jesus) in all places where God was seen, and even most of the places where He was heard; it had to be *because*, to their infected minds, Father-God has no image. If their supposition, that Father-God has no image, is correct, then *Yeshua* (Jesus) would have to be *YHWH*, and He is not. Do we die if we look upon the face of *Yeshua* (Jesus)? No! We live! Yet Moses was told if He saw God's face "with the glory attached" it would kill him. This is one of the clearest illustrations we have of differences between the Father and the Son. One kills us; the other saves us.

God Is Echad

After revealing both His name and His image, God begins to reveal *how* He exists. Consider Deuteronomy 6: 4 *Hear, O Israel: The *LORD our **God is one *LORD*. Gentiles often do not attach the same importance to Deuteronomy 6:4 as do Jews; this verse is the foundation of their religion. Here is how it looks in the Hebrew Scriptures:

> **Hear, O Israel: The *LORD our **God, the *LORD is one. (Shema, Yisrael, YHWH Elohim, YHWH echad.)**

Shema Israel A-do-noi E-lo-he-nu, A-do-noi echad" is the song of the Jews; they are commanded to say it twice each day. Notice that they have substituted *Adonoi* twice for God's name, *YHWH*.

One 259. 'echad, ekh-awd'; a numeral from H258; prop. united, i.e. one; or (as an ordinal) first:--a, alike, alone, altogether...

Some Trinitarian scholars claim that *echad,* like *Elohim,* is plural and that it indicates or implies *several in one.* This meaning conveniently brings *Yeshua* (Jesus) into Deuteronomy 6:4, thereby lending support for the doctrine of the Trinity, however, *echad* is one of several words in Hebrew that are used for the number "one." The *several in one* implication is groundless but is used to cover the infected thinking about the trinity. Here is the Strong's entry:

> 0259 dxa 'echad *ekh-awd'* a numeral from 0258; adj;
> {*See TWOT on 61*} AV-one 687, first 36, another
> 35, other 30, any 18, once 13, eleven + 06240 13,
> every 10, certain 9, an 7, some 7, misc. 87; 952
> 1) one (number)
> 1a) one (number)
> 1b) each, every
> 1c) a certain
> 1d) an (indefinite article)
> 1e) only, once, once for all
> 1f) one...another, the one...the other, one after
> another, one by one
> 1g) first
> 1h) eleven (in combination), eleventh (ordinal)

Once, while visiting with a scholar in Jerusalem, I heard him make this claim of *echad's* plurality. This scholar is a good man and a very good teacher, but he simply repeated what someone else told him. See how simple it is to pass on the infection? It sounded good, but he had not proven it himself! The Lord knows that I've done the very same thing in my life. In fact, most of us, including scholars, church ministers and seminary professors, have done so.

The Jewish View of HaShem (*The Name*)

When textual scholars translate YHWH Elohim, they nearly always use the words LORD GOD. Christian translators follow the Jews, using LORD in place of YHWH. Now let us take a look at what the Jews use for scriptural debates concerning their God (notations following):

Unto thee it was showed, that thou mightest know that the *LORD he is ***God; - <u>there is none else beside him</u>. . . . 39, Know therefore this day, and consider it in thine heart, that the *LORD he is ***God in heaven above, and upon the earth beneath: <u>there is none else</u> (Deu 4:35,39).

Remember the former things of old: for I am ****God, and <u>there is none else</u>; I am ***God, and <u>there is none like me</u> (Isa 46:9),

I am the *LORD, and <u>there is none else</u>, <u>there is no ***God beside me</u>: I girded thee, though thou hast not known me: 6 That they may know from the rising of the sun, and from the west, that <u>there is none beside me</u>. I am the *LORD, and <u>there is none else</u> (Isa 45:5,6).

For thus saith the *LORD that created the heavens; ***God himself that formed the earth and made it; he hath established it, he created it not in vain, he formed it to be inhabited: I am the <u>*LORD</u>; and <u>there is none else</u> (Isa 45:18).

Tell ye, and bring them near; yea, let them take counsel together: who hath declared this from ancient time? Who hath told it from that time? Have not I the *__LORD__? And __there is no*** God else beside me__; a just ****__God__ and a __Saviour__; __there is none beside me__. 22, Look unto me, and be ye saved, *all the ends of the earth: for **I am *God, and <u>there is none else-</u>*** (Isa 45:21).

Did you notice how often we see God declaring there is NO ONE other than Him? *Twelve times!* Basic thought? <u>**There is no other God—no one else like me or beside me—there is none else.**</u> "I am YHWH!"

> ****God** - 410. 'el, ale; short. strength; as adj. mighty; especially the Almighty (but used also of any deity):
>
> ***God** - 30. 'elohiym, el-o-heem'; plur.
>
> *Lord** -3068. YHWH Yehovah, yeh-ho-vaw';

Saviour-**3467. yasha', yaw-shah'; a prim. root; prop. to be open, wide or free, i.e. (by impl.) to be safe; causat. to free or succor:-X at all, avenging,defend, deliver (er)**

There is none holy as the* LORD: *for <u>there is none beside thee</u>: neither is there any rock like our *God* **(1 Sam 2: 2).**

*Wherefore thou art great, O ****LORD **God: *for <u>there is none like thee, neither is there any **God beside thee</u>, according to all that we have heard with our ears* (2 Sam 7: 22).

*O *LORD, there is none like thee, **<u>neither is there any **God beside thee</u>**, according to all that we have heard with our ears* (1 Chron 17:2).

Five more times! Doesn't there seem to be a very straightforward, simple message in all of these scriptures?

"I Am YHWH Elohim And There Is None Else...*And There Is None Beside Me!"*

Do these scriptures leave much doubt in your mind that there is only one Supreme God? It should be obvious that the Jews were taught monotheism, the belief that there is **One** God and Creator of the universe. When you examine these scriptures it is easy to see why most Jews reject the Christian Jesus as the Messiah King, for He is described by Christians as the coequal God. To them, to say *Yeshua* (Jesus) is God is to reject the foundation of Judaism, the First Commandment: *"Hear oh Israel, the Lord our God, the Lord is one, and thou shalt have no other God before me!"*

With both Jews and Christians naturally promoting their respective infected views of God, the translations seem to get a little cloudy. Let me give you what I feel is a clear, summary interpretation of these scriptures. Notice how different it is from what the Christian Church teaches:

I am *YHWH ELOHIM* and there is no one else who is equal to me and there is no one else who is the Father, but me! I am the supreme authority in the entire universe and *everything else, & EVERYONE ELSE,* is subject and submitted to me!

INJECTION 2:
THE TRUTH ABOUT THE HOLY SPIRIT

Is the Holy Spirit the 3rd Person of the Trinity?

In the beginning ***God** *created the heaven and the earth. 2 And the* **Spirit of God** *moved upon the face of the waters. 3 And* ***God** *said, Let there be light: and there was light (Gen 1:1-3).*

God 430. 'elohiym, el-o-heem'; plur. of H433;

Spirit 7307. ruwach, roo'-akh; from H7306; wind; by resemblance breath, i.e. a sensible (or even violent) exhalation; fig. life, anger, unsubstantiality; by extens. a region of the sky; by resemblance spirit, but only of a rational being (includ. its expression and functions):--air, anger, blast, breath, X cool, courage, mind, X quarter, X side, spirit ([-ual]), tempest, X vain, ([whirl-]) wind (-y).

Notice the scripture says *Spirit of God.* What is the difference between the Spirit of God (*Elohim*) and the Holy Spirit?

This verse states that the "*Spirit* of Elohim" not the *Ruach Ha Kodesh,* which is translated *Holy Spirit,* moved on the waters. Is there a difference? Not if you are a Jew or a Modalist. However, if you are a Trinitarian, there is a substantial difference; Trinitarians teach that the Holy Spirit is a separate person of the Godhead and the Spirit of God and the Holy Spirit are not the same. To try to follow this line of thinking is problematic to say the least.

When you get into this study, you begin to realize how Modalism, Oneness, or the Jesus Only movement evolved, and that it often makes more sense than Trinitarianism.

Unfortunately, most Modalists are not Hebrew scholars and only work with English translations. It's ironic that the debates over the Godhead never focused on the person of the Holy Spirit. In Hebrew, *Ruach Ha Kodesh* means *the breath*, or *Spirit of God*. The Greek means the same as the Hebrew; *Hagios Pneuma* means "holy breath," or Holy Spirit.

> **HOLY** 40. hagios, hag'-ee-os; from hagos (an awful thing); sacred (phys. pure, mor. blameless or religious, cer. consecrated):--(most) holy (one, thing), saint.

> **SPIRIT** 4151. pneuma, pnyoo'-mah; from G4154; a current of air, i.e. breath (blast) or a breeze; by anal. or fig. a spirit, i.e. (human) the rational soul, (by impl.) vital principle, mental disposition, etc., or (superhuman) an angel, daemon, or (divine) God, Christ's spirit, the Holy Spirit:--ghost, life, spirit (-ual, -ually), mind.

What Is The Name Of The Holy Spirit?

Many years ago, as a young pastor baptizing new converts, I always used the formula, *"In the name of the Father, and in the name of the Son, and in the name of the Holy Spirit"* according to Matthew 28:19. As I began to study that verse in the Greek, although I knew the name of the Father (*YHWH or Yah-veh or Ye-ho-vah*) and the name of the Son, Jesus, I didn't ever remember hearing the name of the Holy Spirit. At first I thought the Greek had been slightly mistranslated; the correct reading should have been *title of*. Taking out my Greek tool kit, I was surprised to learn that *name* is the correct translation.

No matter how hard I searched, I could not find a name for the Holy Spirit. Do you know why? *There is none!* The way Matthew 28:19 is written, it literally contradicts itself.

You can't baptize anyone in the name of the Holy Spirit because there isn't a name.

Then I realized that in all the descriptions of heaven and the throne room, the Son had a throne as did the twenty four elders and twelve apostles. Where was the throne for the Holy Spirit? There was none. So the third person of my Trinity had neither a name nor a throne! To make matters worse, I realized that if there are three persons, as taught in Trinitarianism, then *Yeshua* (Jesus) is not the Son of the Father, but the Son of the Holy Spirit. After all, was it not the Holy Spirit who overshadowed Mary when she conceived? I suspected that something was seriously amiss and that I was in deeper water than that of the baptismal tank.

Continuing my studies, I discovered that . . . *in the name of the Father and of the Son and of the Holy Ghost...(Mat 28:19)* was not in any of the early manuscripts. Among those who have written about its omission are Kurt Aland, Hans Kosmala *(In My Name),* and David Flusser *(The Conclusion of Matthew).* The consensus of their writings is that the phrase was added after the Council of Nicea. At least knowing that others were being prompted to examine the scripture made me feel much better.

Blasphemy Against The Holy Spirit

If, as Trinitarians claim, the Father, Son, and Holy Spirit are coequals, how is it that blaspheming the Holy Spirit is the *only* unpardonable sin?

> *Wherefore I say unto you, All manner of sin and blasphemy shall be forgiven unto men: but the **blasphemy against the Holy Ghost** shall not be forgiven unto men. 32 And*

*whosoever speaketh a word against the Son of man, it shall be forgiven him: but **whosoever speaketh against the Holy Ghost**, it shall not be forgiven him, neither in this world, neither in the world to come (Mat 12 :31).*

*Verily I say unto you, All sins shall be forgiven unto the sons of men, and blasphemies wherewith soever they shall blaspheme: 29 But he that shall **blaspheme against the Holy Ghost** hath never forgiveness, but is in danger of eternal damnation (Mark 3: 28).*

*And whosoever shall speak a word against the Son of man, it shall be forgiven him: but unto him that **blasphemeth against the Holy Ghost** it shall not be forgiven (Luke 12:10).*

BLASPHEME 987. blasphemeo, blas-fay-meh'-o; from G989; to vilify; spec. to speak impiously:--(speak) blaspheme (-er, -mously, -my), defame, rail on, revile, speak evil.

Did you notice that the verses say nothing about blaspheming *YHWH*, Father God? Only blasphemy against the Son will be forgiven, not blasphemy against the Father.

Trinitarianism lists three coequal persons: Father, Son, and Holy Spirit. Since they are coequal, a sin against one is a sin against all. Yet *Yeshua* (Jesus) says that a sin against Him can be forgiven, and that a sin against the Holy Spirit, "the Spirit of His Father," will not be forgiven in this world or in the world to come.

Thus, according to Scripture, *Yeshua* (Jesus) puts himself lower than the Holy Spirit! How can this be, if the only one that *Yeshua* (Jesus) places Himself under is *YHWH*, Father

God? Neither Modalism nor Trinitarianism can explain this inconsistency.

In fact, the only comprehensible solution to this blasphemy question is that the Holy Spirit is an intricate, inseparable part of the Father; He is not a distinct person,

CRUCIAL POINT: *The Holy Spirit is the Breath of YHWH, inseparable in all ways, omnipresent throughout the universe as the Holy Spirit, The Spirit of the Father, The Spirit of YHWH, the Spirit of God, and horribly translated as the Holy Ghost. "He" is referred to as "He" because "He "is always a complete representative of YHWH and has never been the "third person" of the Trinity! The Father, YHWH, and the Holy Spirit ARE ONE, "echad"!*

but completely *a part of* the Father; He may be the *omni-* part of Him, but He is definitely Him! To teach otherwise, that the Holy Spirit is a *third person*, leads to inconsistency and incomprehensibility.

Where Did the Concept of a "Godhead" Come From?

Did the *Tanach* (Old Testament) teach a Trinity? Did *Yeshua* (Jesus) Himself teach the Trinity? How about the apostles?

Foremost in the teaching of the Trinity concept is the term "Godhead." Godhead does not appear in the Old Testament. It is used only three times in the New Testament: Acts 17:29, Romans 1:20, and Colossians 2:9.

The Greek words for Godhead are *theios* (Acts) and *theiotes* (Romans and Colossians). Both words could have been and should have been translated *God*; most of time they were. Once again, our translators were helping us understand the doctrine of the Trinity.

INJECTION 3:
THE TRUTH ABOUT YESHUA (JESUS)

Who was God Speaking to about Mankind?

*And **God said**, Let **us** make man in **our** image, after **our** likeness (Gen 1:26):*

Now we begin an inquiry about the identity of the one referred to in the above scripture. Is it referring to *Yeshua* (Jesus), and if so, how does He exist with YHWH? What is His relationship to YHWH?

After Rabbi Joseph and I got to Genesis 1:26 he explained the definition of both image and likeness from the Torah. "The only way you can truly understand the Hebrew word for 'image' in today's English," he said, "is a photocopy." Puzzled, I wondered how you photocopy something that can't be seen. The answer soon came — you *don't*!

Rabbi Joseph often took our studies and turned them into sermons for the entire congregation. This was no exception. He told me, "I will finish our lesson this Shabbat." I often wondered if the rest of the congregation knew what he was doing. In the Shabbat service later that week, he taught the standard rabbinic response to the question, "Who was God speaking to on Creation Day?" He declared that God was speaking either to the angels, the animals He had just created, or to Himself merely as a gesture, or figure of speech.

Now, I ask you, do the angels have the image and likeness of God? No! Do the animals? Of course not! Is this just a figure of speech? Does God talk to Himself like old Jews are in the habit of doing?

In Genesis Chapter 1, *He* spoke to *someone* in verses 26-28:

*And **God** said, Let us make man in our **image**, after our **likeness**: and **let them** have dominion over the fish of the sea, and over the fowl of the air, and over the cattle, and over all the earth, and over every creeping thing that creepeth upon the earth. 27, So **God** created man in his own **image**, in the **image** of **God** created he him; male and female **<u>created he them</u>**. 28, And **God** blessed **<u>them</u>**, and **God** said **<u>unto them</u>**, be fruitful, and multiply, and replenish the earth, and subdue it: and have dominion.*

Image 6754. tselem, tseh'-lem; from an unused root mean. to shade; a phantom, i.e. (fig.) illusion, resemblance; hence a representative figure, espec. an idol:--image, vain shew.

Likeness 1823. demuwth, dem-ooth'; from H1819; resemblance; concr. model, shape; adv. like:--fashion, like (-ness, as), manner, similitude.

Make 6213. 'asah, aw-saw'; a prim. root; to do or make, in the broadest sense and widest application (as follows):--accomplish, advance, appoint, apt, be at, become, bear, bestow, bring forth,

From these verses it is clear that *YHWH* has an image and a form. Contrary to most popular teaching, He is devoid neither of shape nor image. God said *Our Likeness* and *Our Image*. The next thing it tells me is that someone, or something, has the same image and likeness that He has.

*In the beginning was **the Word**, and **the Word** was with **God**, and **the Word** was **God**. 2 The same was in the*

beginning with God. 3 <u>All things were made by him; and</u>
*<u>without him was not any thing made that was made.</u> 4 **In***
him was life; and the life was the light of men...14** And **the
***Word** was made flesh, and dwelt among us (and we beheld*
*his glory, the glory as of **the only begotten of the Father**)*
full of grace and truth (John 1:1-3, 14)

These verses tell me that the Father, YHWH, had a
begotten (birthed) Son, Yeshua (Jesus). His Son was with
Him when the earth and man were created because "all
things were made through Him (*Yeshua*), and without Him
nothing was made that was made" (Jn 1:3). From this I must
deduce that in Gen. 1:26 YHWH was talking to His Son,
Yeshua (Jesus) who was and is the likeness and image of His
Father.

"*. . . **the only begotten of the Father**.*" Over and over
again, this term is used in reference to the Son. He is the
only begotten of the Father. The question is *when* was He
begotten? Was He begotten (birthed) before the earth was
created? In other words did He exist somewhere before His
earthly life? Or did He become *the only begotten* when He
was born here on earth? Let's deal with the question of His
pre-existence first.

Was *Yeshua* (Jesus) Pre-Existent Before His Birth on Earth to Mary?

The sixth chapter of John is very direct. Verses 26-65 give us
a clear picture of the relationship between Father and Son,
and where the Son came from. Here are a few examples:

For I came down from heaven, not to do mine own will, but the
will of him that sent me. 39 And this is the Father's will which
hath sent me, that of all which he hath given me I should lose

nothing, but should raise it up again at the last day (Jn 6: 38, 39).

What and if ye shall see the Son of man ascend up <u>where he was before</u> (John 6:62)?

*Jesus said unto them, If God were your Father, ye would love me: **for I proceeded forth and came from God**; neither came I of myself, but he sent me (John 8:42).*

***For the Father himself loveth you, because ye have loved me, and have believed** that I came out from God. **28** I came forth from the Father, **and am come into the world: again, I leave the world, and go to the Father** (John 16:27,28)*

Proceeded-**1831. exerchomai, ex-er'-khom-ahee; to issue (lit. or fig.):--come-(forth, out), depart (out of),**Came-**2240. heko, hay'-ko; a prim. verb; to arrive, i.e. be present (lit. or fig.):--come.**

I came out from God... I came forth from the Father

These two phrases could not make the pre-existence of *Yeshua* (Jesus) any clearer. Contrary to the teaching of some, the Son was ***birthed*** out of the plural Father eons before Mary was born, and before the world was ever created. Furthermore, He was not created out of anything (or out of nothing) as other celestial beings. He was the only one birthed from the Father. Being birthed from a complete, plural being, the Son could only be what the parent *Elohim* was: another plural being.

For as the Father hath life in himself; so hath he given to the Son to have life in himself (John 5:26);

He had life within Himself. What is *Yeshua* (Jesus) talking about and why is he telling us this? It is something that has nothing to do with me, the human race, or even the planet. *Yeshua* (Jesus) is telling us an incredible secret about Himself and the Father. He is showing us that He has this same attribute as the Father, *life within Himself.*

> *These words spake Jesus, and lifted up his eyes to heaven, and said, Father, the hour is come; glorify thy Son, that thy Son also may glorify thee: 2 As thou hast given him power over all flesh, that he should give eternal life to as many as thou hast given him. 3 And this is life eternal, that they might know thee the only true God, and Jesus Christ, whom thou hast sent. 4 I have glorified thee on the earth: I have finished the work which thou gavest me to do. 5 And now, <u>O Father, glorify thou me with thine own self with the glory which I had with thee before the world was</u> (John 17:1).*

This passage conclusively indicates that *Yeshua* (Jesus) was with His Father before the world began. Verse 5, in particular, could not have been written if Yeshua (Jesus) were just a seed in the Father before Mary conceived.

But What Is He?

Now let's look at a particularly unique attribute of *YHWH* — the Seven Spirits of God:

> *John to the seven churches which are in Asia: Grace be unto you, and peace, from him which is, and which was, and which is to come; and from the **seven Spirits** which are before his throne (Rev 1:4).*

*And unto the angel of the church in Sardis write; These things saith he that hath **the seven Spirits of God**, and the seven stars; I know thy works, that thou hast a name that thou livest, and art dead (Rev 3:1).*

*And out of the throne proceeded lightnings and thunderings and voices: **and there were seven lamps of fire burning before the throne, which are the seven Spirits of God** (Rev 4: 5).*

What are we to make of these seven spirits? Does any other being in all existence have seven spirits? The answer is "yes."

*And I beheld, and, lo, in the midst of the throne and of the four beasts, and in the midst of the elders, stood **a Lamb as it had been slain**, having seven horns and seven eyes, **which are the seven Spirits of God** sent forth into all the earth (Rev 5: 6).*

I guess you could say, "Like Father, like Son."

REVIEW: What do we understand about *Yeshua* (Jesus)?

1) He was birthed, not created. He came forth from His Father, YHWH Elohim:

    a) as a pluralistic being

    b) in the same image and likeness of His Father

    c) before our world was created

    d) He has seven spirits and

    e) life within Himself.

    f) He was there, at creation Genesis 1:1, and

    g) was a Co-creator with His Father.

What Did Yeshua (Jesus) Teach?

Yeshua (Jesus) did not teach the Trinitarian concept that He and the Holy Spirit were coequal and coexistent with the Father. He didn't even teach that He was equal to the Father, much less coequal with Him.

> *Ye have heard how I said unto you, I go away, and come again unto you. If ye loved me, ye would rejoice, because I said, I go unto the Father: **for my Father is greater than I** (John 14: 28).*

How can they be coequal if, as the Scripture says, *the Father is greater* than the Son? They can't! *Yeshua* (Jesus) said that everything He did was directed from the Father. His very will was overruled by the Father:

> *Saying, Father, if thou be willing, remove this cup from me: nevertheless **not my will**, but thine, be done. 43, And there appeared an angel unto him from heaven, <u>strengthening him</u> (Luke 22: 42, 43).*

If they are coequal, how do they have separate wills? Why does *Yeshua's* (Jesus') will need to be strengthened?

> *Then said Jesus unto them, When ye have lifted up the Son of man, then shall ye know that I am he, and that **I do nothing of myself; but as my Father hath taught me**, I speak these things. 29, And he that sent me is with me: the Father hath not left me alone; for **I do always those things that please Him** (John 8: 28,29).*

Yeshua (Jesus) was taught of his Father? What would one coequal, coeternal being have to teach another coequal, coeternal being?

How does Modalism (Oneness) deal with this scenario: the Father and the Son communicating with one another as two separate entities? How is it that *Yeshua* (Jesus) is trying to . . . *always do those things that please Him?*

> *I can of mine own self do nothing: as I hear, I judge: and my judgment is just; because I seek not mine own will, but the will of the Father which hath sent me (John 5:30).*

> *For I have not spoken of myself; but the Father which sent me, he gave me a commandment, what I should say, and what I should speak.* 50 *And I know that his commandment is life everlasting: whatsoever I speak therefore, even as the Father said unto me, so I speak (John 12:49,50).*

It is obvious that *Yeshua* (Jesus) was doing and saying what the Father instructed him to do. Never does He imply that He is "co-anything" with the Father. Indeed, by His own words, we see that He is lovingly submitted to the Father, as we all should be.

> *And Jesus came and spake unto them, saying, All power is given unto me in heaven and in earth (Mat 28: 18).*

The term "coequal" means a mutual sharing of everything—power, abilities, and attributes. If *Yeshua* (Jesus) were a coequal of *YHWH Elohim*, wouldn't He already have the power referred to in this verse?

Until you completely examine what *Yeshua* (Jesus) said about Himself and His relationship with YHWH, you cannot define "the Godhead!"

What Did *Yeshua* (Jesus) Teach About The Godhead?

*And Jesus answered him, The first of all the commandments is, **Hear, O Israel; The Lord our God is one Lord**: 30 And thou shalt love the Lord thy God with all thy heart, and with all thy soul, and with all thy mind, and with all thy strength: this is the first commandment (Mark 12: 29, 30).*

It is evident that *Yeshua* (Jesus) taught people exactly what the Torah taught. Yet He went even further in this statement:

Matthew 19:16 *And, behold, one came and said unto him, **Good** Master, what good thing shall I do, that I may have eternal life? 17 And he said unto him, **Why callest thou me good? There is none good but one**, that is, **God**: but if thou wilt enter into life, keep the commandments.*

God - 2316. theos, theh'-os; of uncert. affin.; a deity, espec. (with G3588) the supreme Divinity; fig. a magistrate; by Heb. very:--X exceeding, God, god [-ly, -ward].
Good - 18. agathos, ag-ath-os'; a prim. word; "good" (in any sense, often as noun):--benefit, good (-s, things), well.

The statement in Matthew 19:16 is the strongest one that *Yeshua* (Jesus) makes on the subject of coequality. He not only claims not to be coequal with *YHWH*, but also directly says that the Father, *YHWH*, is the only one that man should even call good! This word "good" has the connotation of holiness and they tied the word master to it. But wasn't He called the *good* shepherd?

I am the good shepherd: the good shepherd giveth his life for the sheep (John 10:11).

The word here for *good* is 2570. *kalos, kal-os'; of uncert. affin.; prop. beautiful, but chiefly (fig.) good (lit. or mor.), i.e. valuable or virtuous (for appearance or use, and thus distinguished from G18, which is prop. intrinsic):--X better, fair, good (-ly), honest, meet, well, worthy.* Once again our translators fail us. Yeshua (Jesus) calls himself the "Good Shepherd," using a totally different word than the word that refers to God's goodness. It ties Him to the role of Shepherd, not Master.

CRUCIAL POINT: Yeshua (Jesus) is so emphatic that He is NOT EQUAL to—nor is He—YHWH, that He refuses to allow them to even call Him Good Master!

Calling them coequal is impossible after reading that scripture. Was *Yeshua* (Jesus) not the Son while He was here on earth? Are we to believe those who teach that He left part of Himself in heaven when he took on a fleshly body and became the perfect sacrifice? How was it that *Yeshua* (Jesus) left part of His memory and kept part of it? It's obvious He remembered being in heaven and the glory He had before He came to earth.

Even in the throne room, we see *Yeshua* (Jesus) not as a coequal, but on the right hand of His Father:

Therefore being by the right hand of God exalted, and having received of the Father the promise of the Holy Ghost, he hath shed forth this, which ye now see and hear (Acts 2: 33).

This is not a coequal relationship, nor is it a coequal throne! Why aren't there three coequal thrones?

In Mark 13: 31, *Yeshua* (Jesus) informs his disciples that He does not know when His return was going to take place:

> *Heaven and earth shall pass away: but my words shall not pass away. 32 But of that day and that hour knoweth no man, no, not the angels which are in heaven, neither the Son, but the Father.*

Those who teach that *Yeshua* (Jesus) was incomplete while on earth say that He didn't know *the hour* at that moment in time, but would know when He ascended back up into heaven. There He would re-assume everything He had left behind in coming to earth and would again become coequal with the Father in every aspect. This may sound well and good, but what scriptural evidence is there for it? None! More infected thinking! Either Yeshua (Jesus) was deity or He was not! How are you partial deity? Did YHWH perform a partial lobotomy on Him before He came to earth and then put that part of His brain back in when He returned?

A final verse denying that *Yeshua* (Jesus) taught coequality with His Father is Matthew 20:23. In it, we find *Yeshua* (Jesus) declaring that it was not up to Him to choose who was going to be on His right hand:

> *And he saith unto them, Ye shall drink indeed of my cup, and be baptized with the baptism that I am baptized with: but to sit on my right hand, and on my left, is not mine to give, but it shall be given to them for whom it is prepared of my Father.*

When *Yeshua* (Jesus) was teaching his disciples to pray, notice how and to whom He instructed them to pray:

After this manner therefore pray ye: Our Father which art in heaven, Hallowed be thy name. 10: Thy kingdom come. Thy will be done in earth, as it is in heaven (Mat 6:9).

The prayer was directed to the Father, not himself. He hallows the Father's name, not his own. He prays for Father's kingdom to come, not his own. He prays for the Father's will to be done, not his own.

Does this sound like coequality? Let the scriptures, especially the words of the only begotten Son of the Father, teach you the truth concerning the Godhead. From these previous examples it is evident that *Yeshua* (Jesus) did not teach the doctrine of a coequal Trinity; it was invented over 300 years later, after the Council of Nicea.

But Scripture Says They Were Equal!

Now, let us look at places in New Testament scripture where the word **equal** appears.

Equal - 2470. isos, ee'-sos; prob. from G1492 (through the idea of seeming); similar (in amount or kind):--+ agree, as much, equal, like.

Let this mind be in you, which was also in Christ Jesus: 6 Who, being in the form of God, thought it not robbery to be **equal** *with God (Phil 2:5,6):*

A better translation, the correct one, would have been *similar to God* or *like God* rather than *equal with God*. Again, it appears that our Trinitarian translators were helping us "understand" the Trinity. **In this verse, the Jews are accusing Him of** *making himself equal with God. Yeshua* **(Jesus) was not making that claim.**

> *And therefore did the Jews persecute Jesus, and sought to slay
> him, because he had done these things on the sabbath day. 17
> But Jesus answered them, My **Father worketh hitherto,
> and I work**. 18 Therefore the Jews sought the more to kill
> him, because he not only had broken the sabbath, but said
> also that God was his Father, **making himself equal with
> God** (John 5:16-18).*

Because they both work on the Sabbath? Because they
both heal on the Sabbath? That makes Him *equal* to God? Or,
does it make Him divine?

These are the only references in the New Testament that
use the word *equal* in reference to the relationship between
the Father and Son! What does that mean? If the doctrine of
the Trinity, three coequals, were taken to court, there
wouldn't be enough *original scriptural documentation* to
support the doctrine; it would be thrown out of court for
lack of evidence.

What About "These Three are One"?

> *For there are three that bear record in heaven, the Father, the
> Word, and the Holy Ghost: and these three are one (1 Jn 5 :7).*

In the original text, the three witnesses were . . . *the Spirit, the
water and the blood*. The phrase from I John 5:7 .... *the Father,
the Word and the Holy Ghost: and these three are one,* was added
by a scribe. Named after Jerome, the translator who
produced the Vulgate (Latin) version of the Bible, this
phrase became known as the Jerome Comma, and does not
exist in any of the manuscripts, even the edited ones.
Theologians who know of the addition usually say nothing
about it. Apparently they are willing to allow forgeries of

this kind into translations if they support their doctrines. Anyone else doing such a thing would be called a heretic.

> *I and my Father are one. 31 Then the Jews took up stones again to stone him. 32 Jesus answered them, Many good works have I showed you from my Father; for which of those works do ye stone me? 33 The Jews answered him, saying, For a good work we stone thee not; but for blasphemy; and because that thou, being a man, **makest thyself God**.---36, Say ye of him, whom the Father hath sanctified, and sent into the world, Thou blasphemest; because I said, **I am the Son of God** (John 10: 30)?*

Again, the Jews are saying He said one thing when, in fact, He said another. Wouldn't He be lying if He said He was not the Son of God?

> *Neither pray I for these alone, but for them also which shall believe on me through their word; 21 That they all may **be one**; as thou, Father, art in me, and I in thee, that they also may **be one in us**: that the world may believe that thou hast sent me. 22 And the glory which thou gavest me I have given them; that **they may be one**, even as **we are one** (John 17: 20):*

One - 1520. heis, hice; (includ. the neut. [etc.] hen); a prim. numeral; one:--a (-n, -ny, certain), + abundantly, man, one (another), only, other, some.

Every single one of the *ones* in John 17:20-22 is identical! Exactly the same! If this makes *Yeshua* (Jesus) coequal with the Father, it makes you and me coequal to the Father as well. I don't know about you, but I am unmistakably not coequal with *YHWH*.

I ask you to take this section of what Yeshua (Jesus) taught and go through it again. Write down each scripture, do the word studies, seek the Lord with all your heart and see what the scriptures and the Holy Spirit say to you.

INJECTION 4:
THE TRUTH ABOUT WHAT THE APOSTLES TAUGHT

*For **there is one God**, and **one mediator between God and men**, the man Christ Jesus; 6 Who gave himself a ransom for all, to be testified in due time (I Tim 2:5).*

Wait a minute! Where did Paul come up with this *one God* idea? Wasn't he a Trinitarian? Being one of the apostles, shouldn't he have at least known the Apostolic Creed? In fact, Paul wrote over and over again about *one God*.

Seeing it is one God, which shall justify the circumcision by faith, and uncircumcision through faith (Rom 3:30).

One God and Father of all, who is above all, and through all, and in you all (Eph 4:6).

*But to us there is but **one God, the Father**, of whom are all things, and we in him; and **one Lord Jesus Christ**, by whom are all things, and we by him (1 Cor 8:6).*

Paul did not have a problem with having one God and calling *Yeshua* (Jesus) Lord! To him it was simple. He didn't try to make them co-anything because he understood their differences.

*Yea, a man may say, Thou hast faith, and I have works: show me thy faith without thy works, and I will show thee my faith by my works. 19 Thou believest that **there is one God**; thou doest well: the devils also believe, and tremble. 20 But wilt thou know, O vain man, that faith without works is dead (James 2:18)?*

If the devils know that there is but one God, how can there be any confusion? If the Trinity doctrine is correct, why, many years after the ascension, is James the half brother of *Yeshua* (Jesus) teaching that there is only one God? Consider Paul's teaching to the church at Corinth:

> *For as in Adam all die, even so in Christ shall all be made alive. 23 But every man in his own order: Christ the firstfruits; afterward they that are Christ's at his coming. 24 Then cometh the end, when he shall have delivered up the kingdom to God, even the Father; when he shall have put down all rule and all authority and power. 25 For he must reign, till he hath put all enemies under his feet. 26 The last enemy that shall be destroyed is death. 27 For he hath put all things under his feet. But when he saith all things are put under him, it is manifest that he is excepted, which did put all things under him. 28 And when all things shall be subdued unto him, <u>then shall the Son also himself be subject unto him that put all things under him, that God may be all in all</u>* (I Cor 15:22).

CRUCIAL POINT: Yeshua (Jesus) is totally submitted to YHWH in every aspect of His existence. Not only does He nor his disciples not teach, or claim, that He is coequal to YHWH, He teaches the opposite—total submission.

If I understand this scripture correctly, all power and authority were given to *Yeshua* (Jesus). How then will He turn around and give them back to the Father? How can coequals do that? How is the Son going to be subject to the Father if he is coequal? If Modalism (Oneness) is correct, how does He submit Himself to Himself? This scripture totally refutes Modalism.

INJECTION 5:
THE TRUTH OF HOW YHWH AND YESHUA EXIST TOGETHER

The Lord gave us I John 2:22-24. *Beware!* There is a spirit that denies the Son. There is also a spirit that denies the Father.

> *Who is a liar but he that denieth that Jesus is Christ? He is an antichrist,* **that denieth the Father and the Son.** 23 **Whosoever denieth the Son, the same hath not the Father: (but) he that acknowledgeth the Son hath the Father also.** 24 *Let that therefore abide in you, which ye have heard from the beginning. If that which ye have heard from the beginning shall remain in you,* **ye also shall continue in the Son, and in the Father** *(I John 2:22).*

Does this say anything about a Trinity? It is understood that there are <u>two</u> sitting in power, not one or three.

According to Modalism (Oneness), the concept of the Godhead can be summarized as follows: *The Father came as the Son and returned as the Holy Spirit.* If this formula is correct, then the Father or the Son, or both, must have lied! How so? *Yeshua* (Jesus) claimed to be the Son when he was really the Father, only in another manifestation, or mode. He wasn't really going back to the Father because He **was** the Father. He wasn't really sending back *another Comforter*; He Himself was going to return, but in another mode! He wasn't really speaking at *Yeshua's* (Jesus') baptism, it was *Yeshua* (Jesus) speaking using some kind of supernatural power.

I understand the Modalists' frustrations with the Trinity doctrine, but in light of the scriptures the Modalist concept just doesn't work. *"ye also shall continue in the Son, and in the Father."*

Are Trinitarianism, Arianism, and Modalism scriptural?

Trinitarianism, Arianism (the belief that *Yeshua* (Jesus) was created not birthed), and Modalism are clearly **not** Biblical teachings. The Father, *YHWH ELOHIM,* and the Son, *YESHUA ELOHIM,* are **not** coequal, coexistent or coeternal.

If *YHWH* is actually three, not one, don't you think *He* would have been the one to tell us in His own Bible: the Torah, the Tanach, or the New Testament? If He is actually a triune being with three distinct persons, why would He say just the opposite?

If *Yeshua* (Jesus) really was coequal, coexistent, and coeternal with the Father, wouldn't *He* have told us? He came to die, so He wasn't afraid to tell them the truth!

The root of our problem is with our understanding of what the word *God* means. To most of us, *God* simply means the Supreme Creator in charge of everything, the final authority. We have the translators to thank for such shallowness. Sadly, they never explained *Elohim.*

My Final Questions

In using the word *saved* in the following questions, I mean truly born-again and regenerated into the spiritual family of God.

- Can an Orthodox Jew serving in an Orthodox congregation be saved?
- Can a Roman Catholic priest be saved while in the Roman Catholic Church?

- Can a Lutheran be saved?
- Can an Islamic Arab be saved?
- Can a Buddhist be saved?
- Can a Baptist be saved?
- Can a Pentecostal be saved?

And now for the most important question of all. Are you saved? Have you been born again? Is your life redeemed by the blood of *Yeshua* (Jesus) and your sins and transgressions against God and man blotted out, never again to be counted against you?

What are you trusting in to have your name written in Lamb's Book of Life? What are you placing your faith in to raise your dead body on resurrection day? Having correct theological doctrines *is not* a prerequisite to being saved. The only thing necessary is your acknowledgement of your own inability to save yourself and your crying out to YHWH to redeem you!

When you see the entire plan of YHWH, you see Him sending His own Son for the sacrificial blood necessary to wash away your personal sins so that He could send His Holy Spirit to dwell inside you and have communion with you. That is *YHWH's* desire for your life: perpetual communion!

If you haven't done this, then call out to God, ask Him for forgiveness, accept *Yeshua* as your personal, acceptable sacrifice to God, and lay down your burden of guilt and shame. Of all the material in this study, this is the only thing that ultimately matters. God loves you, and that is the truth! Everything else will be resolved when we see Him face to face.

Think about this, no man has walked into the Holy of Holies in nearly 2000 years. Back when they did, they entered with the blood sacrifice to cover their sins. I beg you to try this if you have never done so; take the blood of Yeshua (Jesus) apply it to your life and pray the following prayer with me:

Abba Father, I am in no way acceptable to enter your presence but I call on the blood of your only begotten, Yeshua (Jesus) to cover my sins and failures. I ask you to make me a part of the covenant you promised in Jeremiah 31. Make me a priest unto you. Wash me in your Holy Word and Spirit and draw me into that Holy place. Let my eyes see the light of the candlestick of truth. Let me smell the incense of your fragrance and let me taste the shew-bread of life. Forgive me and lift me into Your mercy and Your incredible grace. Regenerate my heart of stone into a heart of love and life. Teach me to walk in Your statutes and write Your laws on my heart. I ask all things in the name of Your Son, Yeshua (Jesus), Amen.

NOW, ONE LAST SACRED COW: *Which Kind Of Pagan Are You?*

 **(BIG INJECTION!)**

How much paganism is acceptable to YHWH?

When we stand before Him, how much of the pagan/heretical sacrilege that we practice in our religions do you think He will excuse?

Which infection do you believe is better:

- To have a reinvented Christian God (Trinity) or a reinvented Jewish God who obeys the commands of the rabbis?

- To observe the pagan Christmas, Easter and Sunday Sabbath or to observe the pagan Jewish holidays?

- To have an edited (and even censored) Christian Bible or a complete fabrication like the rabbinical Talmud?

There's just no easy way to ask, "Are you an infected Jewish pagan or an infected Christian pagan?" So simply answer the question: "Which is better, *the heresy of the Christians or the heresy of the Rabbinic Jews?* Are these silly questions or are they possibly the most important questions of your life?

After studying all this information, which form of infected paganism have you been trying to convert everyone to? I have a horrible feeling hell will be overflowing with those who claim to be Torah observant as well as those who celebrate Easter, Christmas and name Jesus as their Lord and Savior. Zeal and passion without a personal relationship with YHWH is like having a very fast airplane with no wings.

Finally, I want to remove a word and concept from your mind; the word is *convert*! Stop trying to convert people! The Great Commission was to *complete*, not convert. *Yeshua* (Jesus) came to complete (fulfill) the Law, not convert it. Baptism (Mikveh) was for cleansing and regeneration (completion) of the soul, not re-enlistment into another religion. Every time you hear the word convert, substitute *complete* for it. But back to the Great Commission. What do we do with it?

The Great Commission, simply put:

> ➢ GO (Look for opportunities to share)

> ➢ TEACH (kingdom principles, which present God's great plan for the regeneration of the heart)

> ➢ BAPTIZE (Ceremonial cleansing & burial of the old man)

> ➢ MAKE DISCIPLES (Teach people to walk with God) Teach men to have what Moses had: a close, personal relationship with God. Neither Rabbinic Jews nor Christians are having much success in doing that.

Stop converting people to pagan religions and get the *Injection for the Infection* for yourself! Get your spirit regenerated by YHWH's Holy Spirit. *You* press in to the Holy of Holies and become that New Covenant Kingly Priest. THEN, filled with the joy of YHWH, you can help others find a true completion of their faith, their own New Covenant, Kingdom Priesthood.

Remember, *all* religions are infected. All of them! There is not a religion out there teaching men and women to "walk with God!" No...not even yours! You may ask why we have to be infected at all. *Because we've all been raised in it.* We didn't know any better. We've either been members of, or have been attending, infected religious associations all our lives. Who does this scripture apply to:

> *And what agreement hath the temple of God with idols? for ye are the temple of the living God; as God hath said, I will dwell in them, and walk in them; and I will be their God, and they shall be my people.* ¹⁷*Wherefore* **come out from among them, and be ye separate,** *saith the Lord, and* **touch not the unclean thing;** *and I will receive you,* ¹⁸*And will be a Father unto you, and ye shall be my sons and daughters, saith the Lord Almighty (2 Cor 6:16).*

What else needs to be said? Why are we still filling pagan temples called churches and synagogues week after week? Why are we giving them our money and our children? Are you a Believer? What do you believe? Are you a Disciple? Of what?

If you believe *Yeshua* (Jesus) is the Lamb of YHWH, that He came to earth to be the Passover Lamb, that He was offered on the cross for your sins, that He rose from the dead to ascend into the heavenly temple to offer His blood on the four horns of the Alter that is before YHWH so that when you asked for forgiveness *for your own sins and transgressions* that there would be an acceptable offering to YHWH, and that through this act of confession and repentance you are made clean and acceptable to YHWH, then you are living in the New Covenant and have been grafted into the spiritual olive tree of YHWH. You have also been added to the seed of Abraham and heirs according to the promise (Gal 3:24-29). You are *New Covenant Israel* and you need to start acting like Kingdom Priests.

Christians and Jews have both been robbed of this Kingdom Priest right and of its significance. Rabbinic Judaism totally rejected the New Covenant and the Christians replaced it with all their religions, each with its own brand of priests.

It's critical to realize that we do not replace Israel, we are part of Israel. No matter what our physical heritage is, Jew or Gentile, this process grafts us into the promise that YHWH made with Abraham when HE promised that Abraham's seed would be as *the stars in the heaven* and *the sands of the sea*. What this does for the physical descendants of Abraham is purify them, regenerate their hearts and establish them as New Covenant Priests of YHWH. For the Gentiles it does this in addition to adopting them into the lineage of Abraham.

This New Covenant was established to reunite the House of Israel and the house of Judah with YHWH and to make Kingdom Priests out of us all. It was designed to complete the promise made to Abraham by "grafting in" many gentiles into the olive tree and teaching them ALL the commandments and ordnances of YHWH. This New Covenant empowered the disciples through the Spirit to "establish the law" where before in the flesh they always failed.

Too many people focus on what we were instead of what we are becoming: *New Covenant Israel*. "A nation of Holy men and women washed and made acceptable by our maker, our God." We are the workmanship of His hands, His mercy and His grace. In what can we boast?

You can call yourself a *New Covenant Believer*, or a *Disciple of Yeshua* (Jesus), or *New Covenant Israel*. What you have actually become is *New Covenant Israel!* Through the New Covenant you have been added to the children of Israel. But whatever you feel led to call yourself, do it with kindness and joy!

When Moses came down from the mountain learning the ways and commands of the Lord, Exodus 34: 29-35 says his face and skin glowed so much it scared the people to the extent they made him put a veil on. Why didn't they want to go up and get their own glow? Instead, they wanted it covered up so they wouldn't be reminded of their wretchedness!

People who spend time with God look different! How can you teach men to walk with God if *you* don't walk with God? Stop trying to judge, debate with or perform for others—just get in the presence of the Almighty and stay there until you glow. Then, those people God is calling to Himself will be drawn to you and you can help them learn to glow by walking with God, too. We've seen enough used car salesmen with Bibles and grouchy old self-righteous Torah thumpers to last a lifetime.

We need some glowers! *"When you glow, THEN you go!"*

REVIEW: THE CRUCIAL SUMMARY POINTS
(Or...What Do We Now Know?)

SUMMARY:
Who/What is YHWH (God)?

With all that I can understand, knowing that I'm not capable of knowing all of Him or all His ways, this is what I've come to believe about Abba God. *YHWH* is one! One more time, it is written (Deu 4:6):

> **Hear, O Israel: The *LORD our **God, the *LORD is one** (Shema, Yisrael, YHWH   Elohim, YHWH echad.)

> *But to us there is but **one God, the Father***, *of whom are all things, and we in him; and **one Lord Jesus Christ***, *by whom are all things, and we by him (1 Cor 8:6)*

There is One Father, God, and King of the universe who exists with a spiritual body and an omni-Spirit. His name is *YHWH Elohim.*

> *There is **one body***, *and **one Spirit***, *even as ye are called in **one hope** of your calling; 5   **One Lord, one faith, one baptism***, *6 **One God and Father of all***, *who is above all, and through all, and in you all (Ephesians 4: 4-6).*

There is one God-Supreme Power, Who alone is self-existent, Whose Spirit is Holy, Father of all things including *Yeshua* (Jesus).

SUMMARY:
Who/What is The Holy Spirit?

The Holy Spirit is the Spirit of God, literally the breath of the Father. The Holy Spirit is an intricate, inseparable part of Him, not a separate person. The Holy Spirit functions as the power, the comforter, and the teacher of all the children of *YHWH*. By the cleansing of our hearts through the blood of *Yeshua* (Jesus), the Holy Spirit indwells our being, thus allowing us to commune with the Father.

SUMMARY:
Who/What is Yeshua (Jesus)?

MY CONCLUSION:
1) He was birthed, not created, making Him the Son of God. He came forth from His Father, YHWH Elohim; and by that birth, He, too, is *Elohim or God.*
As a...
2) Pluralistic being (just like) the
3) same image and likeness of His Father,
4) before our world was created.
5) He has seven spirits and
6) life within Himself.
7) He was there, at creation (Genesis 1:1), and
8) He was a co-creator with His Father.

Yes, *Yeshua* is also ONE. Both the Father and the Son are *Elohim* (plural), but they are ONE. Not one together, but one individually, by Themselves! That is the point of the Deuteronomy 6:4 scripture. Each of these plural-both male/female beings- are ONE Entity—echad!

- *Yeshua* (Jesus) is God because . . . *He came forth from God* . . . It is obvious that *YHWH* and *Yeshua* (*Jesus*) are both "deity." *Yeshua* (Jesus) was and is *Elohim* because His Father is. What else could He be? Whatever the parents are, so are the children. While *Yeshua* (Jesus) is *Elohim* (God), He is subject to and submitted to the Father, *YHWH*.
- Yeshua came as the Lamb, the Son of God, fulfilling the spring Feasts, redeeming that which was lost.
- He sealed the new covenant with His own blood establishing *The Kingdom of God*, allowing the individual to become regenerated and holy, a Royal Priest unto YHWH.
- Yeshua has earned the right to be *The Messiah King* when 13.) He returns on the day appointed by YHWH, thereby fulfilling the fall Feasts. 14.) He will reign and rule this earth for 1000 years with all power and authority and then 15.) return all that power back to YHWH from whence it came.

Today, He is *my personal* Messiah-Lamb & King, for he came to set *me* free from my bondage of sin. He bathed me in His love and allowed the Spirit of YHWH to wash away my pain and guilt. He made it possible for the Holy Spirit to begin molding and shaping me, making me a holy priest that I might be able to walk into the Holy of Holies and call Him and YHWH, Lord!

He is not the reigning Messiah King of this world (yet), "the Christ," He was never coequal with His Father, YHWH, and is not part of a Trinity Godhead. There is one Lord- Supreme authority, begotten of the Father, YHWH, before time, subject to YHWH, and co-creator with the Father by Whom are all things on this earth and in heaven.

SUMMARY:
Who/What is Man?

Man is a pluralist being, created in the image and likeness of God, to be companions of God, who was divided into male/female beings. Once in a fallen state, having sinned, they could not redeem themselves.

While there are many ethnicities, I believe there are only two kinds of people. Those who are born again and those who are not. I also believe there is only one class of born again people. *What* are they, and *what* should they be called?

> *For he is not a Jew, which is one outwardly; neither is that circumcision, which is outward in the flesh: 29* **But he is a Jew, which is one inwardly; and circumcision is that of the heart, in the spirit**, *and not in the letter; whose praise is not of men, but of God (Rom 3: 28, 29).*

If you have accepted *Yeshua* (Jesus) as your Savior and personal Messiah, and have been born of the Spirit, you are Abraham's seed after the promise. You can call yourself a "New Covenant" Believer in, or a Disciple of, *Yeshua* (Jesus). Whatever you feel led to call yourself, do it with kindness and joy!

> *For by one Spirit are we all baptized into one body, whether we be Jews or Gentiles, whether we be bond or free; and have been all made to drink into one Spirit (I Cor 12 :13).*

SUMMARY:
Covenants

Covenants are the vehicles God chose to define his relationship with and to man.

The covenants we know of are 1) Edenic (Implied), 2) Noahic, 3) Abrahamic, 4) Mosaic, 5) Everlasting, and possibly an addition to the Everlasting Covenant during the promised Millennium period. Covenants like Noah's and David's were personal, as Abraham's was. The Edenic, Mosaic, and Everlasting are national covenants and applicable to the entire nation.

REMINDER: There has never been a covenant between God and a gentile. While gentiles are invited to participate in both the Mosaic and Everlasting covenants, they are made with the nation of Israel (Mosaic) or the House of Israel and House of Judah (everlasting)(Jer 31:31). Never with a gentile!

The Everlasting Covenant

Behold, the days come, saith the LORD, that I will make a new covenant with the house of Israel, and with the house of Judah: 32 Not according to the covenant that I made with their fathers in the day that I took them by the hand to bring them out of the land of Egypt; which my covenant they brake, although I was an husband unto them, saith the LORD: 33 But this shall be the covenant that I will make with the house of Israel; After those days, saith the LORD, I will put my law in their inward parts, and write it in their hearts; and will be their God, and they shall be my people. 34 And they shall teach no more every man his neighbour, and every man his brother, saying, Know the LORD: for they shall all know me, from the least of them unto the greatest of them, saith the LORD: for I will forgive their iniquity, and I will remember their sin no more (Jer 31:31-34).

Hebrews 10:1-18 confirms in vs 16 & 17 that this is the covenant promised in Jeremiah and sealed with Yeshua's

(Jesus') blood. What is not obvious to many is this covenant has eras built in, as well. First era — offering of the Lamb, blinding of the Jews, scattering of the disciples. Next era — gathering of the gentiles. Next era — end the Time of the Gentile, return of the chosen people. Next era — Millennium (these will be the subject of another study).

Know Which Covenant To Walk In

By now you should know that God does not work within religions. He operates within the covenants that He established. It is your responsibility to understand the covenants and to walk in them. Rejoice because you live in this time and because He is revealing His truth to you even through this study. It's not a "Have to!" relationship, it's a "Get to!" Don't let the devil or mistakes steal the joy we have in our walk of Grace. *Shine on!*

SUMMARY:
Religion

Religion is a series of infected vehicles created by infected men to define God and create a salvation system to control men, money and power. There has never been a God named, God sanctioned, or God created religion. I pray that by now you can see that God's only true religion is not a religion at all. It is relationship.

Many practices and customs in Christendom and Rabbinic Judaism, including Messianic Judaism, are pagan in origin. All teach so many false doctrines that, as I stated in the introduction, none are truly a Bible-based religion. They are all infected!

Rabbinic Judaism has redefined God and created a completely new salvation system based on works, good deeds, and obeying rabbinical commands. They redefined the feasts and utilized the basic Hebrew culture to create the lie that they were the "evolved" work of YHWH, God of Abraham.

Rabbinic Judaism is not the "evolved" religion and work of YHWH, God of Abraham. It's not even a biblically based religion. It's completely fabricated by the Pharisees of Babylon as is the Talmud.

Messianic Judaism is today selling Rabbinical Jewish doctrines as manna to the average follower. Rabbinical Feasts! Rabbinical traditions! Rabbinical dress! Rabbinical dog vomit! While there are varying degrees of this from very low to very high, it is the most prevalent part of the movement today.

Messianic Judaism could be an incredible vehicle of restoration if they would repent of the rabbinical heresy and press into YHWH and begin teaching what Yeshua (Jesus) was teaching: the Kingdom of God.

Christianity redefined YHWH, Yeshua (Jesus), and the Holy Spirit. It created the Godhead. It abolished the Hebrew customs and God's feasts. It took on pagan practices and eventually redefined salvation and the priesthood. It also became so pagan that it became a non-biblical religion, as well. Christianity is not the evolved religion of the Hebrew Yeshua (Jesus). It continued to evolve in many different directions. Mormonism, as an example, is a completed process of pagan evolved Christianity. While claiming to be the "rest of the story" it is, in fact, the antithesis of what the Hebrew *Yeshua* (Jesus) came to set up: The Kingdom of God.

FINAL THOUGHTS:

How to Walk With God

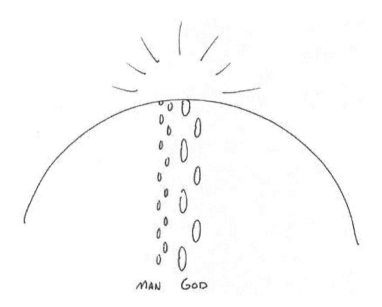

MAN GOD

STEPS TO WALK IN GOD'S NEW COVENANT — YOUR KINGDOM AWAKENING

Let's talk for just a moment.

Before we get into any steps that need to be taken, let's talk about what just happened. You're near the end of the book, and you are at one of several stages right now. You may be very excited and in agreement with most, or all, of the information you've just read. Or you may be in disagreement, and ready to run out to prove me wrong. Or you may be thinking, "What does all of this mean?" Of course, you could be anywhere in between these mindsets.

I realize that what is contained in this book is like having an eighteen wheeler, loaded with information, dumping its contents on your front lawn. It can be overwhelming!

Now, depending on where you are in your walk, the next steps might vary, as they depend on what the Lord has next for *you*. You may be coming from one of many religious paths — Christianity, Rabbinic Judaism, Messianic Judaism, Noahide, Islam, atheism, agnosticism, or any number of other practices. If there are parts of this work you are uncertain of, that's OK. Some of this information may click with you now, or maybe it will take awhile for you to be able to place it into the context of your life and understanding. You may have a great relationship with the Lord, or you may not have one at all. So, it's impossible for me to offer a "cookie-cutter" formula for the path and next steps that are right for you. However, I can and will provide a general direction for those who feel the unction to venture on. We truly believe what the scripture says: "Let every man work out his own salvation with fear and trembling" (*Phil 2-12).*

We will also offer additional teachings and discipleship materials on our web sites for those of you who want to move forward in your spiritual journey. You can order these same materials if you don't have access to the internet.

I love what one man said after reading the manuscript: "I may not agree with all your answers, but I do agree with all the questions." If that's the way you feel, praise the LORD! This book is all about creating a new paradigm for the believer, and causing them to examine carefully what they believe in the light of the truth. I just pray this work leaves you a hunger to actively search out or to deepen your intimacy with YHWH.

Let's Look At Some "What Steps Do I Take First" Suggestions:

"OK, so you've ripped the pagan foundations out from under us—NOW what do I do?" "Where and when do I go to church or synagogue?" "What do I practice and how?" "What are the applicable differences between the Old and New Covenants?" These are common questions for many coming out of the world's religions. Stopping the pagan infected rituals, festivals and traditions is the first step no matter which path you are coming from. It's simply sweeping out the house. Then, we need to fill the house, room by room, with His Spirit, His Festivals and His Traditions—remembering that He has an individual plan for your particular "home." Keep in mind, we are replacing a religion that created a set of rules to make you holy, with a personal relationship with the Lord God Almighty, in which *He* makes you Holy. This is both an event and a process.

With the two witnesses—the Word and Father's Holy Spirit—all truth will be established. Ask, Seek and Knock! This is the New Covenant, the Kingdom you live in. HE answers and HE writes His commandments on your heart.

> **CRUCIAL POINT:** *Whenever that legalistic spirit of condemnation, self-righteousness and arrogance comes in, it stinks up the entire room. Ask yourself this as you walk toward God, "Am I turning into a flower or a stink bug?"*

Have To? Or *Get To?*

There is one thing I really want to make clear, so I'll say it again: Under Mosaic law, *we had to do it*; under New Covenant grace, *we get to do it!* Yes, I know that the Old Covenant was not without grace (Heb. 9:15). I'm not a Dispensational teacher. But the grace revealed in the New Covenant is the ultimate in power and perfection—note each time we are told it is a "better" covenant. There is such a sweet, flowery fragrance in our blood-bought liberty under this walk of grace. Let's not let Satan stink it up by turning it into legalistic drudgery.

ARE YOU READY FOR A NEW COVENANT AWAKENING?

I believe that our Protestant forefathers started down the road towards the ultimate restoration of truth, but that path was diverted into what we know today as the Reformation. The Reformation was a step in the right direction, but it was only a partial step. The solution is not to refine, revise, or update our denominations and sects. When something is rotten at its core, a little tweak here or there won't do—we need something more radical. We need the Restoration and reestablishment of YHWH'S New Covenant Kingdom. *We need to return to His covenant, walk in His ways, and be*

His people. We need to keep His statutes, celebrate His festivals and be His kingdom priests. We need to have a *New Covenant Awakening!*

It's time we realized that the epidemic has robbed us all! Robbed us of our priesthood, our inheritance, our rights, our blessing, our power, our authority and even our identity! I don't even know if I'm using the right word — should I be saying robbed or *tricked?* We've been raised in this infected environment while most of our forefathers gradually traded our inheritance of the Kingdom/New Covenant for their own Kingdom of the Church. Satan has tricked us in so many ways. If you're rabbinic then you've been tricked into sitting around and arguing over what color blue your *tzitziot* should be; if you're Christian you are probably still wasting time, energy, and money celebrating all the Christian pagan holidays instead of enjoying the Feasts of the Lord.

Theologians have invented, and continue to invent, doctrines and arguments that make excuses for their ineffective, powerless, and legalistic ways, and then these "teachings" are institutionalized, putting large groups of people under bondage to dead religious systems. What does this have to do with the New Covenant? *"They were tricked and we've been robbed!"* We can't raise the dead, heal the sick, or cast out demons because we are entrenched in doctrines and dogmas that give an intellectual explanation for our rebellious infected lives. What does the Word say? "Come out from among them!"

> *And what agreement hath the temple of God with idols? for ye are the temple of the living God; as God hath said, I will dwell in them, and walk in them; and I will be their God, and they shall be my people.* [17]*Wherefore* **come out from among them, and be ye separate,** *saith the Lord, and* **touch not the unclean thing;** *and I will receive you,* [18]*And will be a Father*

unto you, and ye shall be my sons and daughters, saith the
Lord Almighty (2 Cor 6:16)

CRUCIAL POINT: *Do not be deceived, YHWH will not be mocked or compromised. He will not mix His house with paganistic ways (Christian, Rabbinic or Pagan), so we must come out from among them be separated unto YHWH! We MUST do It His Way, and within His New Covenant.*

If, while you have been studying this material, you have come to the conclusion that you have been unwittingly involved in any pagan practice(s), then there is a simple way to deal with it. "Turn from your wicked ways." This is both an event and a process.

> ***If my people, which are called by my name, shall humble***
> ***themselves, and pray, and seek my face, and turn from their***
> ***wicked ways;*** *then will I hear from heaven, and will forgive*
> *their sin, and will heal their land. 15 Now mine eyes shall be*
> *open, and mine ears attend unto the prayer that is made in this*
> *place. (2 Chr 7:14-15)*

What Is The Correct Way To Stop the Paganism?

Let's not deny reality: leaving behind long-practiced traditions is not only difficult; it can also result in persecution and rejection by others. But although there is a price to be paid, the final result is worth it all—a people cleansed, tested and looking more like *Yeshua* (Jesus) than ever. Like Him, we must be willing to make sacrifices for the truth in order to meet the needs of others. I have seen people lose their joy in these new found revelations because of personal rejection. Don't let that happen to you. Although the truth offends many, live to please the Lord while always being gracious to others.

ADDITIONAL TEACHING AND SPIRITUAL EXERCISES AVAILABLE

If you have the desire to take additional spiritual steps, we offer a 5-step process that may be of benefit to you. This is apart from assuming anything about your spiritual condition or standing with YHWH. It is *an exercise* for those who feel the need to address spiritual issues in your life. If you are currently not participating in any pagan practices, have a healthy understanding of the New Covenant and are walking in Kingdom principals, you may not feel the need for additional material. On the other hand, some of you may be led to review the material in order to see what may be applicable to your needs. Teachers or leaders may want to lead groups, classes, fellowships or congregations through all, or part, of this exercise. This is a simple way to assist those of you who feel convicted to make changes, and who want to utilize His gifts and power in a deeper way. Many are crying out, "There must be more to this than what I've experienced." It can be repeated as you feel the need. It also serves as a record and date to reaffirm your faith, encouraging you to stand when you are being tried.

These exercises are not a "cure all," but simply steps in the right direction to reinforce your faith and assure your victory. Some of you may even want to be baptized again (or for the first time) in the name of Yeshua. What I can tell you is this: if you agree that these things are true but do nothing, it will be like a garden that you want to plant. If you don't plow up the soil and actually sow seed, no new life will ever come forth, and there won't be any fruit to harvest. So do something! Reach out to YHWH. He's already reaching out to you. Begin to seek him in earnest, and follow the leading of the Lord YHWH!

Basic Steps Back to Reestablishing the Priesthood:

1. Repenting and renouncing the pagan gods and break all rights they have on us and our families.
2. A formal divorce from all demonic forces.
3. Betrothal to Yeshua.
4. Commitment to walk in YHWH's New Covenant,
5. Declaring ourselves New Covenant Kingdom Priests.

There will soon be individual lessons on specific subjects you can either download or order on our websites: www.russandbrenda.com or www.rockingthefoundations.com or www.newcovenantisrael.org

I pray that you find and walk in *your personal New Covenant Awakening*!

SUGGESTIONS TO HELP YOU GET STARTED

When sweeping pagan practices out of the house, it's critical to replace these old, infected traditions with living, Spirit-led traditions that actually bring you closer to YHWH. Below, we have notes on the Feasts and the Sabbath with scriptures and suggestions that may be helpful. Trusting completely in YHWH and walking *only as He directs*, bathe these thoughts and ideas in prayer and do them as you are inspired.

KEEPING SABBATH

If you keep the Sabbath because I do, then you are keeping it unto me instead of unto God. If the Lord convicts you to keep the Sabbath, then you should. This is a question that one should take to the Lord on an individual basis. However, I believe this to be a *Primary Injection* for the Infection, and the beginning of the return to biblical doctrines and the basis on which all covenants are built. It is impossible to return to "Biblical Truths and Hebraic Roots" without observing the Lord's Sabbath.

I know Christians who go to church on Sundays and keep the Sabbath holy by not doing things they feel should not be done on the Sabbath. Is there anything wrong in that? I do not believe it is wrong to go to church or synagogue on any day. I have, however, included some notes on the following pages for those who want to start keeping the true biblical Sabbath. *My advice would be to learn to keep the Sabbath before you start trying to observe the other feasts.* The Sabbath is the first of the Feasts and is foundational to all the other teachings and feasts. The Sabbath is in every feast; if you are not keeping the Sabbath correctly then you will not be keeping the feasts correctly, either.

The single most important thing for you to do is to seek God with your whole heart. Ask Him directly for His Holy Spirit of Truth to teach you all things, and determine to knock on the door of His Holy Word until it is opened to you.

STEPS TOWARD KEEPING THE SABBATH:
My Personal Recommendations

If you want to begin to keep the Sabbath, here are some steps to help you start. Because not everyone has the opportunity to "keep a completely biblical Sabbath," do what you can within your own ability. The biblical Sabbath starts Friday evening at sundown (when you can see 3 stars in the sky) and ends Saturday evening at sundown. While there are many rabbinical websites that will give the exact moment of sundown in just about every place on the planet, may I suggest that you begin a tradition that works with you and your family's lifestyle? It may begin at 5 PM or later. You may not be able to gather until after sundown, but there are steps you can individually take until you can meet.

WE CAN ALL DO THESE 3 STEPS WHEREVER WE ARE:

1. **Acknowledge the Sabbath** as the Lord's Day; He is the Creator of our world. Not only is this first, I believe it is foremost.

2. **Ask forgiveness for breaking his Sabbath** and ask the Lord to remove any curse which could have come on you and your family for breaking the Sabbath. I don't believe we are all cursed, but it would be a good exercise for any of us.

3. **Say a prayer around sundown.** It may be as simple as, *"Lord God, I acknowledge you as Creator of our world and I thank you for allowing us to have a Sabbath in which to rest and meditate on you."* Those of you who have to work could add to your prayer, *"Father, I have to work and I pray for a job or position that will allow me to have Sabbath off. Until then, I will acknowledge you as Lord of my life, Lord of my Sabbath. Even while working, I honor you this Sabbath day."*

Of course, you can add anything that helps to attain a spirit of worship and helps you enjoy your Sabbath. The Sabbath is something we *get to do*! It is a time of rejoicing and joy. Stay away from those who try to make it a burden and a chain around your neck. Under the *Covenant of Grace* we joyfully walk into the things of God and are *allowed to do* all the things the Children of Israel could not do under their *Covenant of Law*. Those of you who have to work on Sabbath can make it your day of "special ministry." While doing your duties to your employer, you can make an extra effort to be joyful because you have a job and can help provide for your family. You can make it a special time when you try to reach out to your fellow workers and encourage them, lift their spirits and try to emotionally and spiritually meet their needs. There are ways to make this work no matter what your circumstances. I don't care if you are a prison guard, a health care worker or whatever; if you want to keep the Sabbath unto the Lord there is a way to make it work!

Develop some traditions that help you and your family celebrate the beauty of the Sabbath. Jewish families traditionally light a Shabbat candle with the mother lighting the candle and saying a blessing. (In their traditional blessing, they claim they were commanded to do this. However, the rabbis are the only ones who commanded them to do it. It is a bit ironic that they were told not to "kindle a fire" in their houses on Shabbat *(Exo 35:3)*, and yet they chose fire as their tradition.) If possible, have a special family time or dinner. Sometimes it's difficult, especially with children involved in school activities that frequently take place on Friday nights. Maybe Saturday at lunch or dinner celebrating the close of Sabbath would work. Be creative! Come up with your own way of honoring the Lord on His day. As you do you will walk closer to Him and He will walk closer to you. Find ways to make the Sabbath a special day. Do it with flowers, music, stories, strolls, or with studies; but do something that you and your family enjoy doing together that includes celebrating the Lord as Creator of the universe. KEY WORD: *DO!*

4. Let's Do "The Don'ts": Keeping it Holy:

- **Don't work!** Do the best you can here. Ask God to show you how best to keep this special day.
- **Don't cook!** It's easier than you think. Either prepare the day before by cooking whatever will keep for the next day, or have cold cuts, salads, sandwiches, fresh fruits and veggies. Pick up a box or bucket of fried chicken on the way home Friday evening. There are so many ways not to cook. Just choose to stop cooking on the Sabbath.
- **Don't clean!** Don't wash the dishes, laundry, or the floors until Saturday after sundown. That's something you could do even if you have to work on Sabbath. Those who don't have to work, don't! If you are traveling, consider hanging a "do not disturb" sign outside your hotel room to give the maid a break, too!

I went to work for a Baptist preacher years ago. One of my conditions in accepting a position as a VP in his company was I would be allowed my Sabbaths off. (Not everyone can get that, I realize.) He said he respected my position on the Sabbath and had no problem with it. As time went on, nearly a year later, he was planning his annual banquet and sales promotional campaign for Friday night, all day Saturday, with the final dinner and sales awards Saturday night. I told him I would be able to join the festivities Saturday evening after sundown when the Sabbath ended. He was shocked. Since I was the VP of Marketing, it was critical for me to be there! He couldn't figure out any other way to get everyone together. What could he do? I suggested he start his event Saturday evening and go through Sunday because I never met anyone who claims to have a Sunday Sabbath who ever kept it holy. This took him aback, but he finally agreed.

> **CRUCIAL POINT:** People who don't keep the Sabbath on the Sabbath...don't keep the Sabbath.

Even people who really believe the Sabbath was changed from Saturday to Sunday and have never heard the truth, don't keep it Holy, or unto the Lord. There may be a rare exception here and there, but in my experience, it's *very* rare. I don't know a single person who does. If you try to teach people how to keep the Sabbath holy, they cry out, "You're putting us back under the Law!" If teaching how to keep the Sabbath is putting us back under the law, so is teaching not to commit murder and adultery. You'll find all three in the same set of Ten Commandments. Should we have a meeting to amend them to the Nine Commandments, or just vote on which ones we want to keep and how we want to keep them? Fact is, your religion and mine already had that meeting.

There are records of the first and second century Christians not being able to keep the Sabbath because of pagan cultures. Many chose to fast on Sabbath just to honor the Lord. I'm not suggesting that you or anyone fast, I'm just giving examples of people not having the opportunity to celebrate Sabbath but doing something to acknowledge Him on His day. Can you see the Lord smiling on His children as they made the attempt to please Him?

STEPS TOWARDS KEEPING THE FEASTS OF THE LORD

You may find that some of the Feasts of the Lord come easy, while others take time and creativity to work them into your life and/or that of your family's.

Remember that this is a process! It takes time and discipline. I remember my first few Sabbaths. As a hopeless work-a-holic, I was pacing the floor. "Do you know what all I have to do? Do you realize what I could be getting done? God, do you know how many people are dying and going to hell while I sit here on my keester, doing nothing?"

If you don't get anything else out of this study, please get

> **CRUCIAL POINT:** *It's not what we accomplish while we're here, it's what we become.*

this: God didn't need us to help Him create this world, to make eagles fly, or to make fish breathe under water. I think He can finish what He started with our just working six days a week. We often take ourselves way too seriously and don't realize how blessed we are to have a Lord and Master who planned in advance for us to have a day off every week. Therefore, get happy and shut it down!

On the practical side, we will do some additional teaching on the website, and I plan to write another book about the Feasts of the Lord and how to keep them.

> *Wherefore, my beloved, as ye have always obeyed, not as in my presence only, but now much more in my absence, **work out your own salvation with fear and trembling**. 13 **For it is God which worketh in you both to will and to do of his good pleasure. 14 Do all things without murmurings and disputings: 15 That ye may be blameless and harmless, the sons of God, without rebuke**, in the midst of a crooked and perverse nation, among whom ye shine as lights in the world (Phil 2:12-15);*

We have the greatest of all covenants to live under. **You're a priest, so be one!** *(1 Pet. 2:9).* Go by faith into the Holy Place and commune with the Holy One. Learn from Him the ways in which to worship Him and **then** let no one else, especially yourself, condemn you for how you worship *your* Lord.

All the things we do, or don't do, we do unto the Lord. It's separating out a day when *all* that we do, or don't do, is unto Him. It's another way to worship Him and express our love and gratitude to and for Him. *We get to do this!* It's our heritage. It's our privilege and it's our right! *It's walking towards Him.*

Here are a few scriptures to remind us of how the Lord felt when He was dealing with the children of Israel concerning His Sabbath and Feasts:

> *Bring no more vain oblations; incense is an abomination unto me; the new moons and sabbaths, the calling of assemblies, I*

*cannot away with it is iniquity, even the solemn meeting.
14Your new moons and your appointed feasts my soul hateth:
they are a trouble unto me; I am weary to bear them. 15And
when ye spread forth your hands, I will hide mine eyes from
you: yea, when ye make many prayers, I will not hear: your
hands are full of blood (Isa 1:13).*

*Blessed is the man that doeth this, and the son of man that
layeth hold on it; that keepeth the sabbath from polluting it,
and keepeth his hand from doing any evil. 3Neither let the son
of the stranger, that hath joined himself to the LORD, speak,
saying, The LORD hath utterly separated me from his people:
neither let the eunuch say, Behold, I am a dry tree. 4For thus
saith the LORD unto the eunuchs that keep my sabbaths, and
choose the things that please me, and take hold of my
covenant; 5Even unto them will I give in mine house and
within my walls a place and a name better than of sons and of
daughters: I will give them an everlasting name, that shall not
be cut off. 6Also the sons of the stranger, that join themselves
to the LORD, to serve him, and to love the name of the LORD,
to be his servants, every one that keepeth the sabbath from
polluting it, and taketh hold of my covenant; 7Even them will I
bring to my holy mountain, and make them joyful in my house
of prayer: their burnt offerings and their sacrifices shall be
accepted upon mine altar; for mine house shall be called an
house of prayer for all people. 8The Lord GOD which gathereth
the outcasts of Israel saith, Yet will I gather others to him,
beside those that are gathered unto him (Isa 56:2).*

*If thou turn away thy foot from the sabbath, from doing thy
pleasure on my holy day; and call the sabbath a delight, the
holy of the LORD, honourable; and shalt honour him, not
doing thine own ways, nor finding thine own pleasure, nor
speaking thine own words: 14Then shalt thou delight thyself in*

the LORD; and I will cause thee to ride upon the high places
of the earth, and feed thee with the heritage of Jacob thy father:
for the mouth of the LORD hath spoken it (Isa 58: 13).

Thus saith the LORD; Take heed to yourselves, and bear no
burden on the sabbath day, nor bring it in by the gates of
Jerusalem; 22Neither carry forth a burden out of your houses
on the sabbath day, neither do ye any work, but hallow ye the
sabbath day, as I commanded your fathers. 23But they obeyed
not, neither inclined their ear, but made their neck stiff, that
they might not hear, nor receive instruction. 24And it shall
come to pass, if ye diligently hearken unto me, saith the
LORD, to bring in no burden through the gates of this city on
the sabbath day, but hallow the sabbath day, to do no work
therein; 25Then shall there enter into the gates of this city
kings and princes sitting upon the throne of David, riding in
chariots and on horses, they, and their princes, the men of
Judah, and the inhabitants of Jerusalem: and this city shall
remain for ever. 26And they shall come from the cities of Judah,
and from the places about Jerusalem, and from the land of
Benjamin, and from the plain, and from the mountains, and
from the south, bringing burnt offerings, and sacrifices, and
meat offerings, and incense, and bringing sacrifices of praise,
unto the house of the LORD. 27But if ye will not hearken unto
me to hallow the sabbath day, and not to bear a burden, even
entering in at the gates of Jerusalem on the sabbath day; then
will I kindle a fire in the gates thereof, and it shall devour the
palaces of Jerusalem, and it shall not be quenched (Jer 17:21).

Moreover also I gave them my sabbaths, to be a sign between
me and them, that they might know that I am the LORD that
sanctify them. 13But the house of Israel rebelled against me in
the wilderness: they walked not in my statutes, and they
despised my judgments, which if a man do, he shall even live

in them; and my sabbaths they greatly polluted: then I said, I would pour out my fury upon them in the wilderness, to consume them. [14]*But I wrought for my name's sake, that it should not be polluted before the heathen, in whose sight I brought them out.* [15]*Yet also I lifted up my hand unto them in the wilderness, that I would not bring them into the land which I had given them, flowing with milk and honey, which is the glory of all lands;* [16]*Because they despised my judgments, and walked not in my statutes, but polluted my sabbaths: for their heart went after their idols.* [17]*Nevertheless mine eye spared them from destroying them, neither did I make an end of them in the wilderness.* [18]*But I said unto their children in the wilderness, Walk ye not in the statutes of your fathers, neither observe their judgments, nor defile yourselves with their idols:* [19]*I am the LORD your God; walk in my statutes, and keep my judgments, and do them;* [20]*And hallow my sabbaths; and they shall be a sign between me and you, that ye may know that I am the LORD your God.* [21]*Notwithstanding the children rebelled against me: they walked not in my statutes, neither kept my judgments to do them, which if a man do, he shall even live in them; they polluted my sabbaths: then I said, I would pour out my fury upon them, to accomplish my anger against them in the wilderness (Eze 20:12).*

I will also cause all her mirth to cease, her feast days, her new moons, and her sabbaths, and all her solemn feasts. [12]*And I will destroy her vines and her fig trees, whereof she hath said, These are my rewards that my lovers have given me: and I will make them a forest, and the beasts of the field shall eat them.* [13]*And I will visit upon her the days of Baalim, wherein she burned incense to them, and she decked herself with her earrings and her jewels, and she went after her lovers, and forgat me, saith the LORD (Hos 2:11).*

To please Him, which allows us *TO WALK WITH HIM,* is our final goal! How can we fail if that is all that we ever work toward?

Let God be true and every man a liar!

✖ *A SPECIAL NOTE OF INSTRUCTION ABOUT OUR MISSION AND PURPOSE:*

Walking with God is a process. We walked away, but most of us want to leap back. While our walking away was a much slower process, realize this: you can't fix everything at once. Go step by step and learn to WALK IN each concept and precept. Master each step before running to or through the next step. *Line upon line. Precept upon precept.* It's like building a rock house. Each stone has to fit firmly and tightly in place before you set the next one in place or your entire building will collapse. Sometimes you have to spend a lot more time fitting and chipping one stone to make it fit while other times the stone will fall right into place.

Zeal is a wonderful thing but it often causes people to run when they should walk. Please bathe everything in prayer and fast as often as you can before you make any decisions to change your spiritual direction or advise others. We are not clones, nor all called to walk the same path at the same time. We are only told we, as His Body, will all arrive at the same place *(Eph 4:13).* In the New Covenant, we are *all* priests of the Most High God. Build a firm foundation based on truth and love and walk as God Himself instructs you to walk. Don't condemn yourself or others for what has happened in the past. Don't condemn yourself or others as you learn to walk in the light you are given. Whatever you do, do not condemn others for not having the same revelation you have. Father hates a haughty spirit.

I pray that this teaching encourages you to seek God with all your mind, heart and spirit. I pray that nothing I have shared is a stumbling block or an offence to anyone. If I have repeated anything that is historically inaccurate I ask for forgiveness and welcome feedback. If I have misunderstood or miscommunicated anything, I ask for forgiveness. Most important to me, if I've offended you in any way, I beg your forgiveness. If I have caused you to dig deeper, I rejoice. Take the time to pray and seek the Holy Spirit on all of these things, especially on the way in which the Father and the Son exist. Ask, Seek and Knock!

Get your injections and Walk with God!

Shalom Aleichem,

Russ Houck,
(aka Dr. Pappy)